RTI for Reading at the Secondary Level

WHAT WORKS FOR SPECIAL-NEEDS LEARNERS

Karen R. Harris and Steve Graham
Editors

Strategy Instruction for Students with Learning Disabilities
Robert Reid and Torri Ortiz Lienemann

Teaching Mathematics to Middle School Students with Learning Difficulties
Marjorie Montague and Asha K. Jitendra, Editors

Teaching Word Recognition:
Effective Strategies for Students with Learning Difficulties
Rollanda E. O'Connor

Teaching Reading Comprehension to Students with Learning Difficulties
Janette K. Klingner, Sharon Vaughn, and Alison Boardman

Promoting Self-Determination in Students with Developmental Disabilities
*Michael L. Wehmeyer with Martin Agran, Carolyn Hughes,
James E. Martin, Dennis E. Mithaug, and Susan B. Palmer*

Instructional Practices for Students with Behavioral Disorders:
Strategies for Reading, Writing, and Math
J. Ron Nelson, Gregory J. Benner, and Paul Mooney

Working with Families of Young Children with Special Needs
R. A. McWilliam, Editor

Promoting Executive Function in the Classroom
Lynn Meltzer

Managing Challenging Behaviors in Schools:
Research-Based Strategies That Work
Kathleen Lynne Lane, Holly Mariah Menzies, Allison L. Bruhn, and Mary Crnobori

Explicit Instruction: Effective and Efficient Teaching
Anita L. Archer and Charles A. Hughes

Teacher's Guide to ADHD
Robert Reid and Joseph Johnson

Vocabulary Instruction for Struggling Students
Patricia F. Vadasy and J. Ron Nelson

Preparing Effective Special Education Teachers
Nancy Mamlin

RTI for Reading at the Secondary Level:
Recommended Literacy Practices and Remaining Questions
Deborah K. Reed, Jade Wexler, and Sharon Vaughn

Inclusive Instruction:
Evidence-Based Practices for Teaching Students with Disabilities
Mary T. Brownell, Sean J. Smith, Jean B. Crockett, and Cynthia C. Griffin

RTI for Reading at the Secondary Level

Recommended Literacy Practices and Remaining Questions

Deborah K. Reed
Jade Wexler
Sharon Vaughn

THE GUILFORD PRESS
New York   London

© 2012 The Guilford Press
A Division of Guilford Publications, Inc.
72 Spring Street, New York, NY 10012
www.guilford.com

Printed in the United States of America

This book is printed on acid-free paper.

Last digit is print number: 9   8   7   6   5   4   3   2   1

Library of Congress Cataloging-in-Publication Data

Reed, Deborah K.
  RTI for reading at the secondary level: recommended literacy practices and remaining questions / Deborah K. Reed, Jade Wexler, Sharon Vaughn.
       p. cm.—(What works for special-needs learners)
  Includes bibliographical references and index.
  ISBN 978-1-4625-0356-8 (pbk.)
  1. Reading—Remedial teaching.   2. Reading (Secondary)   3. Response to intervention (Learning disabled children)   I. Wexler, Jade.   II. Vaughn, Sharon.   III. Title.
  LB1050.5.R444 2012
  372.43—dc23
                                                                        2011048252

About the Authors

Deborah K. Reed, PhD, is Assistant Professor in the Department of Educational Psychology and Special Services at The University of Texas at El Paso. She is a former middle and high school teacher who developed the Texas Adolescent Literacy Academies based on multi-tiered reading instruction and intervention. In 2010 Dr. Reed received the Outstanding Researcher of the Year Award from the Council for Learning Disabilities. Her publications have appeared in *Scientific Studies of Reading, Learning Disabilities Research and Practice, Reading Psychology, Learning Disability Quarterly, Research in Middle Level Education,* and *Journal of Adolescent and Adult Literacy.*

Jade Wexler, PhD, is Assistant Professor in the Department of Special Education at the University of Maryland. A former high school special education reading teacher, she was the 2010 recipient of the Albert J. Harris Award from the International Reading Association. Dr. Wexler has served as a member of the editorial board for *Learning Disability Quarterly,* and her publications have appeared in *Reading and Writing: An Interdisciplinary Journal, Journal of Youth and Adolescence, Exceptional Children, Journal of Learning Disabilities, School Psychology Review,* and *Learning Disabilities Research and Practice.*

Sharon Vaughn, PhD, is H. E. Hartfelder/Southland Corporation Regents Chair of Human Development and Executive Director of the Meadows Center for Preventing Educational Risk at The University of Texas at Austin. She has served as president of the Division for Learning Disabilities of the Council for Exceptional Children, and she was Editor-in-Chief of the *Journal of Learning Disabilities* and Co-Editor of *Learning Disabilities Research and Practice.* Dr. Vaughn is the recipient of

numerous awards, including the Jeannette E. Fleischner Award from the Division
for Learning Disabilities of the Council for Exceptional Children, the Distinguished
Researcher Award from the Special Education Research Special Interest Group of
the American Educational Research Association, and the Distinguished Faculty
Award from The University of Texas. With funding from U.S. government grants,
she is currently investigating effective interventions for students who have reading difficulties and for students who are English language learners. Dr. Vaughn is
the author of more than 25 books, 230 peer-reviewed articles, and 65 book chapters
addressing intervention practices for students with learning difficulties and disabilities.

Acknowledgments

This work was supported by awards to the Meadows Center for Preventing Educational Risk at The University of Texas at Austin from the Institute of Education Sciences, the U.S. Department of Education, the Reading for Understanding Research Initiative (Grant No. R305F100013), and the Eunice Kennedy Shriver National Institute of Child Health and Human Development (Grant No. P50 HD052117). The opinions expressed are our own and do not represent the official views of the Institute of Education Sciences, the U.S. Department of Education, the Eunice Kennedy Shriver National Institute of Child Health and Human Development, or the National Institutes of Health.

Contents

Prologue: Response to Intervention with Secondary Students

Why the Issues Are Different Than with Elementary Students

SHARON VAUGHN AND JACK M. FLETCHER

Vellutino, Scanlon, Small, and Fanuele (2006) reported on an intervention that was provided to kindergarten students at risk for reading difficulties and then continued in first grade for those students with persistent reading problems. They evaluated subgroups of students according to their *response to intervention* (RTI): They determined which students met expected reading benchmarks and released them from treatment, and then examined the consequences of providing continued treatment for those students who maintained risk status. This work, as well as research on layered interventions for persistently at-risk students (O'Connor, 2000; O'Connor, Fulmer, Harty, & Bell, 2005) and on tiers of instruction for students at risk for reading problems (Vaughn, Linan-Thompson, & Hickman, 2003), helped to frame the ways in which RTI models were defined. In addition, RTI at the early elementary grades was influenced by work investigating screening and progress-monitoring measures (Fuchs & Fuchs, 1998; Stecker, Fuchs, & Fuchs, 2007) as ways to recognize students at risk early in schooling and determine whether the treatments were having the desired impact. As a result of this growing body of research,

Jack M. Fletcher, PhD, is a Hugh Roy and Lillie Cranz Cullen Distinguished Professor of Psychology at the University of Houston. His research interests focus on learning disabilities and brain injury in children, including definition and classification, neurobiological correlates, and intervention. He currently is Principal Investigator of a Learning Disability Research Center grant funded by the National Institute of Child Health and Human Development. He was the 2003 recipient of the Samuel T. Orton Award from the International Dyslexia Association.

primarily in early reading, RTI was perceived as a viable means of preventing reading and math difficulties (Fletcher & Vaughn, 2009; Vaughn & Fuchs, 2003).

However, the issues centering around RTI become quite different as students move through the grades, when there is less focus on prevention and more on remediation. Over the last several years, we have improved our understanding of critical elements of RTI—screening, assessment, and intervention—as these relate to secondary students (Barth et al., in press; Denton et al., 2011; Tolar et al., 2011; Vaughn et al., 2008; Vaughn, Cirino, et al., 2010; Vaughn, Wexler, Leroux, et al., 2011). Our current thinking is that RTI for secondary students is different in some fundamental ways from RTI at the elementary level.

IDENTIFICATION AND SCREENING FOR AT-RISK READERS IN SECONDARY GRADES

Whereas universal screening for reading and math difficulties is accepted practice within RTI frameworks at the early elementary level, universal screening for reading problems at the secondary level may be accomplished through extant data sources and in most cases may not require additional testing. By the time students reach the sixth grade, schools have considerable information about which students demonstrate reading difficulties (e.g., criterion-referenced tests, previous diagnostic tests, and state reading assessments). Our recent studies and the observations of Fuchs, Fuchs, and Compton (2010) indicate that these data sources can provide reliable information to determine which older students are at risk for reading problems and require further intervention.

If these measures are employed as screening tools, their use may not simply be a matter of passing or failing, and some scrutiny may be required to determine the level of performance associated with risk status. Since most of the reading assessments involve comprehension, some follow-up assessments may be needed to identify the components of reading that require intervention, but these follow-ups can be brief. In general, this approach conserves resources for intervention, which should always be the highest priority for students who are struggling. We think that the best way to identify the majority of students who need additional intervention at sixth grade and above is consistently low achievement in an academic area of significance, despite overall strong instruction at the classroom level and previous research-based interventions.

TIERS OF INTERVENTION FOR OLDER STUDENTS WITH READING DIFFICULTIES

Fundamental to the successful implementation of RTI with younger students is the implementation of increasingly intensive tiers of intervention to respond to students' instructional needs, based on their lack of response to previously implemented research-based interventions. Recent evidence and our clinical experience suggest that secondary students with low reading achievement can be assigned to less or more intensive interventions based on their current reading achievement scores, rather than being moved from less intensive to more intensive interventions based on their response. We agree with Fuchs et al. (2010) that both empirical and practical evidence supports this view. Empirically, we can distinguish more from less impaired learners; group them on the basis of their diagnostic *academic* profiles (e.g., word reading and comprehension); and then assign them (according to these profiles) to more or less intensive interventions that take into account their levels of decoding, fluency, and reading comprehension levels. Students with significant reading difficulties whose growth and level of performance based on previous interventions have been low are the most challenging (e.g., Denton, Fletcher, Anthony, & Francis, 2006; Vaughn et al., 2009).

This finding raises the question of what instructional practices make sense for older students with intractable reading impairments. We think that there are many issues to consider—including the relative impact of language impairment, memory problems, attention problems, and other factors related to self-regulation, as well as the extent to which these can be understood empirically and effective treatments implemented. At this point, there is a need for studies to focus on intervention for students at any grade level who are identified as inadequate responders, since previous intervention studies probably included students who had not had adequate instruction. We think, though, that there is some evidence that even students with intractable reading difficulties benefit from extensive and intensive treatments, even if they do not close the gap with their same-grade peers (Vaughn, Wexler, Leroux, et al., 2011).

In summary, the RTI models used in elementary schools are unlikely to be precisely similar to those used in secondary schools, for several critical reasons: (1) prevention is the focus in early elementary grades, and remediation is the focus in secondary grades; (2) at the early elementary level there is a high interest in identifying at-risk students early, and at the secondary level students at risk for reading problems are typically known from past data sources; and (3) using increasingly intensive interventions at elementary grades provides for a system that is responsive to students' needs, whereas at the secondary level the needs of students are more reliably defined and interventions can be designed initially to address their reading difficulties. The purpose of this book is to expand further on these key issues related to effective implementation of RTI at the secondary level. Of course, the models and interventions defined are based on what is currently the best knowledge, the suggested practices will require reconsideration as this knowledge accumulates and expands.

This chapter is adapted from Vaughn and Fletcher (2010). Copyright 2010 by the National Association of School Psychologists. Adapted by permission.

Introduction

Over the last decade, multi-tiered reading instruction and RTI have received considerable attention in lower elementary grades, thanks in part to the national effort to address early literacy through Reading First (Part B, Subpart 1, of Title I funding in Public Law 107-110, the No Child Left Behind Act of 2001). The research basis on effective reading instruction dates back a great deal longer—perhaps 25 years or more—but efforts to examine delivering that instruction in a layered fashion that grows increasingly individualized have developed much more recently (O'Connor, Harty, & Fulmer, 2005). These layered approaches to instruction were designed to meet several important goals.

First, they were designed to systematically shore up classroom instruction, so that more students would be provided with research-based approaches to learning to read. Second, they were designed to screen students early and provide them with supplemental interventions as needed. For example, if a second-grade student demonstrated very low scores on vocabulary and comprehension, additional interventions focused on these elements would be provided. Third, this layered approach to intervention was conceptualized as a data source to facilitate identification for learning disabilities (LD). For students who did not respond adequately to classroom instruction (Tier 1) with supplemental intervention (Tier 2), these data would be considered as relevant to interpreting more formal assessments and identifying students as having LD.

By design, RTI offered an alternative to the previous model, which required students to experience academic failure at a level sufficiently discrepant from their

IQ before they could be provided withsupplementary services to remediate the problems they were experiencing. The IQ–achievement discrepancy had been the prevailing practice for identifying students with LD, including reading disabilities, despite questions about the validity of this approach (e.g., Fletcher et al., 1994; Share, McGee, & Silva, 1989; Speece & Case, 2001; Stanovich & Siegel, 1994). What researchers recommended, instead, was an examination of how students responded to high-quality instruction (e.g., Fuchs & Fuchs, 1998; Speece & Case, 2001; Vellutino et al., 1996). This involved looking at both the level of a student's performance (as compared to the grade level or developmental benchmark) and the rate of progress the student was making (Speece, Case, & Molloy, 2003). Research conducted with elementary students helped establish a variety of procedures for using this alternative model, including how often to collect data, what type of data to collect, the effectiveness of certain types of instruction, how large or small the group size should be for students who were experiencing difficulty, and what dosage and duration of supplemental instruction might be necessary to make a difference in a student's level of performance and rate of growth.

Thus the role and function of RTI began to evolve in elementary school settings where students spent all day, primarily with one teacher who had some flexibility in how to arrange the schedule and apportion the instructional time. The Individuals with Disabilities Education Improvement Act of 2004 (IDEA 2004; U.S. Department of Education, 2004) specifically allowed districts to adopt RTI not only for determining special education eligibility, but also for providing preventative instruction to students who were struggling though not yet identified for special education. Some states went further in requiring RTI, not simply offering it as a permissible choice along with the severe-discrepancy model (Zirkel & Thomas, 2010).

Although elementary schools, particularly grades K–3, were busily working out the details of RTI implementation, the vast majority of leaders and teachers in middle and high schools had never heard of RTI and were unprepared for how to implement RTI practices at the secondary level. In fact, there is reason to believe that when RTI was integrated into IDEA 2004, few individuals responsible for its integration considered whether or how RTI would be implemented at the secondary level (Fletcher, Coulter, Reschly, & Vaughn, 2004). In 2005, when districts were launching RTI, some decided to develop and implement RTI models from elementary through secondary grades. In many cases, these districts were designing their own RTI models at the secondary level, aligning them with the instructional elements they perceived as effective at the elementary level.

RTI at the secondary level is considerably different from RTI at the elementary level, for many reasons that are fundamental to secondary instruction. For example, whereas elementary students often have one or two academic teachers, secondary students may have five or six. Scheduling at the elementary level is largely controlled at the classroom level by teachers. Secondary RTI implementation requires consideration of the fact that most students change classes frequently throughout the day; often do not have the same teachers for their core academic courses as their classmates do; are enrolled in courses based on graduation requirements for certain credits or Carnegie units; and are further constricted in scheduling by the placement of uniquely offered elective courses and/or co-curricular activities occurring during the school day (e.g., athletics classes, marching band, etc.). These logistical issues work against large experimental studies needed to determine whether and how RTI should be implemented, because such research requires students to be randomly (and strictly) assigned to treatment or comparison conditions for potentially large blocks of instructional time.

In the absence of sounder guidance, it is perhaps understandable why some districts attempted to move the RTI models developed for elementary schools into middle and high schools. However, this has created consternation among teachers and administrators, as well as acknowledgment among researchers that the ill-fitting procedures need to be rethought (Fuchs et al., 2010). We think it is important to state that the features of effective instruction inherent in RTI are not what is disputed (see Chapters 2 and 4 for more information on effective instruction). Rather, the problems center around how to effectively organize and implement the structural components of RTI (see Chapter 1 for an overview) in a secondary setting, as well as what the purpose of RTI might be when it is used with adolescents for whom the time of "early identification" has already passed.

Practitioners and researchers alike agree that middle and high school students should receive high-quality instruction in general education classes, but the question for many is this: How do we bolster the quality of this instruction to enhance overall reading for learning? In this book, we pose possible answers to this question by providing instructional guidance on how to teach vocabulary and comprehension across the content areas, as a means of preventing many students from experiencing difficulty.

There is also little disagreement that students with considerable needs in reading require additional reading intervention. Instead, the concerns are how to organize the instructional schedule to provide this reading intervention, what the content of the reading instruction should be, and who should provide it. Again, in this book we tackle these difficult issues, which cannot be addressed adequately with embedded vocabulary and comprehension support alone.

The basic tenets of a tiered approach to instruction, including a comprehensive analysis of performance data collected at regular intervals, are the basic tenets of RTI that apply at all grade levels. Over the past several years, we have developed, implemented, and evaluated through experimental studies the efficacy of procedures and practices for implementing RTI at the secondary level (Vaughn, Cirino, et al., 2010; Vaughn, Denton, & Fletcher, 2010; Vaughn & Fletcher, 2010; Vaughn, Wanzek, et al., 2010; Vaughn, Wexler, Roberts, Barth, Cirino, et al., 2011). We have also designed professional development (e.g., Reed et al., 2009) for secondary teachers to enhance their classroom reading instruction, and we have developed and implemented both Tier 2 and Tier 3 interventions. We intend to display in this book our practical understanding of what it takes to implement effective RTI practices in a secondary setting. Some of the frequently asked questions we address include the following:

- Which teachers are responsible for Tier 1? Is it the English teachers? Is it only for inclusion or co-taught classes?
- How do you deliver a "90-minute core" of reading instruction when a class is only 45 minutes long? Does this mean that all English classes have to be double-blocked?
- Do we have to have intervention classes if our state is meeting Adequate Yearly Progress goals or the state's criteria for acceptable school performance?
- How do we know who needs intervention and in what areas?
- What types of assessments are we supposed to give, and how often do we give them?
- What do we do with all the assessment results?
- How do we know what to teach in intervention? Is there a certain program we're supposed to use?
- Are interventions occurring in the regular/general education class? How does one teacher deliver the regular instruction plus intervention?
- Who teaches the intervention classes?
- Does intervention happen every day? Can it be before or after school?
- Is there a certain length of time that intervention has to last?
- How do we schedule all these classes?
- What do we do about changing students' schedules when there is no other class available at that time?
- Who will teach us about RTI, and where do we go if we have more questions?

These questions (and more) may have occurred to you as well. The chapters of this book have been planned to provide answers to some of the most pressing issues middle and high schools face when implementing RTI in the area of reading. We have chosen to focus on this subject area because students' vocabulary and comprehension skills (as well as the complementary skill of writing) affect their ability to learn and succeed in all content areas (Torgesen, Houston, Rissman, Decker, et al., 2007). Therefore, a great deal of the information is specific to the research base for reading instruction and intervention with adolescents. However, other information pertains to the processes and procedures of RTI in general and may be applied to multi-tiered instruction in other areas, such as math or behavioral support. Where appropriate, we have indicated the information that can be more broadly applied.

Because some states and school districts have more aggressively pursued implementing RTI at the secondary level than others have, we assume that you, our readers, will have differing levels of prior knowledge about the model and about reading instruction. For some of you, the information in this book may seem very different from what you have been told about RTI, because we advocate for practices that are uncharacteristic of how the framework is applied in elementary schools. For others, all the information—including even what *RTI* stands for—will be new. Still others of you will be somewhere in between with a little knowledge about RTI and/or adolescent literacy, but not enough information to put all the pieces together in a functional, coherent whole.

Given the breadth of information provided here and the wide range of backgrounds that our readers bring to the task, we have structured the book to facilitate reading it in different sequences. Let's start by looking at the order and contents of the chapters:

- **Chapter 1** ("RTI in Reading: An Overview"): why we need to apply RTI in the area of reading for adolescents; what traditional RTI is and includes; how RTI differs at the secondary level; how RTI intersects with special education; and what the benefits are of moving to an RTI model.
- **Chapter 2** ("Step 1: Implementing Effective Tier 1 Instruction"): what effective instructional practices support students' literacy, how to select materials or strategies for Tier 1; how to use screening assessments; what professional development is needed to support teachers in implementing Tier 1; how to create a school environment conducive to learning; and how to establish a team to oversee RTI in the area of literacy.
- **Chapter 3** ("Step 2: Establishing Interventions in Reading"): how to determine which students need reading intervention, what methods for scheduling intervention courses are possible in middle and high schools; how Tier 2 differs from study skills classes; how Tier 2 will differ from Tier 3 if multiple intervention tiers are provided; what group sizes are most appropriate for intervention; how assessment data can be used to place students into intervention tiers; what methods can be used to diagnose the specific needs of students who are struggling with reading and to monitor their progress in those areas; and what to consider when selecting an intervention teacher.
- **Chapter 4** ("Step 3: Guidelines for Tiers 2 and 3"): how to provide effective instruction in intervention classes; how to use formal and informal progress monitoring to guide instructional decisions; what can make instruction more intensive and individualized; how to select intervention materials and programs; what roles different personnel fulfill in an RTI model; and how to provide professional development to support the intervention tiers.
- **Chapter 5** ("Step 4: Refining Implementation of RTI"): what is negotiable and non-negotiable in the design and implementation of RTI at the secondary level; how to communicate the non-negotiables; how to determine when a school is ready to improve its implementation plan; and how to use a case study of a high school to evaluate implementation and to plan for overcoming roadblocks and taking next steps.

- **Appendices A–C:** sample bell schedules and master schedules from middle and high schools of different sizes and configurations.
- **Appendix D:** samples of literacy strategies applied to content-area material.
- **Appendix E:** samples of literacy strategies used in reading intervention.
- **Appendix F:** resources for additional information on RTI and RTI-related topics.

Now let's take a look at some of the options for proceeding through this book, so that you can determine what might be best for you. We list them by your possible role and background:

- You serve in any role at a school that is about to begin RTI implementation, and you know very little about RTI: Read the chapters in order.
- You are familiar with the concept of RTI, and you are a general education teacher who does *not* have responsibility for reading intervention: Read Chapters 2 and 5, and review the appendices.
- You are familiar with the concept of RTI, and you are a reading intervention teacher: Review Chapter 2 before reading Chapters 3–5 and the appendices.
- You serve in any role at a campus that has been involved in implementing RTI, *or* you have been involved in an in-depth study of RTI: Select particular topics within the chapters that reflect your current questions or interests.
- You are an administrator: Read Chapters 1 and 5, as well as Appendices A–C and F.

Throughout the book, we provide many cross-references to other chapters or sections, so that if you have skipped ahead to a particular topic or chapter, you can link back to information you might need to fill in any gaps in your knowledge that arise. We have tried to recreate in static print format a reading experience that is akin to reading online with hypertextual links to pertinent supporting information. If at any point you need more information than we have been able to provide here, refer to the websites in Appendix F, which are categorized by type of resource.

We know from firsthand experience that implementing the essential components of an RTI framework at the secondary level requires considerable time, effort, and resources. We hope that this book serves as a valuable guide for success.

CHAPTER 1

RTI in Reading

An Overview

The purpose of this book is to provide information relevant to implementing RTI within secondary settings—both middle and high schools. As stated in the Prologue, we recognize that RTI at the secondary level differs in some fundamental ways from RTI at the early elementary level. One significant way is that elementary RTI focuses on prevention, whereas with secondary students the focus is more on remediation. Also, using RTI as a data source to facilitate identification for LD is unlikely to occur in the same way at the secondary level, as in the primary grades, if it occurs at all.

This book also addresses RTI primarily with a focus on reading, for three reasons: Reading is (1) the academic area of highest need for older students, contributing to their success in school and in postsecondary experiences; (2) the academic area that most enables success in other content areas, such as science and social studies; and (3) the area where the vast majority of students with learning problems and LD have difficulties.

WHY IS RTI NEEDED IN THE AREA OF READING AT THE SECONDARY LEVEL?

Over the past two decades, researchers and educators have worked together to resolve the significant problem of how we teach students to read and how we prevent reading difficulties. Considerable progress has resulted. We have a better understanding of how students learn to read, how to identify students early with reading difficulties, and how to remediate basic reading problems (Fletcher,

Lyon, Fuchs, & Barnes, 2006). Although there is more room for linking research to practice in early reading, we are much better informed about many issues related to early reading development, including agreement about the importance of oral language and vocabulary development, the critical role of phonological awareness, the importance of phonics instruction in assisting students in mapping sounds to print, and ways to improve fluency with a focus on reading comprehension (Rayner, Foorman, Perfetti, Pesetsky, & Seidenberg, 2001). We even have a much improved arsenal of measures to identify and assess reading difficulties, as well as to monitor students' progress (see Appendix F for a list of websites and other resources related to reading assessment).

With so many improvements in our knowledge about early reading, what are the remaining issues to tackle? As your experiences in the classroom may indicate, a significant remaining problem is the number of students who learn the basic foundation skills of reading but make inadequate progress in reading complex words, reading fluently, and reading to understand. This problem is further accentuated by a growing population of students with inadequate background knowledge to understand and connect learning from content-area texts.

WHAT IS THE READING PERFORMANCE
OF SECONDARY STUDENTS?

National and international studies reveal that significant numbers of adolescents and young adults do not adequately understand complex texts, such as those materials that they are asked to read for schoolwork. In fact, the reading for understanding of many secondary students is so low that it impedes their school success, their access to postsecondary learning, and their opportunities to succeed within our increasingly competitive work environment (Biancarosa & Snow, 2004; Kamil et al., 2008). Many of the jobs that high school graduates would have performed three or more decades ago required little literacy knowledge; however, this is no longer the case. Whether you are a police officer, a nurse, a sales attendant, or a business-person, reading and understanding increasingly complex texts have become part of your job. Even if you are not employed outside the home, literacy is necessary to complete forms, follow medical instructions, and stay well informed to responsibly conduct your duties as a citizen.

The National Assessment of Educational Progress (NAEP) is the only test given to a sample of students across the United States and across grade levels in which all states are required to participate. So how have U.S. children and adolescents been doing on reading over time? The trend in 4th- and 8th-grade performance from 1992 to 2009 shows that average NAEP reading scores have increased slightly—from 217 to 221 and from 260 to 264, respectively (National Center for Education Statistics, 2009). However, this trend in improvement does not continue for high school students. For 12th-grade students, a significant *decrease* from 1992 was reported (from a score of 292 to 288), with about 26% of students scoring below the basic reading level (National Center for Education Statistics, 2010). The low results for high school students were across reading areas, including reading for information, reading to perform a task, and reading for literary experience.

In addition to the low overall performance for high schoolers on reading, there continue to be significant gaps between the performance of students classified as European American/white and those classified as Hispanic or African American/ black. These low performance levels on national reading tests create concern, for several reasons. First, students with low literacy are less likely to be engaged in school. For example, 55% of students with low literacy levels do not graduate from high school (National Commission on Adult Literacy, 2008). Graduating from high school is a low bar for what is needed for economic success. Second, students with low literacy do not adequately comprehend text. This is a significant problem for these students, as it means either that they are unable to read text related to content learning, or that teachers bypass text by reading aloud or using alternative sources such as audiovisual media. Third, students who struggle with reading do not read for pleasure or for information at the same rate as those who read well.

Students make the most rapid growth in reading during elementary school, and reading growth declines considerably over time with high school students making the least growth (Bloom, Hill, Black, & Lipsey, 2008). Recently, reports by the ACT (2009) revealed that only 50% of ACT-tested students are ready to read and understand college-level text, with more students "on track" in 8th and 9th grades than in 12th grade. The 2006 report states that "the clearest differentiator between students who are college ready and students who are not is the ability to understand complex text" (p. 12). Of high concern is the finding that males, African Americans, Hispanic Americans, Native Americans, and students from families with incomes less than $30,000 are most at risk for having very low reading comprehension (ACT, 2006, 2009). Finally, the Programme for International Student Assessment (PISA) indicated that the United States ranked 21st among the 30 member countries of the Organisation for Economic Co-operation and Development (OECD) on literacy-related outcomes (OECD, 2007).

DOES READING DIFFER IN ELEMENTARY AND SECONDARY SCHOOLS?

Much of what we know about effectively teaching older students with reading difficulties we have learned from studies with younger students. However, a growing research base provides guidance to instructional strategies found to be effective with adolescents (for syntheses of this research base, see, e.g., Edmunds et al., 2009; Scammacca et al., 2007; Wexler, Vaughn, Edmonds, & Reutebuch, 2008). Learning to read is not "different" for older students, but once students know how to read, several aspects of promoting reading comprehension vary with older students.

In 1983, Chall and Jacobs conducted a seminal study in which they documented the continued regression in reading skills of low-income students with low vocabulary. Over time, the low vocabulary and concept development of these students impaired their understanding of text to such an extent that reading comprehension was significantly compromised. Though it is unlikely that starting vocabulary development in the secondary grades can adequately compensate for the significantly low vocabulary of such students, learning what words mean and how to learn the meaning of unfamiliar words encountered when reading text is essential to instruction of secondary students. Because understanding the words that are read is essential to comprehension, most successful methods of instruction with older students combine vocabulary learning with comprehension instruction.

Shanahan and Shanahan (2008) describe some of the significant differences between reading development for younger students and reading development for secondary students by highlighting two key elements that are the same (basic literacy and intermediate literacy) and one key element that is different (disciplinary literacy). A description of each of these and how they influence instruction with older readers is provided in Figure 1.1.

Basic literacy refers to those basic processes that are necessary for learning to read. For most students this includes segmenting and blending the sounds of language (phonemic awareness); mapping these sounds to print and understanding the common rules related to sound–print relationships (phonics); reading words accurately, with adequate speed, and with expression (fluency); and knowing what words mean (vocabulary) so that understanding of text results. Basic literacy skills are necessary across elementary and secondary populations, and though the activities may vary by age, the actual ways in which students acquire these key elements are similar. It is highly unlikely that older students will require phonemic awareness, and it is also likely that they will have most if not all of the basic phonics skills. However, many older readers with reading difficulties lack advanced word-reading skills and will benefit from instruction that involves multisyllable words and learning to read and understand academic vocabulary.

Intermediate literacy refers to the strategies and practices that promote understanding of text. These include knowing the academic vocabulary related to the text, as well as understanding the meaning of the words and concepts within the text. Intermediate literacy also refers to those comprehension strategies that help readers understand what they read including monitoring understanding, thinking about the main idea and summarizing key ideas. Intermediate literacy is similar in readers from about second grade through adulthood. Thus much of what we know about teaching practices related to intermediate literacy with younger students can be adapted and applied to older readers.

Disciplinary literacy refers to a more mature type of literacy development that is unique to older readers. It includes understanding of genre, academic vocabulary, word use, and sources related to the text they are reading. The required reading of secondary students focuses on the acquisition of disciplinary knowledge—for instance, terms and ideas in math (e.g., *equals, sine, pi*), social studies (e.g., *Fascists*), and science (e.g., *cell, energy*), to name just the major disciplinary areas studied. It also focuses on acquisition of the norms for using words (e.g., *or* and *and* in Boolean algebra mean something very special in mathematics, as does *force* in science). In addition to these terms and key words, the genres related to providing information in disciplines vary, as does the importance of the source. Historians are very interested in what sources are used to derive information, and they appreciate reading original sources as a means of verifying and understanding history (e.g., actual letters from a pioneer family).

FIGURE 1.1. Basic, intermediate and disciplinary literacy. Based on Shanahan and Shanahan (2008).

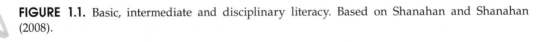

WHAT IS RTI?

 Stop and Think

As you read this section, keep in mind that the information defines RTI as it has been researched in elementary schools and extended into secondary settings. Think about what aspects of this traditional model might be a challenge for you to implement in middle or high school. Look for explanations throughout this book on how RTI at the secondary level differs from the typical elementary model.

The NAEP, PISA, and ACT data indicate that the ways we previously have organized and designed courses in middle and high schools are not equipping many students with the advanced reading skills they need to be successful in life. This need to rethink the school model systemically is linked to the growth of RTI. The term *response to intervention* refers to a framework for providing instruction to students with learning and behavior difficulties that is based on universal screening, assessment, and ongoing supplemental interventions, which increase in intensity to meet students' specific needs. In other words, RTI is a schoolwide service delivery system that is multi-tiered, including all students initially in general education and providing increasingly intensive interventions for students who are not making adequate progress, potentially leading to special education placement. There are many approaches to RTI, and it is best considered as a set of processes rather than a single model, with variations in how the processes are implemented (Fletcher & Vaughn, 2009). Because RTI is implemented schoolwide, it involves school building leaders as well as general and special education teachers.

RTI may be conceptualized in different ways, some having four or more tiers of instruction. For the purpose of this book, we are describing the RTI model as having three tiers of instruction, because this is the most common approach and is well represented in the research (Compton, 2006; Fuchs & Fuchs, 2007). Figure 1.2 provides an overview of a three-tiered model as it was originally conceived for and researched in elementary schools. The percentages in the figure are suggestive and are addressed further in Chapter 2. What is important to note here is that each successive tier of instruction has fewer students. Let's examine the basic premises behind each of the three tiers, so that we can begin our look at RTI on the middle and high school level with a common understanding of a traditional three-tiered model.

Tier 1 includes all students and is typically considered general education. For example, it is expected that all but a very few students will participate in math, science, and English language arts/reading (hereafter abbreviated as ELAR) successfully and will benefit from the instruction provided. It is also assumed that 80% or more of the students will be able to read and understand grade-level text, so that they can read for pleasure and read to learn within their content-area classes (National Association of State Directors of Special Education, 2006). Tier 2 typi-

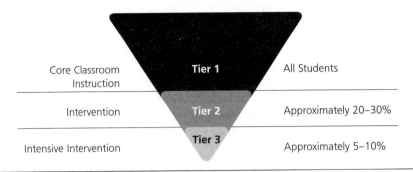

FIGURE 1.2. Three-tiered intervention model. Adapted with permission from the University of Texas Center for Reading and Language Arts. (2005). *3-tier reading model: Reducing reading difficulties for kindergarten through third grade students.* Austin, TX: Author.

cally includes about 20% of students. These students are also participating in Tier 1 instruction in math, science, and social studies, but they require supplemental instruction to improve their reading. These students may receive an additional class each day for 30–50 minutes to supplement their reading of multisyllable words, learn increasingly complex vocabulary, and acquire proficiency in reading strategies. Even fewer students (5–10%) require more intensive Tier 3 interventions. These interventions are for students with significant needs in reading. These students are unlikely to read words accurately and fluently and have a difficult time accessing and understanding the reading texts in their content areas. Most of these students are more than two grades behind their peers.

As mentioned, these percentages represent accepted hallmarks, but may not adequately reflect your school context. If you are troubled by them, take a moment to read pages 27–29 in Chapter 2, to better understand how other indicators can improve our interpretation of how well the tiers are functioning. Otherwise, let's continue reviewing what happens in each tier as the model has traditionally been applied. You will notice other references to upcoming chapters embedded throughout the next section. These are provided to link you with more detailed information about how some elements of the three tiers are adjusted for the organizational structures and academic demands of middle and high schools.

HOW DO THE TIERS OF READING INSTRUCTION/INTERVENTION DIFFER?

Primary Instruction, Tier 1

What distinguishes Tier 1 from all of the other tiers of instruction? The primary distinction is that *Tier 1 (primary instruction)* involves all students in the classroom with an intention of providing them with the most effective instruction or behavior supports. For example, in a seventh-grade ELAR class, the instruction provided to all of the students in the class is referred to as Tier 1 instruction.

In Tier 1, general education teachers provide evidence-based instruction to all students in the class (see Chapter 2 for more information on Tier 1 at the secondary level).

Secondary Intervention, Tier 2

Secondary intervention, or Tier 2, is provided for those students with reading difficulties. Tier 2 interventions are typically delivered to small groups, with the intention of providing additional instruction that will allow the students to make adequate progress in Tier 1 instruction without further intervention. Tier 2 interventions *supplement* rather than supplant the ELAR program provided in Tier 1 general education classrooms. Yet the support that students receive in Tier 2 is still under the domain of general education. It is *not* special education. Teachers continue to monitor the progress of students while they are receiving Tier 2 support (see Chapter 3 for more information on Tier 2 at the secondary level). Tier 2 interventions are provided for a duration (e.g., one or more semesters) that allows students adequate time to respond to the instruction (Gersten et al., 2008; National Research Center on Learning Disabilities, n.d.). After this time, educators examine progress-monitoring data and other data to answer the following questions for each student:

- Is the student making good progress?
- Is the student making some but not sufficient progress, thereby necessitating that he or she continue Tier 2 intervention?
- Is the student making very little progress, thereby requiring him or her to be provided with a more intensive intervention (i.e., Tier 3)?

Once it is determined that a student has made sufficient progress to be successful in Tier 1 alone, he or she no longer receives the supplemental intervention provided in Tier 2.

Tertiary Intervention, Tier 3

Tertiary intervention, or Tier 3, is provided to those students who continue to experience difficulties and show minimal progress during secondary or Tier 2 interventions. Some adolescents may be placed directly into tertiary intervention (see Chapter 3 for more information on placing students into Tier 2 or 3, as well as how to distinguish these levels of intervention). Typically, however, the majority of students who require intervention benefit from secondary intervention and do not require tertiary intervention. Tertiary intervention is typically provided for a longer time period and more frequently than secondary intervention. Usually students who are provided with tertiary intervention are not also provided with secondary intervention, but remain within their primary intervention (Gersten et al.,

2008). Tier 3 students receive explicit instruction individually or in small groups of up to six students. (See Figure 1.3 for a description of how Tiers 2 and 3 might be implemented.) Depending on the number of tiers in the RTI model, this tier may or may not be special education. Many states require consideration of how well students respond to intervention when special education status is being identified and reviewed. More information on how special education intersects with a three-tiered model is provided on pages 19–21 of this chapter and in Figure 1.4.

- **Implement universal screening to identify students at risk for reading problems.** Develop procedures for screening all students to determine students at risk for reading. Consider using students' performance on state-level tests the previous year as a means of identifying students who require additional reading intervention.
- **Determine whether students who need additional reading instruction would benefit from Tier 2 or Tier 3.** Students who need additional intervention but are close to meeting grade-level reading criteria can be placed in Tier 2. Students with more significant reading problems (i.e., more than two grade levels behind peers) can be placed in Tier 3 and provided more intensive interventions.
- **Determine students' instructional needs.** Determine students' knowledge and skills related to relevant reading skills/knowledge expected at their grade level. For example, for reading it may be several of the following elements: word reading, word or text fluency, vocabulary, spelling, and comprehension.
- **Form same-ability, small groups.** For secondary intervention, form groups of students with similar learning needs. Group sizes should be as small as local resources will allow. For tertiary interventions, even smaller group sizes are appropriate to maximize opportunities to respond.
- **Provide daily, targeted instruction that is explicit, is systematic, and provides ample practice opportunities with immediate feedback.** Identify the instructional content in small instructional units (e.g., 3–5 minutes per unit) for each lesson.
- **Focus on the reading or math skills that have the highest impact on learning, based on students' current performance.** Model examples of what you want students to do before providing students with opportunities to practice. Scaffold instruction and make adaptations to instruction in response to students' needs and to how quickly or slowly students are learning.
- **Follow a systematic routine.** Use clear, explicit, easy-to-follow procedures, and sequence instruction so that easier skills are introduced before more complex ones.
- **Pace instruction quickly, so that students are engaged and content is covered.** Maximize students' engagement, including many opportunities for students to respond.
- **Provide ample opportunities for guided initial practice and independent practice.** Monitor students' understanding and mastery of instruction frequently. Adapt instruction so that items are more difficult for some students and easier for other students.
- **Include frequent and cumulative reviews of previously learned material.** When students do not demonstrate proficiency, reteach.
- **Ensure that students are reading texts at the appropriate level of difficulty.** Levels of accuracy in reading text need to be very high when students are reading independently. Comprehension is impaired when students struggle too much with reading the words. When students are reading text with teacher guidance and support, lower levels of accuracy may be appropriate. Reading accuracy

(cont.)

FIGURE 1.3. Implementing effective interventions: Tiers 2 and 3. Based on Vaughn and Bos (2009).

levels vary from source to source. Remember to provide students with opportunities to read a variety of text types, including texts similar to those required in classroom reading. To calculate reading accuracy, divide the number of words read correctly by the total number of words read. Take the following into consideration:

- *Independent level:* Texts in which no more than approximately 1 in 20 words is read incorrectly (accuracy level: 95–100%).
- *Instructional level:* Texts in which no more than approximately 1 in 10 words is read incorrectly. Students need instructional support from the teacher (accuracy level: 90–94%).
- *Frustration level:* Texts in which more than 1 in 10 words is read incorrectly (accuracy level: less than 90%).

- **Provide many opportunities for struggling readers in Tier 3 to acquire and use word-reading strategies, especially for multisyllable words.**
  - Have students practice reading words and texts at the appropriate level of difficulty (usually instructional level under the direction of the teacher).
  - Include the reading of word cards or words in phrases or sentences to increase word recognition fluency (often used with high-frequency and irregular words, and words that contain previously taught letter–sound correspondences or spelling patterns).
  - Include comprehension instruction that introduces new vocabulary words, incorporates graphic organizers, and teaches students to think about words they don't know or don't understand.

- **Include writing to support reading and spelling.** Have students apply what they are learning about letters and sounds as they write letters, sound units, words, and sentences. Involve parents so that they support students' efforts by listening to them read and practice reading skills.

- **Conduct frequent progress monitoring (e.g., every 1–2 weeks) to track student progress and inform instruction and grouping.**

FIGURE 1.3. *(cont.)*

Stop and Think

> Remember that the components of Tiers 2 and 3 described in Figure 1.3 were developed for younger students. As discussed in Chapter 4, there are limitations on monitoring the reading progress of adolescents. Notably, available instruments are unlikely to detect changes in the reading skills of middle or high school students over a short time span, such as the 1- to 2-week interval mentioned in Figure 1.3 that separates administrations of progress-monitoring assessments for elementary students.

ARE WE REQUIRED BY LAW TO USE RTI?

Perhaps one of the biggest challenges is determining whether a student has a reading problem that can be readily remediated through appropriate Tier 1 instruction and perhaps secondary intervention, or whether the problem is more significant and requires special education. One of the significant influences of RTI is that it is designed to help resolve some of the major issues involved in identifying students with reading disabilities/LD. The overview provided in Figure 1.4 compares identification of students with LD prior to IDEA 2004 to the present identification process with RTI.

Prior to IDEA 2004	RTI
No universal academic screening.	All students are screened.
Little progress monitoring.	Progress monitoring assesses whether students are reaching goals—multiple data points are collected over an extended period of time across different tiers of intervention.
"Wait to fail" model—students were frequently not provided with interventions until they had qualified for special education.	Students are provided with interventions at the first sign that they are struggling; there is an increased focus on proactive responses to students' difficulties.
Focus on within-child problems or deficits.	Ecological focus. Systems approach to problem solving, focused on instruction and interventions varying in time, intensity, and focus.
Clear eligibility criteria (i.e., a child either did or did not qualify for special education services). Categorical approach—targeted, intensive interventions were typically not provided unless a student was found to be eligible for special education.	Tiered model of service delivery, with interventions provided to all students who demonstrate a need for support, regardless of whether they have a disability label.
Multidisciplinary team was mostly made up of special education professionals; individual students were typically referred by classroom teachers with academic and/or behavioral concerns.	Problem-solving (or intervention) teams include general and special educators; teams consider progress-monitoring data and evaluate all students who are not reaching benchmarks.
Reliance on assessments, particularly standardized tests.	Collaborative educational decisions are based on ongoing school, classroom, and individual student data; adjustments to instructions/interventions are based on data.
Assessment data were collected during a limited number of sessions.	Multiple data points are collected over time and in direct relationship to the intervention provided.
"Comprehensive evaluation" consisted mainly of formal assessments conducted by individual members of the multidisciplinary team; often the same battery of tests was administered to all referred children.	"Full and individualized evaluation" relies heavily on existing data collected throughout the RTI process; evaluation includes a student's response to specific validated interventions and other data gathered through observations, teacher and parent checklists, and diagnostic assessments.
LD construct of "unexpected underachievement" was indicated by low achievement as compared to a measure of a child's ability (i.e., IQ–achievement discrepancy).	LD construct of "unexpected underachievement" is indicated by low achievement and insufficient response to validated interventions that work with most students ("true peers"), even struggling ones.

FIGURE 1.4. Identifying students with LD: Identification prior to IDEA 2004 and with RTI. Adapted from Klingner, J. K. (2009). Response to intervention. In S. Vaughn & C. S. Bos (Eds.), *Strategies for teaching students with learning and behavior problems* (7th ed., p. 67). Upper Saddle River, NJ: Pearson. Copyright 2009 by Pearson Education, Inc. Adapted by permission of Pearson Education, Inc.

STOP *Stop and Think*

Do you know whether your state or district requires the implementation of RTI at the secondary level? If so, do you know whether there are differences between how RTI is implemented at this level and how it is implemented in elementary schools? What questions do you have for state or district leaders that would help your campus successfully implement RTI in middle and high schools?

Simply stated, federal regulations do not require the use of RTI; however, you may be working in a state that does require use of RTI. Also, it is possible that your district guidelines require implementation of RTI. Specifically, the federal regulations cite the following:

1. The state may not require the use of severe discrepancy between intellectual ability and achievement for determining whether a student has a specific LD.
2. The state must permit the use of a process based on response to intervention.
3. The state may permit the use of alternative research-based procedures for determining whether a student has an LD.

Links to information on state requirements can be found in Appendix F.

WHAT IS THE ROLE OF READING ASSESSMENT?

The two types of assessment that are fundamental to the implementation of RTI are screening and progress monitoring. These occur within the overall system of assessments a school administers.

Screening

Screening within RTI is the use of a universal tool to determine whether any students are at risk for learning problems. It is typically used for detecting reading problems, as well as problems in math or even behavior. Effective screening tools provide a reliable and valid measure that can be easily and quickly administered to large numbers of students. To screen older students for reading problems, we may ask them to read a passage at grade level and then respond to questions. These data sources allow us to identify students with difficulties and then to provide them with additional instruction as needed. Within an RTI model, screening is typically conducted at the beginning and middle of the year. With secondary students, state-level assessments can often be used as screening measures; this issue is explored more thoroughly in Chapter 2.

Progress Monitoring

Progress monitoring involves frequent and ongoing measurement of student knowl-edge and skills, and provides relevant student data for evaluating instruction. Used with a few students or the entire class, progress monitoring is essential to effective implementation of RTI, because it allows instructional decision makers (e.g., classroom teachers) to determine the rate of growth students are showing and to determine whether additional intervention is needed—and, if so, what kind of intervention. This is done by plotting data gathered over time to see the rate and level of progress a student is making. To see sample graphs, turn to Figure 4.2 in Chapter 4, which explores the use of progress monitoring in Tiers 2 and 3 in more detail. For the purposes of our RTI overview, we address the most common ques-tions about progress monitoring in Figure 1.5.

 Stop and Think

> *So far in this book, very clear differences in the use of screening and progress-monitoring measures have been mentioned for application with secondary students as compared to elementary students. In what ways do these types of assessments seem easier to use with adolescents, and in what ways do they seem more challeng-ing? As discussed in Chapter 4, there are limitations to monitoring the progress of adolescents, so this aspect of RTI will take careful consideration. Figure 1.5 will stimulate your thinking about these issues.*
>
> *Figure 1.5 explains the use of progress monitoring for adolescents. Why are assessments administered less frequently for adolescents than they are for younger students? Why might the types of assessments need to be different for students in kindergarten through third or fourth grades as compared to adolescents? For more information on progress monitoring at the secondary level, see Chapter 4.*

WHAT ARE THE BENEFITS OF PROGRESS MONITORING?

According to the National Center on Student Progress Monitoring (n.d.), there are many benefits to using progress monitoring, including these:

- Increased learning, because instructional decisions are based on student data.
- Improved information about students who are on target to meet account-ability standards.
- Increased information to improve communication about students' progress with family members and other professionals.
- Higher expectations for low-achieving students.

Why use progress monitoring?
- To track students' learning.
- To determine students who need further instruction or intervention.
- To arrange grouping structures so that students have more opportunities to learn from peers and the teacher (e.g., student pairs, small groups).
- To design instruction that meets individual students' needs (e.g., support learning of key ideas, concepts, vocabulary).
- To identify students who need additional interventions in reading.

How is progress monitoring done?
- Assess all students periodically on what you are teaching (e.g., main idea, cause-and-effect relationships), and provide additional instruction to students who are behind a level. Given the limitations on the availability of reliable and valid instruments for secondary students, the assessments to which we refer are considered informal curriculum-based measures that are usually teacher-made. See Chapter 4 for more guidance on the construction of such progress-monitoring measures.
- Use school-level or classroom-based assessments to identify students who need extra help and to create goals for learning. Once you determine which students require extra help, you can plan appropriate instruction or identify students who need intervention in addition to classroom learning.
- Consider using standardized measures for more formal progress monitoring such as maze measures (see *www.progressmonitoring.com* and Chapter 4 for information on appropriate standardized measures for older students).
- Assess progress by comparing learning goals with actual student progress. Students who are making adequate progress should still be assessed approximately three times a year to ensure that they are learning and continuing to achieve at grade level.

FIGURE 1.5. Using progress monitoring.

WHAT ARE THE ADVANTAGES OF MOVING TO AN RTI APPROACH?

The goal of any RTI approach is to raise the achievement levels of all students by providing differentiated instruction and increasingly intensive supplemental instruction to students with reading difficulties, and by using ongoing screening and progress monitoring to determine which students need interventions and how they are progressing. There are several key advantages to using RTI. One such advantage is that RTI assists educators in identifying and treating students with learning difficulties/LD. Perhaps among the most hotly debated issues in special education are the criteria for identifying individuals with LD. Beyond the scope of this book are the numerous articles, chapters, books, and speeches lamenting the traditional methods of identifying students with LD, which require a discrepancy between IQ and achievement as a criterion (see also Figure 1.4, which contrasts the identification of LD before and after IDEA 2004). In addition to concerns about the disproportionate representation of minorities (e.g., Donovan & Cross, 2002) are issues related to the "wait to fail" outcome, in which students must wait until they are old enough and far enough behind before they meet traditional eligibility requirements.

In response to the ongoing concerns about eligibility for special education and identification of LD, the U.S. Department of Education in 2002 held meetings and a summit to reach consensus on these issues (Bradley, Danielson, & Hallahan, 2002). The results of the meeting can be summarized as follows (Vaughn & Klingner, 2007): (1) LD is a valid construct that exists across the lifespan, with a prevalence as high as 6%; (2) students with LD require a special education, which may be conceptualized within a multi-tiered system as Tier 3 or Tier 4; (3) IQ–achievement discrepancy is not an adequate criterion for identification; (4) RTI is the most promising conceptual framework for identifying and treating students with LD; and (5) we know more about effective interventions than is often evident in practice.

A second advantage to using RTI is that students are provided with research-based instruction. Thus, when students make less than adequate progress in their core classroom (e.g., ELAR), we know that it is not because they have had inadequate instruction, but rather because they need supplemental instruction. This provides an opportunity for Tier 2 (secondary intervention) or Tier 3 (intensive tertiary intervention) to be provided.

A third advantage to using RTI is that it provides for a schoolwide conceptual framework for organizing key principles of instruction (e.g., preteaching and reviewing vocabulary across disciplines, providing advanced organizers of the big ideas of learning before teaching), as well as for providing increasingly intensive layers of intervention (Tier 2 and Tier 3) to supplement instruction for students with academic needs.

A fourth advantage is that all students are screened and monitored for their growth in reading, and this information provides a schoolwide plan for how to improve instruction, monitor student success, and inform the students and parents of progress.

WHAT ARE THE BENEFITS OF IMPLEMENTING RTI?

In summary, the potential benefit of implementing RTI is that through a schoolwide effort, leaders, teachers across content areas (e.g., science, math, ELAR), and specialists (e.g., reading and special education teachers) work cooperatively with common goals and procedures for identifying students who require additional instructional support, monitoring their progress, and providing supplemental instruction to meet their needs.

 Stop and Think

> *As stated in the Prologue and at the beginning of this chapter, RTI at the secondary level is not geared toward prevention and is unlikely to be a data source for facilitating identification of LD in the same way as it does in the primary grades. Therefore, how can you understand the four advantages described in terms of their impact on or benefit for middle and high schools? The following chapters may help you focus your thinking.*

HOW IS RTI AT THE SECONDARY LEVEL DIFFERENT FROM RTI AT THE ELEMENTARY LEVEL?

RTI was developed as a means of preventing academic and behavior problems through the early identification of youngsters who demonstrate these difficulties and the rapid provision of interventions needed within a range of intensity. This approach assures that students' challenges are corrected and that adequate progress is made. With an emphasis on prevention, RTI has been organized, designed, and implemented primarily at the early elementary level, to address the needs of young children in kindergarten through third grades. However, because of what many educational leaders perceive as a systems approach to screening, monitoring, and providing appropriate ranges of supplemental supports to meet students' needs in the primary grades, they are beginning to apply this same systems approach with older students in the upper elementary grades (grades 4 and 5), as well as secondary settings (grades 6–12).

Now that we have provided a common understanding of the traditional RTI model, we devote the remainder of the book to exploring how these components can be adapted for implementation in middle and high schools. Before moving on, take a moment to reflect on the information in this chapter by responding to the reflection questions. At the end of each subsequent chapter, you will also find reflection questions to check your understanding of the concepts and help you consider how you might apply them in your own school setting.

REFLECTION QUESTIONS

1. How might an RTI model implemented with a focus on reading improve outcomes for students?
2. Why is there a need to implement an RTI model focusing on reading at the secondary level?
3. Can you describe the core components of a three-tiered RTI model as it was originally developed for elementary students and indicate how they might be different for secondary students?
4. Can you distinguish the differences among Tiers 1, 2, and 3?
5. How does RTI help reduce some of the major issues centering around identifying students with reading disabilities/LD?
6. What are the advantages of implementing an RTI approach?
7. Describe the differences between reading development for younger students and reading development for secondary students.

CHAPTER 2

Step 1

Implementing Effective Tier 1 Instruction

You may have seen images of three-tiered models that use layers of a triangle to represent the narrowing scope of each successive tier (as Figure 1.2 does). This type of image has been a very popular graphic, in part because it helps you visualize the way intervention classes are dependent on the strong foundation provided by Tier 1. Without that high-quality core instruction, an RTI system cannot be supported. These models may have been conceived originally for elementary schools, but the basic principle of Tier 1 is the same for secondary schools. Put simply, here are the goals of this tier:

1. To ensure that all students, regardless of background or special population status, are provided *high-quality instruction* in every core academic class (i.e., ELAR, mathematics, social studies, science).
2. To *prevent* students from being referred for Tier 2 or Tier 3 interventions inappropriately or unnecessarily because the quality of instruction was inadequate.
3. To engage all campus teachers in a constructive and productive dialogue about *monitoring students' progress* and effectively implementing practices designed to improve outcomes.

How does this conceptualization of Tier 1 differ for secondary students from Tier 1 at the elementary level? Fundamentally, the idea that Tier 1 provides appropriate and research-based instruction designed to advance academic performance for all students is the same (see Chapter 1 for more introductory information on

Tier 1 in a traditional RTI model). What you will note as different is that at the secondary level the focus of Tier 1 is across the academic curriculum (including math, science, ELAR, and social studies), whereas at the elementary level the focus is typically on reading and/or math.

We want to acknowledge that meeting social studies standards, for example, in a social studies class, while also supporting the reading skills of students at multiple levels in a short 50-minute period, is no small task. We are advocating for strong core academic instruction that enables students to access and learn from the texts. We are not recommending that content-area teachers neglect their content standards or become reading interventionists. That is simply an unreasonable expectation, which is partly why Tiers 2 and 3 exist: to create an appropriate setting staffed by individuals properly trained in reading intervention to deliver the supplemental instruction some students will need to overcome reading difficulties. We address those matters in Chapters 3 and 4. In this chapter, we focus on the components of Tier 1 that will make interweaving vocabulary and comprehension instruction with content learning more feasible and successful.

 ### Stop and Think

Providing Tier 1 literacy instruction and support within content-area classes is one way in which RTI at the secondary level is distinct from RTI at the elementary level. Why do you think vocabulary and comprehension instruction are emphasized as important to strong core academic instruction across the content areas? In what ways are vocabulary knowledge and understanding of text important to students' success in math, science, and social studies, as well as ELAR? For additional resources on Tier 1 at the secondary level, see the websites provided in Appendix F.

You may recall from Chapter 1 that a commonly accepted hallmark of a strong core program is having 80% or more of the student body meeting academic targets with Tier 1 instruction alone (Fletcher & Vaughn, 2009; Reschly, 2003). In fact, many effective Tier 1 programs are distinguishable by the low numbers of students receiving Tier 2 or Tier 3 interventions. A school or district may want to use this indicator as a way to judge whether it needs to strengthen its Tier 1 programs. For example, if a school has identified that a majority of students are in need of Tier 2 and/or Tier 3 intervention, this should be a red flag that the faculty and staff need to spend time improving the Tier 1 core instruction.

ⓘ USEFUL INDICATORS OF STRONG TIER 1 CORE INSTRUCTION*

Having 20% or less of the student body in intervention is not the only means for evaluating Tier 1, and in certain situations it may even be misleading. Consider the following scenarios, which illustrate (1) a school exceeding the suggested percentages and (2) a school where the percentage of students meeting academic targets is very low:

1. About 95% of the students at School A are already demonstrating basic proficiency with grade-level standards. However, the handful of students at each grade level who are below proficiency can only be helped through compensatory education, such as after-school tutoring, test preparation courses, or pull-out programs. There is no system in place to catch these kids before they fail. Rather, school personnel must wait until the inevitable happens before the students can be offered remediation, because, "Really, our school is doing just fine."

2. Across town at School B, it is a challenge to raise passing rates on state assessments and 4-year completion rates to the target 80% level. For the last 2 years, the school has been on an improvement plan, because 40% of the students are not meeting grade-level standards. The school has made great strides in raising the quality of core academic instruction. Although it received additional funding from the state to support these efforts, the teachers cannot feasibly help the hundreds of students who need supplemental assistance outside the regular classes. "There are just too many of them!"

Does either scenario sound familiar to you? Are you a School A teacher who is frustrated about missing opportunities to intervene before it's too late? Or are you a School B teacher who is teaching your heart out, but you just can't make progress fast enough to catch the moving target of minimum proficiency standards? If either is true at your school, you know why examining passing rates on grade-level assessments is not always the most useful hallmark for evaluating Tier 1.

*This symbol ① will alert you to important information that further clarifies RTI processes at the secondary level.

An alternative way to look at what constitutes a strong core is by identifying the elements needed to create and maintain Tier 1 as a proactive approach to instruction. We can do this by using exemplar school campuses as a guide for the kinds of features we would expect to see in other schools with high implementation of Tier 1. What are some of the features observed in schools with effective implementation of Tier 1 (National High School Center, National Center on Response to Intervention, & Center on Instruction, 2010)?

- Effective instructional practices in every classroom
- Cross-curricular literacy supports
- Regularly administered screening assessments
- Environments conducive to learning
- Literacy leadership teams overseeing RTI

We address these features in this chapter in the order given above. Many are interrelated, so it can be difficult to explain them in isolation. Whenever doing so is appropriate, we refer to other sections of this chapter or to other chapters in the book. As noted in the Introduction, you are encouraged to treat those as the static print versions of hyperlinks and flip to the information you need to support your developing understanding. Before we begin an in-depth exploration of matters specific to content-area literacy and reading intervention, let's review the general instructional practices found to be most effective at increasing student achievement.

HIGH-QUALITY CORE INSTRUCTION: EFFECTIVE INSTRUCTIONAL PRACTICES

Tier 1 is defined by high-quality instruction in all classes. The core curriculum for middle and high schools is not contained in a 90-minute reading block, as it is in elementary schools. Rather, it encompasses the use of reading and writing in all content-area classes in order for students to learn from texts and build conceptual knowledge. Because the students in a general education class can represent a broad span of ability levels, it is not uncommon for teachers to feel torn between accomplishing their content-area standards and teaching literacy skills (RAND Reading Study Group, 2002). How can you meet these competing demands in a 50-minute period?

If it is overwhelming to you, do not feel alone. This is a challenge for most secondary teachers, because the preservice training for middle and high school tends to be dominated by the content and instructional practices for a particular subject or domain (Heller & Greenleaf, 2007; Reed & Groth, 2009). For example, if you are going to be a math teacher, you learn about practices and key concepts specific to teaching mathematics. Most traditional and alternative certification programs provide only cursory information on adapting this content or utilizing different strategies to meet the needs of students at varying ability levels. Content-area teachers are known for considering themselves masters of their disciplines and exhibiting discomfort with anything that seems to fall outside those confines. You may have heard such pleas as "That's not my area," or "I'm not a reading teacher."

 Stop and Think

> *Unlike elementary teachers, middle and high school teachers do not all consider themselves reading teachers. Tier 1 at the secondary level emphasizes vocabulary, comprehension, and writing instruction that is integral to learning content and successfully demonstrating understanding of important concepts. Rather than asking content-area teachers to address reading, Tier 1 involves core academic teachers in implementing effective instructional practices despite the subject area. The basic features of effective instruction are described below and extended in Chapter 4.*

Fortunately, several features of instruction have been found in research to be highly effective at improving student achievement across subject areas. The strategies are fairly straightforward, but can be deceptively simple. We encourage you to implement these habitually and not to assume that you can jump over earlier steps to save time and get to the assignment more quickly. Remember, this is about *effective* instruction. If implemented faithfully, the practices will also prove *efficient*, because they will save time typically spent on reteaching and remediation. However, carefully progressing through the phases can feel very inefficient at first. The phases of effective instruction, summarized in Table 2.1, need to be considered when you are planning instruction in any course. Information on the specific features for reading intervention is added in subsequent chapters.

Let's examine each of these features to make sure we have a common understanding of what each entails. Whenever appropriate, we provide examples to illustrate the features in action.

1. *Communicate clear expectations* for what your students should know and be able to do, as well as how they should accomplish this (Vaughn & Bos, 2009). This includes explicitly stating the objective of your lesson, as well as modeling the procedures for all activities, perhaps multiple times (Housand & Reis, 2008). A high school science teacher, for example, might begin a lesson by saying:

"Today we are going to categorize living organisms into groups based on their characteristics. To do this, we are going to use a special graphic organizer called

TABLE 2.1. Features of Effective Instruction for All Classes

1. *Communicate clear expectations.*

2. *Model expectations with overt demonstrations* of thoughts and actions ("I do").

3. *Break the task into small steps, and provide feedback* after each step ("We do"). Gradually increase the number of steps or the length of work completed between feedback periods.
   • Offer feedback that specifically identifies what to continue and what to change.
   • Provide many opportunities for students to discuss their developing understanding.

4. *Plan for follow-up instruction* ("You do"), to include:
   • Teaching self-monitoring and fix-up strategies.
   • Supplementing background knowledge.
   • Providing real-world applications.

5. *Incorporate student engagement,* such as:
   • Offering some choice in materials, activities, and/or products.
   • Making connections to other lessons and content.

6. *Provide distributed practice.*

7. *Differentiate instruction* by:
   • Utilizing different groupings of students.
   • Making the curriculum appropriately challenging across ability levels.

a *semantic feature analysis* [Bos & Anders, 1992], which includes the names and characteristics of the taxonomic groups from your textbook reading. We will use the semantic feature analysis to make sure we understand all the terms and concepts we have read and how they relate to each other. It will also help us compare the differences and similarities in the characteristics that define each taxonomic group. You will notice that the taxonomic groups are written down the far left-hand column, and the characteristics or features are written across the top. We will examine one row or taxonomic group at a time and use the information in our textbook to help us determine if it exhibits each feature. If it does, we will put a plus sign in the box under that feature. If it does not exhibit the feature, we will put a minus sign in the box."

	Prokaryotic	Eukaryotic	Single-cellular	Multicellular	Microscopic	Autotroph	Live in harsh conditions	Cell walls contain cellulose
Archaea								
Bacteria								
Protists								
Fungi								
Plants								
Animals								

2. *Demonstrate* what you want your students to do and how you want them to learn. You may have heard this referred to as the "I do" phase of instruction (Archer, Isaacson, & Peters, 1988). One of the critical differences between teaching your students how to do something and assigning them to do it is the extent to which you demonstrate the work while talking through what is happening, what you are doing, and how you are processing information. In other words, you think aloud while you are modeling each step. Our high school science teacher from the example above might do the following:

"Let me show you how I would complete the first row, on *archaea*. I see from the diagram in the book that archaea do not have a cell nucleus, so I know that means they are *prokaryotes*. I can put a plus sign under the first characteristic or feature, and that also means I can put a minus sign under *eukaryotic*. Eukaryotes do have a cell nucleus, so organisms must be one or the other but cannot be both. That is similar to the next two features: *single-cellular* and *multicellular*. The organism has to be one or the other, because either it is made of just one cell or it is made of many cells together. I see on page 284 that archaea are described as 'single-celled microorganisms.' That tells me I can put a plus sign under *single-cellular* and a minus sign under *multicellular*. A microorganism is one that is unicellular, not necessarily microscopic. I remember reading about some microorganisms that are *macroscopic* or visible to the naked eye, so I don't know if archaea are *microscopic* yet. Let's keep looking in our chapter. . . . "

The teacher would continue talking aloud as he or she she modeled how to complete the semantic feature analysis for the entire row on *archaea*, as shown below.

	Prokaryotic	Eukaryotic	Single-cellular	Multicellular	Microscopic	Autotroph	Live in harsh conditions	Cell walls contain cellulose
Archaea	+	−	+	−	+	+/−	+	−
Bacteria								
Protists								
Fungi								
Plants								
Animals								

Note. The +/− symbol under *Autotroph* indicates that archaea can be autotrophs or heterotrophs.

3. Next, *break the task into small steps* for students to complete. After each step, *provide your students immediate feedback* that highlights specifically what was done correctly and what needs to be changed to improve performance. This is the "We do" phase of instruction (Archer et al., 1988), which potentially lasts for the longest period of time. You might compare it to an apprenticeship period, in which the students receive teacher- and peer-assisted guidance as they acquire and refine their new knowledge and skills. You gradually increase the length and/or number of steps completed between feedback periods. Throughout the practice opportunities, involve your students in discussing their developing understanding of the content and processes with you and their peers (Alfassi, 2004; Applebee, Langer, Nystrand, & Gamoran, 2003). You may need to scaffold the text you are using to practice the skill or to vary the activity you are using, depending on the students' progress.

In our high school science example, the next step would be for the teacher to complete the row on *bacteria* together with the students by carefully guiding the students in locating information in the text to determine whether or not bacteria exhibit each characteristic. For each plus or minus sign entered on the grid, students would have to explain their reasoning, using evidence from the text. Then the teacher might complete the next row on *protists* with the students by having them attempt to mark the plus and minus signs for two to three features at a time before discussing the rationales for their marks and moving on to evaluating the next two to three features for protists.

4. As you identify areas with which your students are having difficulty, *provide follow-up instruction* to ensure that everyone is able to handle the work inde-

pendently in the final ("You do") phase (Archer et al., 1988). This requires that you teach your students self-monitoring skills to identify when their understanding has broken down, as well as problem-solving strategies to repair the breakdown (National Institute of Child Health and Human Development, 2000). These are strategies for stopping and checking their work, reading, or other activity along the way. How will they know if they are doing it correctly? What can they do if they detect they have made a mistake, lost the understanding of the text, or encountered some obstacle? The science teacher in our example might have students ask themselves: "Can I find supporting information in a paragraph or diagram? Do I know another way to describe the feature or a different name for it? Can I think of an organism in the taxonomic group that will help me figure out whether members of that group could have the feature or not?"

You may also need to provide supplemental lessons to build missing or replace inaccurate background knowledge. This would be true, for example, if the science teacher in our example discovered that the students did not understand that autotrophs make their own food and were confusing them with heterotrophs. Similarly, you can create real-world or otherwise meaningful applications for the students' new knowledge and skills (Graves, Cooke, & Laberge, 1983; Langer, 1981, 1984; Neuman, 1988). These are authentic experiences that help students connect information to their everyday lives and to see the usefulness of the knowledge and skills beyond your classroom. The science teacher in our example might have students find examples of organisms in current science news articles and discuss the significance of the taxonomic groups to which they belong. For example, he or she could ask students how the characteristics of the organisms affect the environment or our food supply (positively and/or negatively).

5. *Student engagement*, or active involvement, can be motivating for students—particularly those who tend to struggle. To further support students' motivation, offer certain choices in the materials, activities, and/or products (Guthrie et al., 2004). This does not mean that "anything goes." You need to set appropriate parameters so that the learning goals are accomplished. You might offer small choices within an assignment, such as in what order they can complete components. Help students make good choices by explaining what the options entail, and provide feedback relative to their choices.

6. Finally, *plan for distributed practice* as you begin to connect the content of one lesson to other lessons (Alfassi, 2004). Without returning to the information and procedures multiple times, students are not likely to retain them for long. Even when trying to remember what they learned, many students will consider your lessons as discrete, "one and done" activities. Therefore, helping students make connections across lessons and structuring ways to recursively review concepts will foster deeper learning.

7. To the extent that "intervention" is provided within Tier 1, it is most likely to occur in the form of *differentiated instruction*. This involves making purposeful

changes or adaptations to the instructional activities, student groupings, materials, or lesson products, with the goal of making the content accessible to students of all ability levels. Our science teacher, for example, might have students who were excelling add other characteristics to the semantic feature analysis. Students who were struggling to complete the grid, meanwhile, could be given simplified language or pictures to support the features.

 ### Stop and Think

The examples of effective instruction given above are based on a science lesson, but should be considered applicable to all core academic classes. Take a moment to consider how the seven features would apply to a course you teach. The particular content would need to change, but the basic instructional practices should remain the same. To learn more about the elements of RTI that are "negotiable," see Chapter 5.

ⓘ COMMON MISUNDERSTANDINGS ABOUT DIFFERENTIATION AT TIER 1

Although the term *differentiation* is used frequently in schools, we have found that teachers have different understandings of what it means. When this term is applied to general education classes in Tier 1, we have observed two common misunderstandings of it. The first is that instruction for "all students" is sometimes interpreted exclusively as "whole-group instruction." When you are introducing new content through direct teaching and modeling, whole-group instruction is certainly appropriate. However, students benefit from practice opportunities that involve working in small groups. Collaborative grouping creates more opportunities for your students to discuss content, build on the collective knowledge of their peers, hear and see different models of language use, actively engage in classroom activities, and receive corrective and immediate feedback from peers (McMaster, Fuchs, & Fuchs, 2006; Saenz, Fuchs, & Fuchs, 2005; Vaughn, Klingner, & Bryant, 2001).

Another benefit of small-group instruction concerns the second common misunderstanding about Tier 1. Some teachers, particularly those who are more accustomed to older models of special education service delivery, assume that differentiated materials, activities, and lesson products are only for those students with an individualized education program (IEP). In fact, adaptations for support and enrichment should be made for *all* students, as necessary, to provide an appropriate level of challenge. When you purposefully group your students, it is easier to adapt your instruction by planning different reading materials, instructional focus areas, and/or levels of complexity in an activity or assignment for each group.

Regardless of whether or not students receive modifications or other instructional adaptations, they are to be afforded the fundamental skills, concepts, and objectives needed to maintain growth in the content area (Carnine & Carnine, 2004; Foorman & Torgesen, 2001). That is the purpose of differentiated instruction: to make the core curriculum accessible to every student. Otherwise, a student who is working to overcome a difficulty with reading, for example, will be denied the opportunity to learn science. The student will fall further behind peers and lack the background knowledge necessary to accelerate academic achievement even after building reading proficiency.

What does differentiation look like in practice? Box 2.1 describes how one content-area teacher planned for differentiation.

BOX 2.1. DIFFERENTIATED INSTRUCTION IN A U.S. HISTORY CLASS

Ms. Inkanish was teaching a lesson on U.S. mobilization for World War II (WWII) to her U.S. history class. She had seven students who were identified as having reading difficulties serious enough to make their comprehension of the textbook challenging. Two of these students (Students A and B) were enrolled in an intensive intervention, where they were learning word identification skills. The other five students (Students C, D, E, F, and G) were enrolled in a less intensive intervention, where they received supplemental assistance with their reading fluency and comprehension.

The history teacher also had two students who were English language learners (ELLs). One, Student H, was at an emergent level of English reading and writing proficiency, significantly below grade level. The other (Student I) was at an intermediate level, meaning that he had sufficient skills to demonstrate his academic knowledge with assistance.

Ms. Inkanish had the following starting point for the week's lesson plans, but needed to develop the instructional activities, sequence (including connections across lessons), and appropriate adaptations (including scaffolding and differentiated instruction):

Objective: Explain what happened to the economy and to different groups of people as the United States got ready for and started fighting WWII (adapted from State Standard I-B.5).
Target vocabulary: *war mobilization, internment, defense industries, domestic policy, inflation, security measures*
Resources/materials: Textbook Chapter 25, Sections 3 and 4 on domestic policies and the economy; supplementary readings on the U.S. internment camps and on recruitment of women as well as racial and ethnic minority groups into the workforce; streaming videos.
Assessment of learning: (writing prompt) Explain how the United States mobilized for WWII. Based upon the results, do you think the United States did a good job mobilizing? Why/why not?

To differentiate the lessons in the unit and meet the needs of her students at different levels of reading ability and language proficiency, Ms. Inkanish decided to begin by building students' background knowledge. She had students watch a streaming video on U.S. mobilization for WWII that included Spanish subtitles. To help students focus on the key ideas in the video that related to the lesson objective, she provided them with a graphic organizer:

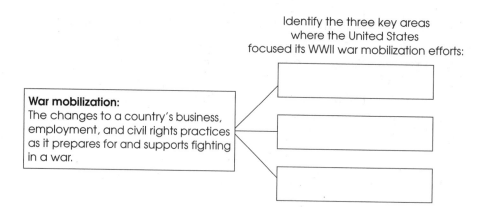

Ms. Inkanish had given a copy of the graphic organizer to Student H the day before viewing the video, so that she would have time to look up the word in her English–Spanish dictionary. Each of the key areas students were to identify was explicitly mentioned in the video and supported by a title graphic that appeared on the screen. After students viewed the 10-minute video, Ms. Inkanish modeled how she identified one of the key ideas in the video (the "I do" phase): "I heard the narrator say, 'There were many important changes to domestic policies that moved the United States away from isolationism,' and then the subtitle even flashed on the screen. The emphasis the narrator put on 'domestic policies' when he said 'important changes,' and the supporting subtitle used in the clip, tell me that this is a key area to include on our graphic organizer."

She wrote this in the top box of the graphic organizer she had projected on the screen at the front of the room. Ms. Ikanish then asked the students to help her complete the next box (the "We do" phase). "Tell me another one of the areas mentioned in the video where the United States focused its WWII war mobilization efforts," she prompted the students. As students offered the other key areas, Ms. Inkanish typed them into the graphic organizer and asked students to share what they learned: "What did you see and hear in the video about why this area was considered important?"

She also encouraged students to compare what they had learned from the video to what they learned in other lessons: "Have we studied any other historical event during which the United States took a similar approach?" By doing this, she was incorporating student engagement by making connections to other lessons and content. After soliciting an idea from a student and recording it in the graphic organizer, she had partners explain why they thought this was or was not a "key idea" to include. This offered students many opportunities to discuss their developing understanding.

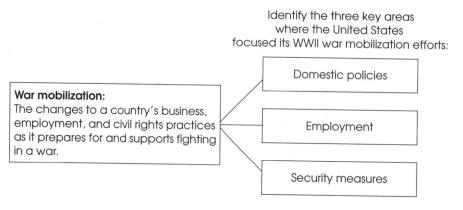

After approximately 12 minutes of this discussion, Ms. Inkanish divided the students into six groups of five students each, as follows:

Group 1	Group 2	Group 3	Group 4	Group 5	Group 6
Student A (word-level)	Student B (word-level)	Student C (fluency and comprehension)	Student D (fluency and comprehension)	On-grade-level student	On-grade-level student
Student H (emergent)	Student E (fluency and comprehension)	Student I (intermediate)	Student F (fluency and comprehension)	On-grade-level student	On-grade-level student
Student G (fluency and comprehension)	On-grade-level student	On-grade-level student	On-grade-level student	On-grade-level student	On-grade-level student
On-grade-level student	On-grade-level student	On-grade-level student	On-grade-level student	Above-grade-level student	Above-grade-level student
On-grade-level student	On-grade-level student	On-grade-level student	On-grade-level student	Above-grade-level student	Above-grade-level student

The groups were asked to gather additional information on one of the three key areas where the United States focused its WWII mobilization efforts. Groups 1 and 2 were assigned a short passage about employment issues during the WWII mobilization effort. The passage was written on a lower readability level and was available in electronic format with embedded hyperlinks for word pronunciations, definitions, and illustrations or visual cues. In addition, the text could be copied and pasted into the translation program, so Student H could choose to read all or portions of the passage in her native language. In addition, Ms. Inkanish provided these groups with a cause–effect organizer:

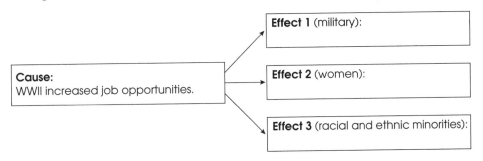

The clues to the effects, noted in parentheses, were only provided on the papers of Students A, B, and H.

Groups 3 and 4 were assigned a slightly longer and moderately challenging passage on the security measures adopted by the U.S. government during WWII. Although just under three pages long, this text included its own glossary to support students' understanding of the terms used. In addition, it had several photographs of internment camps. Ms. Inkanish provided these groups with a different cause–effect graphic organizer:

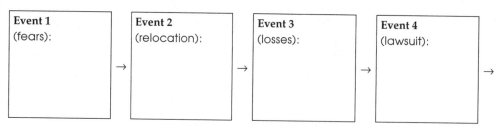

| Event 1 (fears): | | Event 2 (relocation): | | Event 3 (losses): | | Event 4 (lawsuit): | |

The clues to the events, noted in parentheses, were only provided on the paper of Student I initially, but Students C, D, and F were told that they could request clues if necessary. Only Student D requested the parenthetical clues.

Groups 5 and 6 were assigned a slightly more challenging reading on the domestic policies of the United States as it mobilized for WWII. This was found in Sections 3 and 4 of Chapter 25 in the textbook, so some terms were given in boldface and defined in the glossary. There was also an overview at the beginning of the chapter, as well as "stop and check" questions at the end of the chapter. Students were not required to answer the questions, but Ms. Inkanish told them that the questions might help them consider what information was most important. These groups were asked to create a graphic representation of the cause–effect relationships among the economic conditions in the country and the U.S. policies and agencies created to mobilize the economy for the war effort. Ms. Inkanish offered sample templates to these groups if they needed ideas for how to create a cause–effect graphic organizer. Only students in Group 5 asked to review the samples.

Students worked in their groups for the rest of the period that day and the first 15 minutes of the period the next day. Then Ms. Inkanish asked Groups 1, 3, and 5 to share their information with each other, while Groups 2, 4, and 6 did the same. She made sure that all students had printed copies of each passage and graphic organizer.

For the third day of the unit, Ms. Inkanish had students generate questions as a homework assignment. They were to formulate questions about information that was confusing, that had something in common across the passages, or that had noticeable differences from one passage to the next. Ms. Inkanish distributed a list of stems such as these to help students formulate their questions:

- What does _____ mean/refer to in the sentence on page ____: "_____"?
- How is _____ from passage _____ related/similar to _____ from passage _____?
- Why is _____ in passage _____ not like/different from _____ in passage _____?

Students came to class with at least three questions, and worked on finding answers to the questions with different partners as Ms. Inkanish rotated students through a sequence of pairings. They completed four rounds of question answering with four different partners.

On the fourth day of the unit, Ms. Inkanish prepared her students for the writing assignment that would assess their learning. They would be asked to evaluate U.S. efforts to mobilize for WWII, using the information they had read and discussed. Ms. Inkanish distributed a prewriting template to help students organize their ideas.

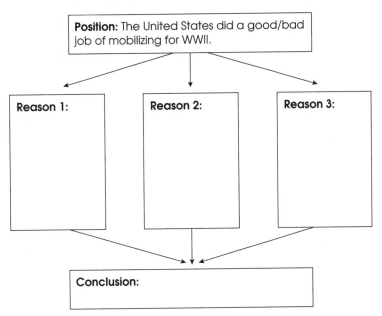

Ms. Inkanish had previously modeled completing this template when the class had written an essay together, using information from a previous unit. Therefore, she was able to review the procedures before assigning partners of slightly different ability levels to work on generating the ideas for the template. With the assistance of a more capable peer, Students C–G and Student I were able to complete the work successfully. However, Ms. Inkanish pulled together Students A, B, and H (the students with word-level difficulties and the ELL student at an emergent level of English proficiency) to provide extra assistance with the prewriting activity.

When everyone was ready to draft their essays on the fifth day of the unit, Ms. Inkanish gave Students A through I a list of vocabulary words from the unit, as well as transitional phrases. Students A, B, and H were also provided with sentence stems for starting each of the five paragraphs. For example, the stem to start the concluding paragraph was: "I believe that _____, _____, and _____ support the position that _____." Students H and I were encouraged to draft their papers in Spanish before attempting to write the information in English. Finally, all students were able to use a computer from the mobile laptop station.

STOP *Stop and Think*

The example of differentiated instruction provided in Box 2.1 is based on a social studies class, but should be considered applicable to all core academic classes. Take a moment to consider how you might apply the ideas to differentiate a lesson in a course you teach. You might also consider incorporating some strategies taught in the reading intervention tier(s) as a form of differentiation for students who are struggling with the literacy demands of the content area. For suggestions, see Appendix E.

CROSS-CURRICULAR LITERACY SUPPORTS

In addition to the practices considered to be generally effective, three-tiered models for literacy instruction and intervention include specific supports for vocabulary, reading comprehension, and writing. Core literacy instruction in middle and high schools helps students read and write like historians, scientists, mathematicians, and literary critics. Because each discipline has unique ways of using language to communicate important ideas and concepts, students may struggle with the literacy demands of all subjects or only one subject area.

In elementary schools, the same teacher typically delivers the instruction for all content areas and can monitor how students are handling different text genres and formats. Because middle and high schools are departmentalized, every teacher (not just the ELAR teachers) plays a necessary role in Tier 1. It is essential that they weave scientifically based vocabulary and comprehension strategies into their daily instruction. Tables 2.2 and 2.3 compare and contrast Tier 1 literacy instruction components at the elementary level (Table 2.2) with the components at the secondary level (Table 2.3).

For RTI to be considered a "schoolwide approach," it is important to adopt a few specific instructional routines that can be implemented in all core academic classes to support students' reading and learning from content-area texts (Deshler et al., 2001; Jacobs, 2008). When all teachers agree to incorporate a select, manageable set of vocabulary and comprehension instructional routines, they can support each other in planning lessons and share the burden of helping students become accustomed to using the practices (Bryant, Linan-Thompson, Ugel, Hamff, & Hougen, 2001; Sturtevant & Linek, 2003).

So which vocabulary and comprehension strategies should your school select, and how many of them does the school need? There are many content-area literacy programs and strategies available (see suggested resources in Appendix F), but you will want to identify those with the best evidence of effectiveness. This is usually not an easy task. First, it is important to understand what qualifies as a research or evidence base for an effective literacy practice. Every commercially available program and professional development package claims to have research support. Therefore, you have to become a good consumer of the programs and the available research by learning to scrutinize the material according to accepted guidelines for high-quality research (Stanovich & Stanovich, 2003). In addition to checking the reports available through the U.S. Department of Education's What

TABLE 2.2. Elementary Tier 1 Literacy Instruction

Focus

For all students

Program

Scientifically based instructional practices focusing on phonemic awareness, phonics, fluency, vocabulary, and comprehension

Grouping

Whole class and flexible groups

Time

Uninterrupted 90-minute block

Assessment

Screening assessment/benchmark

Interventionist

General education teacher

Setting

General education classroom

Note. Adapted with permission from the University of Texas Center for Reading and Language Arts. (2005). *3-tier reading model: Reducing reading difficulties for kindergarten through third grade students.* Austin, TX: Author.

TABLE 2.3. Secondary Tier 1 Literacy Instruction

Focus

For all students

Program

Scientifically based vocabulary and comprehension strategies

Grouping

Whole class and flexible groups

Time

All content-area classes, all day

Assessment

Screening assessment/benchmark

Interventionist

General education teacher

Setting

General education classroom

Note. Adapted with permission from the University of Texas Center for Reading and Language Arts. (2005). *3-tier reading model: Reducing reading difficulties for kindergarten through third grade students.* Austin, TX: Author.

Works Clearinghouse (available at *ies.ed.gov/ncee/wwc*), you can evaluate the extent to which research on a strategy or program:

- Was independently conducted (i.e., the study was not done by the authors or developers of the strategy).
- Used reliable and valid standardized measures to report findings.
- Included a comparison group of similar ability levels and demographics that did not participate in the program or receive the recommended instructional treatment.
- Utilized participants of similar ages (and, ideally, of similar demographics) as the students in your school who will receive the program or instruction.
- Was published in a professional journal that utilizes a rigorous review process (preferably a "blind" review by other researchers) to ensure the quality of the methods and increase the confidence in the findings.
- Reported effect sizes to demonstrate how well the program or instruction improved student performance over typical practice or whatever instruction was provided in the comparison condition.

Selecting Materials

The following checklist can be used to evaluate textbooks and other instructional materials for their appropriateness in supporting the literacy needs of adolescents at Tier 1. It is unlikely that any one textbook or resource will include all the elements listed, but better texts will include more of the items. The checklist can provide a quick reference to any missing components of vocabulary, comprehension, and writing support in the materials you select. Wherever an item is checked "no" on the list, you will need to plan supplemental lessons or activities that will address those needs.

	Yes	No
Vocabulary		
1. Does the text identify a small set of words that are critical for comprehension of each passage/chapter?		
2. Does the teacher's edition suggest how to adjust the target set of words for students of lower and higher ability levels?		
3. Does the teacher's edition or ancillary material provide explicit instruction in and activities for analyzing words by prefixes, roots, and suffixes?		
4. Is each word initially defined with a student-friendly definition and an example of the word in context?		
5. Does the teacher's edition or ancillary material provide explicit instruction in and activities for using contextual analysis to infer word meanings?		
6. Does the teacher's edition or ancillary material suggest ways in which words can be related or contrasted?		
7. Are there suggestions for ways to provide multiple exposures to vocabulary words?		
8. Does the teacher's edition or ancillary material provide explicit instruction in and activities for how to use dictionaries to confirm and deepen knowledge of word meanings?		
9. Are there suggestions for how to encourage discussion and use of targeted words?		
10. Does the teacher's edition suggest how to support students who are struggling to learn the target words?		
Comprehension		
1. Does the teacher's edition suggest how to explicitly teach comprehension skills, such as previewing, finding the main idea, summarizing, and drawing conclusions?		
2. Does the text or supplemental material include methods for activating and building students' prior knowledge of concepts related to those addressed in the passage?		
3. Are there suggestions for how to encourage discussion about the key concepts before, during, and after reading?		

4. Is there specific guidance in the text for students to generate and answer their own questions about what they are reading?		
5. Are the questions provided in the text or supplemental material at different levels of complexity?		
6. Does the teacher's edition suggest how to support the learning of students at lower and higher ability levels by: • Offering alternative texts/passages to read? • Requiring collaboration with peers? • Providing intervention and extension activities?		
7. Does the text or supplemental material consistently organize the information in a given passage in a common text structure (description, sequencing/procedural, cause–effect, problem–solution, persuasion/position–reason, compare/contrast)?		
8. Does the teacher's edition or ancillary material provide graphic organizers for organizing and relating key information from a passage?		
Writing		
1. Are writing prompts provided that require students to: • Synthesize information? • Communicate ideas to a specific audience? • Demonstrate learning of subject matter concepts?		
2. Does the teacher's edition or ancillary material provide explicit instruction in and activities for prewriting (to include brainstorming, planning, and collaborating/researching)?		
3. Does the teacher's edition or ancillary material provide explicit instruction in and activities for how to draft a one-paragraph response versus a multiparagraph essay?		
4. Does the teacher's edition or ancillary material provide explicit instruction in and activities for how to review a draft for mechanics and content?		
5. Are model responses provided?		
6. Are there suggestions for how to encourage discussion and collaboration among students as they review and revise drafts?		
7. Does the teacher's edition or ancillary material provide explicit instruction in and activities for how to combine sentences?		
8. Does the teacher's edition or ancillary material provide explicit instruction in and activities for how to finalize and publish a written response?		

Stop and Think

Identifying appropriate supplementary instructional materials can be challenging if your school or district does not already provide a curriculum bundle (a compendium of the key ideas, guiding questions, state standards, examples, and resources teachers should use for planning instruction). Additional resources can be found at the websites listed in Appendix F. Note that all items are free of charge.

If you are curious about some of the instructional strategies referenced in the descriptors on the checklist, please refer to Appendix D. There you will find samples of vocabulary and comprehension strategies as they might be applied to the different content areas as well as to reading intervention classes. Having an idea of what the strategies look like when applied to content might better prepare you to evaluate materials.

Supporting Content-Area Teachers in Providing Tier 1 Instruction

Once you have narrowed the pool of possible programs and strategies to those that have a better evidence basis, the next step is to consider which will best meet the needs of all content area teachers. If the strategies are to be implemented schoolwide, they need to be easily integrated into lessons across the academic core: ELAR, mathematics, science, and social studies. Some strategies may be useful in ELAR and social studies where long passages of connected text are more common, but less practical for a mathematics class where word problems are the more likely "texts."

We have found that vocabulary or concept instruction is a reasonable and effective entry point into content-area instruction. All courses have vocabulary and concepts with which students need to be familiar in order to meet the learning goals. In fact, most teachers tell us that the sheer numbers of words they think their students do not know is overwhelming. To make the Tier 1 literacy support relevant, you might start by helping teachers determine which words or concepts in their courses merit direct instruction and which just need to be provided to students so they can focus on the content. From there, we have found that teachers are receptive to learning two or three fairly simple evidence-based instructional routines for introducing unfamiliar multisyllable words and fostering increasingly deep knowledge of the words over distributed practice. Some suggestions for these initial efforts with vocabulary include the following:

- Ways for teachers to classify words into content-specific, academic, and common words.
- Routines to help students break multisyllable words apart by syllables and/or morphemes (prefixes, roots, and suffixes).
- Opportunities to explore examples and nonexamples of words being used in different contexts.
- Opportunities to compare and contrast related words.

These are reasonable ways to initiate Tier 1 literacy support, but creating awareness of vocabulary words and teaching students to use two or three word-learning strategies will not be enough to make all texts accessible to all students. More will need to be done to address specific vocabulary needs within subject areas, as well as to expand the support to encompass reading comprehension and writing. But your experience with overly ambitious professional development initiatives is probably consistent with ours. Trying to do too much too quickly is a recipe for disaster under typical circumstances, but this is even more true when planning Tier 1 instruction, because many content-area teachers feel ill prepared to provide literacy instruction or to adapt the supports to the unique needs of their disciplines (Kosanovich, Reed, & Miller, 2010).

We suggest taking an incremental approach and offering teachers sufficient time and professional resources to build confidence and success with the new practices. Schools that have had greater success at integrating literacy across the curriculum report doing these things:

- Drawing on the teachers' perceived needs and responding to the unique literacy issues of the content areas (Reed, 2009; Siebert & Draper, 2008).
- Ensuring time for collaborative planning and access to materials (Bryant et al., 2001; Deshler et al., 2001).
- Providing some form of skilled facilitation and ongoing support (Bryant et al., 2000; Nichols, Young, & Rickelman, 2007; Reed & Groth, 2009).

(i) THE APPLICATION OF LITERACY STRATEGIES ACROSS CONTENT AREAS

Resources for cross-curricular literacy strategies and programs are provided in Appendix F, but it is important to note that using a set of agreed-upon vocabulary and comprehension supports across content areas does not mean that the routines and strategies will be rigidly implemented. Each discipline has unique needs and styles of communicating information that become increasingly complex through the grade levels (Shanahan & Shanahan, 2008). Disregarding those specific concerns can make content-area teachers resistant to, and perhaps resentful of, the schoolwide approach. To be able to capitalize on the consistency and efficiency created by adopting a few common literacy practices across the curriculum, you also need to plan for assisting teachers with making the instruction appropriate for their particular courses.

For example, a two-column note-taking procedure for monitoring text comprehension can be implemented in different ways, depending on the kind of thinking and the organization of information required for the discipline. When reading a novel for ELAR class, students might record the main ideas in the left column and elaborating or clarifying details in the right column. When reading an article about a scientific experiment or discovery, students might record the observations in the left column and the scientist's interpretations of those observable facts in the right column. In mathematics, students might record particular concepts or theorems in the left column and explanations or examples of problems in the right column. Finally, in social studies, students might record events or an individual's position points in the left column and the historical, geographical, and cultural influences on those events or positions in the left column. In this way, all teachers would be implementing a common structure for comprehension support, but it would be tailored to the purposes and goals of each content area.

Fidelity Observations

Although some of these types of subject-specific changes to literacy strategies and routines are needed, there usually are key components of the strategies related to the features of effective instruction that should not be altered. The literacy leadership team overseeing the work (described in the last section of this chapter) will need to monitor the fidelity with which adopted strategies are implemented. We want to emphasize that this is not done to catch teachers doing something wrong so they can be punished. Rather, *fidelity observations* guide the leadership team in interpreting student data (e.g., whether progress or lack of progress can be attributed to instruction) and identifying areas for future professional development or individualized assistance.

It is our belief that most teachers do not lie awake at night plotting ways to undermine Tier 1 or the effectiveness of cross-curricular literacy instruction. It is much more likely that teachers are doing the best they know how to do and would appreciate feedback and structured assistance in refining their implementation. Without clearly defined fidelity protocols, observations will tend to be more evaluative and will generate data that cannot be compared across classrooms or time. A sample fidelity observation tool can be found in Figure 2.1.

You will notice that the fidelity observation tool in Figure 2.1 includes sections that correspond to the areas of cross-curricular literacy support (vocabulary and text comprehension) and some of the features of effective instruction introduced in this chapter. The descriptors are general enough to be used with a variety of strategies and in different content areas; however, you may wish to add components that are more specific to particular strategies or programs adopted for Tier 1. More explanation of and resources for fidelity observations at Tiers 2 and 3 are provided in Chapters 4 and 5. As we discuss in those chapters, the tool in Figure 2.1 can also be customized to include the specific strategies or programs adopted for use in the intervention classes.

 Stop and Think

> *The fidelity observations described in this section include indicators that are stated rather generally. This is to enable their use across content areas and to maintain the focus of teachers and observers on the features of effective instruction, rather than the nuances of a content area. Fidelity observations in elementary schools are often much more specific, because they are conducted during the 90-minute reading block as opposed to during math, science, or social studies instruction.*

Descriptive information		
Date:	Monitor:	Site:
Weekday:	Observer:	District:
Period(s):	Length of observation:	Observation round:

Components	Start time	End time	Implementation quality				N/A
			4	3	2	1	
Vocabulary instruction							
A portion of the period is dedicated to explicit vocabulary instruction.							
Evidence of multiple exposures to vocabulary exists.							
Direct and explicit strategy instruction							
Direct instruction in how to use explicit comprehension strategies is provided.							
Students are provided time to independently practice the comprehension strategies.							
Extended discussion of text meaning and interpretation							
A specific discussion protocol is utilized.							
Follow-up questions are asked to extend comprehension discussions.							
Motivation							
Goals are explicitly stated.							
Goals are connected to other disciplines.							
Goals are connected to students' lives outside of the classroom.							

(cont.)

FIGURE 2.1. Fidelity observation guide for use in all tiers of instruction. Adapted from Edmunds, M., & Briggs, K. (2003). The Instructional Content Emphasis Instrument: Observations of reading instruction. In S. Vaughn & K. L. Briggs (Eds.), *Reading in the classroom: Systems for the observation of teaching and learning* (pp. 31–52). Baltimore: Brookes. Copyright 2003 by Paul H. Brookes Publishing Co., Inc. Adapted by permission. Also adapted from Kamil et al. (2008) and Wexler, Vaughn, & Roberts (2010).

Student engagement	15 min.	30 min.	45 min.
Indicate overall student engagement at specified intervals throughout the class period.			

Indicators of Engagement

Count students as engaged if they are following along or are focused on activity, but not necessarily vocally participating.

4   High engagement =   Almost all (90% or more) students are actively engaged in learning activity (reading, writing, listening, talking about relevant topic).

3   Medium engagement = Most (75% or more) students are actively engaged in learning activity (reading, writing, listening, talking about a relevant topic).

2   Low engagement =   More than half (51–74%) staring out the window, engaging in idle chatter, fiddling with materials, inappropriately moving about the classroom.

1   No engagement =   Most students (75% or more) are *not* engaged; entire class participating in activities not associated with class content.

Quality Indicators and Descriptors

4 Excellent	3 Average	2 Weak	1 No occurrence of component
Uses language that is direct and explicit.	Inconsistently uses language that is direct and explicit.	Uses language that is indirect and implicit.	Component applicable to lesson content, but teacher fails to attempt.
Models many examples.	Provides some examples.	Provides no models or examples.	
Provides sufficient and varied opportunities for practice.	Provides many opportunities for practice with little variation. Practice opportunities do not seem to be based on student need.	Provides insufficient opportunities for practice with no variation.	
Provides immediate corrective and descriptive feedback.	Provides inconsistent feedback.	Provides little feedback, nonspecific feedback, or no feedback.	

(cont.)

FIGURE 2.1. *(cont.)*

4 Excellent	3 Average	2 Weak	1 No occurrence of component
Adjusts time to meet students' needs.	Uses time appropriately. Use does not always seem based on student need, yet still seems adequate for given activity.	Demonstrates poor use of time. Use is not differentiated and seems unrelated to student need or task difficulty.	
Constantly monitors student performance.	Monitors some students, or monitors all students for some activities.	Demonstrates lack of monitoring or monitoring of very few students.	
Scaffolds tasks and materials to meet student needs.	Uses scaffolding inconsistently and does not always tailor it to student needs.	Scaffolds inappropriately or insufficiently.	
Uses appropriate pacing, including wait time.	Uses inconsistent pacing that varies from appropriate at times to too fast or too slow and provides insufficient wait time.	Demonstrates poor pacing—either too slow or too fast, with not wait time provided.	

FIGURE 2.1. *(cont.)*

SCREENING ASSESSMENTS

In addition to fidelity data, student data are important to informing the Tier 1 core instruction. The role of assessment at this level of the RTI model is to monitor all students to ensure that they are on track to meet grade-level standards, which in turn can give you important information about the effectiveness of your Tier 1 instruction. The standards are established by your state, and students are assessed during annual criterion-referenced testing to determine whether they meet the standards. We encourage you to use these data as an integral part of the universal screening system, because (1) the tests are routinely administered and do not require procuring other resources; and (2) the data typically offer a confidence interval or range of scores considered to be "on the bubble" between passing and not passing, which can be used to capture a wider range of students needing support.

This makes the annual state assessment an efficient screening tool, or a means of identifying students who do not appear to be meeting or maintaining performance targets. It is important to keep in mind, however, that these tests are administered toward the end of the year. This means that the results come too late to permit you to adjust instruction or consider supplemental interventions that would prevent failure. Perhaps your school or district has already acknowledged this limitation and instituted interim benchmark or short-cycle assessments to help you gauge your students' progress toward the summative test. If you do not currently use benchmarks, you might explore options for administering formative assessments three to four times per year to gather information on how students are performing in the core content areas. (Assessment resources are provided in Appendix F.)

In the elementary grades, these formative measures usually provide the first opportunity for teachers to determine who is struggling. By the time students reach you in middle or high school, it is usually apparent who is having difficulty reading and writing. You may not have detailed information on what is causing each student's difficulty, but that is the role of the diagnostic assessments used in intervention. Tier 1 screening measures only need to alert you that a student may be struggling with reading. A well-planned and coordinated system of assessment will prevent students from "slipping through the cracks."

What if benchmark assessments are not an option for you? Or what if you find that the benchmark data are not very accurate at identifying students in need of intervention? The informal assessments you typically use may be a useful source of screening data. High-quality classroom tests can be used to gauge how well your students understand the specific texts used in the course. These assessments are referred to as *curriculum-based measures* (CBMs), because they are tied to the particular content students are learning. In ELAR classes, the CBMs are more likely to be directly connected to comprehension and vocabulary objectives. However, CBMs for mathematics, science, and social studies courses can also provide information on students' progress in developing the vocabulary of each content area and improving their reading comprehension in the area's unique texts.

It is possible, for example, that an incorrect answer to a science question was due to a student's lack of technical vocabulary knowledge or understanding of the style of language used to communicate scientific information, rather than to his or her deficiencies with science skills. If CBM results are analyzed to consider the contribution of students' reading skills in combination with their content knowledge and skills, the data can help you more quickly identify those in need of reading support, as opposed to support in the specific content area. The literacy leadership team (described in the last section of this chapter) will need to plan for professional development (described in the next section) that can build teachers' capacity to look at their CBM data in this way.

Regardless of the screening assessment(s) you use, keep in mind that the goals are (1) to gauge students' overall academic reading ability, and (2) to distinguish students for whom Tier 1 instruction is sufficient from students for whom an additional class in reading (i.e., reading intervention) may be necessary.* As you know, students' performance can change over the course of a year. Some students who

---

*Remember that although our focus in this book is on reading, these recommendations regarding screening assessments in an RTI framework can also be applied to a mathematics focus area.

were doing well in the first month or even semester of school can begin to struggle as the content and texts become increasingly complex (Biancarosa & Snow, 2004; Perfetti, Landi, & Oakhill, 2005). That is why we encourage groups of teachers to work together to examine student data from benchmarks or CBMs once a quarter or once a trimester. The sooner students can be identified as having learning problems, the more likely it is that reading and/or academic failure can be prevented by adjusting instruction appropriately. Scheduling considerations associated with these periodic evaluations are addressed in the next chapter.

 Stop and Think

> *For more information on how screening at the secondary level differs from that at the elementary level, review Chapter 1 and the assessment resources provided in Appendix F.*

PROFESSIONAL DEVELOPMENT FOR LITERACY IN ALL CONTENT AREAS

As we have indicated above, professional development is essential to building the capacity of those who are responsible for carrying out the components of RTI. Like many educators who are involved in this process, you may be wondering where you should start. What should your priorities be? What do administrators and teachers need to know, and what are the more effective ways of providing support?

Overall, professional development needs to be thoroughly planned, to be provided incrementally in a logical sequence, and to include adequate follow-up support for teachers to address their specific concerns and needs. The checklist that follows suggests critical topics for professional development in content-area literacy.

Has the faculty demonstrated mastery of:

	Yes	No
Effective instruction		
1. Setting clear objectives for what students should know and be able to do?		
2. Modeling what to do, when, and how?		
3. Establishing the purpose for using learning strategies?		
4. Gradually releasing responsibility for completing work to students?		
5. Offering distributed practice in skills and strategies?		
6. Providing follow-up instruction to students?		
7. Offering reasonable choices in students' learning?		
8. Differentiating instruction to meet the needs of students with diverse ability levels and language proficiencies?		

Vocabulary		
1. Identifying words for instruction?		
2. Analyzing words by syllables and morphemes?		
3. Directly teaching new words?		
4. Using contextual analysis to infer word meanings?		
5. Providing examples and nonexamples of word meanings and applications?		
6. Relating and contrasting words?		
7. Providing multiple exposures to words?		
8. Using a dictionary to confirm and deepen knowledge of word meanings?		
9. Encouraging word consciousness and the use of words in different contexts?		
10. Scaffolding vocabulary instruction with word-learning strategies?		
Comprehension		
1. Explicitly teaching comprehension skills such as previewing, finding the main idea, summarizing, and drawing conclusions?		
2. Activating prior knowledge and/or building background knowledge?		
3. Fostering discussion about key concepts before, during, and after reading?		
4. Teaching students to generate and answer their own questions about what they are reading?		
5. Asking questions at different levels of complexity?		
6. Supporting the learning of students at lower and higher ability levels by: • Offering alternative texts/passages to read? • Incorporating collaboration with peers? • Providing intervention and extension activities?		
7. Teaching students to recognize common text structure (description, sequencing/procedural, cause–effect, problem–solution, persuasion/position–reason, compare/contrast)?		
8. Creating and using graphic organizers for organizing and relating key information from a passage?		
Writing		
1. Developing and providing writing prompts that require students to: • Synthesize information? • Communicate ideas to a specific audience? • Demonstrate learning of subject matter concepts?		
2. Teaching prewriting (to include brainstorming, planning, and collaborating/researching)?		
3. Teaching students to draft one-paragraph responses and multiparagraph essays?		
4. Teaching students how to review a draft for writing mechanics and content?		

5. Using writing models?		
6. Fostering discussion and collaboration among students to review and revise drafts?		
7. Teaching students how to combine sentences?		
8. Teaching students how to finalize and publish a written response?		
Assessment		
1. Organizing data?		
2. Interpreting benchmark assessment data?		
3. Planning or modifying instruction based on assessment data?		
4. Communicating assessment results to students, parents, and other stakeholders?		

In addition to the major headings in the checklist above, teachers may need professional development in fostering an environment conducive to learning. This topic is addressed in the next section, but we want you to understand that behavior and other issues related to teachers' ability to deliver strong Tier 1 instruction may be added to the checklist to meet the needs of your school.

When a school is first implementing RTI, the staff as a whole may be the subject of the checklist. Any element checked "no" is a possible topic for professional development. In these early stages, certain sessions are generally provided to all teachers to bring everyone up to a minimum level of skill in effective Tier 1 literacy instruction or to introduce a starting area for such instruction (e.g., the vocabulary recommendation we have given previously in the "Cross-Curricular Literacy supports" section). Keep in mind that some sessions will need to be repeated from year to year as new teachers and support staffers join the school.

In the past, we have devoted a full day (in the summer or during the back-to-school professional development time) to preliminary information, according to the following schedule:

8:00–8:30: Explanation of why we are undertaking this work in RTI for literacy

8:30–9:45: Overview of effective instruction

9:45–10:00: Break

10:00–10:30: Time for groups of teachers to plan lessons incorporating effective instruction (with facilitators present for guidance)

10:30–11:00: Selecting vocabulary words for instruction

11:00–11:30: Time for groups of teachers to work together on identifying vocabulary words for instruction in their course materials (with facilitators present for guidance)

11:30–12:30: Lunch

12:30–1:00: Breaking apart multisyllable words

1:00–1:30:   Time for groups of teachers to plan lessons incorporating the instructional routine(s) for breaking apart multisyllable words (with facilitators present for guidance)

1:30–1:45:   Break

1:45–2:45:   Generating examples and nonexamples of vocabulary word use/application

2:45–3:15:   Time for groups of teachers to plan lessons incorporating instruction in generating examples and nonexamples (with facilitators present for guidance)

3:15–3:30:   Explanation of the follow-up plan

After this initial session, individual teachers or small groups of teachers may need a specially designed professional development plan to support their implementation or the unique requirements of a content area. For example, a math teacher may require specialized professional development on how to adapt comprehension strategies for use with word problems. Other areas of support may be identified in the fidelity observations (described above in the "Cross-Curricular Literacy Supports" section) and noted on a checklist completed for a single teacher or small group of teachers. Therefore, the follow-up plan (referred to in the 3:15–3:30 time slot on the sample schedule) should include these components:

- One faculty meeting devoted to explaining the fidelity observations (see Figure 2.2 for suggested explanations), and subsequent faculty meetings to update the teachers on the progress toward implementing the schoolwide practices.
- Weekly meetings among small groups of teachers to plan lessons and examine student data. These can occur before/after school or during daily planning times.
- Monthly visits by a consultant or literacy expert within the district, who can address literacy issues specific to each department.
- Professional development days distributed throughout the year to introduce one or two new literacy instructional routines/strategies at a time. These can be departmentalized sessions or may be delivered on a whole-group basis if the practices are appropriate (with only slight adaptation) for all content areas.
- Structures for providing in-class modeling of or coaching on the new practices, as well as for observing peers delivering the instruction.

Consider the sample professional development schedule, suggested follow-up activities, and checklist as starting points from which a professional development plan appropriate for your school's faculty can be devised. Like students, teachers

Who conducts them?

Members of the RTI literacy leadership team who have been trained in the proper implementation of each component of the program, strategy, or instructional practice being observed.

What are they?

A means to (1) monitor the implementation of an adopted program, strategy, or instructional practice, to ensure that classroom instruction is closely aligned with the intended procedures, methods, and content; (2) gather data on the school's overall progress in implementing the program, strategy, or practice; and (3) gather data on the areas in which to provide teachers with further support.

When are they done?

Weekly at first, and monthly thereafter for those teachers who achieve and maintain 80% or better mastery of all instructional components.

Where are the data kept?

In a secure electronic or hard-copy file accessible to members of the RTI literacy leadership team who are responsible for planning professional development, ordering necessary materials, and evaluating the school's progress.

Why are they important?

Many programs, strategies, and instructional practices fail to achieve desired results because they are not implemented in the ways the developers and researchers intended. Just as students need feedback on how they are performing, teachers also need very specific information about how well their instruction aligns to the procedures, methods, and content. Conducting classroom observations also communicates to the students and faculty that the initiative is important and ongoing.

How is the information used?

Data are used to (1) plan subsequent professional development for individuals as well as groups; (2) purchase additional resources or tools that would improve the quality and efficiency of implementation; and (3) evaluate the effectiveness of the adopted program, strategy, or instructional practice.

FIGURE 2.2. Fidelity observations.

have differing degrees of background knowledge in and experience with Tier 1 literacy instruction. It is important to consider their levels of expertise with the topics outlined on the checklist before making any decisions.

 Stop and Think

The description of professional development takes into consideration that teachers from all core content areas will be participating. Although all teachers may participate together when initially learning about a vocabulary or comprehension strategy, they will need more individualized assistance in tailoring the application of that strategy to a particular content area. We want to emphasize, again, that combining literacy and content instruction is no easy task and requires extensive support. This non-negotiable of RTI at the secondary level is addressed in Chapter 5.

MAKING THE SCHOOL ENVIRONMENT CONDUCIVE TO LEARNING

Many middle and high school administrators comment that without a systematic, schoolwide plan, issues related to discipline (e.g., classroom behavior, tardies, dress code violations) can consume their attention each day (Education Trust, 2005). Similarly, teachers report that they spend the majority of any collaborative planning time discussing matters unrelated to instruction (Conley, Fauske, & Pounder, 2004; Reed & Groth, 2009). Despite the best intentions, our jobs can become a game of Whack-a-Mole (i.e., continually pounding down problems as they surface, without a plan to prevent them in the future) if there is not a well-designed plan in place to keep the focus of teachers and students alike on academics. Given these types of concerns, it has been suggested that schools integrate three-tiered reading and behavior models (Horner, Sugai, Todd, & Lewis-Palmer, 2005; Stewart, Benner, Martella, & Marchand-Martella, 2007). Many schools experiencing more success with an academic focus have implemented *positive behavior support* (PBS), a decision-making framework for improving student behavior (Morrissey, Bohanon, & Fenning, 2010; Sugai & Horner, 2009).

In a nutshell, PBS refocuses the "discipline plan" away from relying on a series of punishments to react to problem behavior, so that attention and resources are placed on directly teaching acceptable behaviors and providing frequent positive reinforcement (Dunlap, Carr, Horner, Zarcone, & Schwartz, 2008; Lewis, Jones, Horner, & Sugai, 2010). When problem behavior occurs, a well-functioning PBS system works to identify and alter the triggers (referred to as *antecedents*) to that behavior within the context(s) in which the behavior is exhibited. For example, rather than writing up a student named Maria for being off task during group work, a PBS system would start with the assumption that Maria is getting something out of this behavior. So what's the real issue? Is Maria avoiding a particular type of assignment or content because she doesn't feel confident doing this in front of peers? Is there someone in her group that she doesn't like or that she is trying to impress? Does she have low blood sugar at this time of day? Is she hoping to get sent out of class on a referral so that she can stroll the hallway or see a particular person in the office? Or does she just not know what is expected of her?

To continue with this example, the primary level of PBS would involve preventing Maria from being off task by directly teaching the expected behavior during group work. Therefore, teachers would need to explicitly state, model, and provide practice opportunities for the following:

- How to move into the group
- What materials to bring
- Where to find other resources that might be needed
- How loudly/softly to talk
- What each person's role is in the group
- What product is expected from each person and from the group as a whole

- How much time there is to complete the activity or parts of the activity
- Whether there is a choice to work independently on all or part of the activity
- How to respond to group members' questions and suggestions
- How to disagree appropriately and respectfully with a group member
- What it looks and sounds like when a group is on task and working together versus off task and/or not working together
- How to let a teacher know of any problems

This probably seems like a long list of things to teach before students can even work on the actual content of the assignment. Unfortunately, the list is probably not even complete. Even though you may wish that students came to middle or high school already knowing these skills, the time you spend explicitly teaching and modeling the skills during the group work will pay off later when you have less stress and, more importantly, more successful students.

As multitiered instruction in reading does, PBS involves secondary prevention strategies (e.g., social skills training and academic support), as well as tertiary interventions for students who need additional structure. In each phase, students are involved in self-monitoring their progress toward the behavior goals; this not only motivates the students, but reduces their reliance upon external control. In essence, PBS institutes a 3-tier model around behavior in much the same way that the three-tiered model described in this book is structured for literacy. Websites offering more complete resources for understanding and implementing PBS are listed in Appendix F.

Our purpose here is not to teach you how to create a PBS system, but to make you aware of this as one model for eliminating chaos within the school. To create an environment conducive to learning, everyone in the system needs to understand "the way business is done here." If too much time, attention, and energy are diverted to dealing with discipline, no one in the building can focus properly on academics. No matter what system you choose to implement, remember that the intent should be to take away discipline as a possible distracter. The fewer discipline problems with which schools have to deal, the more they can focus on the primary goal: creating a strong Tier 1 where research-based instruction is being effectively delivered.

Although behavior problems are one of the most common obstacles to creating a conducive learning environment, they are not the only distracter. Many factors beyond behavior are related to a conducive learning environment. You need to examine your own school to determine what is diverting time and attention away from academics. Here are a few questions to ask:

1. Are administrators spending more time in the office or at school functions than in classrooms where instruction is happening?
2. Are teachers frustrated with the lack of ready access to student assessment data?

3. Do you have to stop a meeting where teachers and administrators are looking at the curriculum and the assessment data, so that everyone can go outside to watch the new football scoreboard being installed in the stadium (or some similar event)?

4. Does someone have to stand in the hallway with a bullhorn before school to yell at students to get into their classrooms?

5. Are parent–teacher meetings dominated by talk of the best design for the new school shirts or whether driver's education will be offered in summer school?

6. Does every professional development day feature a motivational speaker?

7. Is it more common to find your teachers disciplining students than providing instruction?

If you have answered "yes" to any of the questions above, you may need to work on shifting the focus within your school to academics. We tell students and the larger school community what we think is most important in the ways we choose to spend our time each day and in the kinds of things that get our attention or dominate our conversations. It is one thing to put up a poster that states "We're here to learn," and another thing to show students a genuine learning environment.

 Stop and Think

> *Similar to multi-tiered reading instruction, PBS can be implemented at both the elementary and secondary levels. Some of the same differences linked to changing of classes and teachers throughout the day will apply to implementing RTI for behavior as to implementing it for reading. If you look to an elementary model for guidance on PBS, be aware that some of the organizational components may need to be adapted.*

"I CAN'T DO THIS ALONE": THE IMPORTANCE OF AN RTI LITERACY LEADERSHIP TEAM

By now, you may be thinking to yourself, "This sounds great, but what can I do to change things all by myself?" Another distinguishing characteristic of schools that have had greater success with implementing RTI is the presence of strong instructional leadership (Canter, Klotz, & Cowan, 2008; Torgesen, Houston, & Rissman, 2007). This typically includes the principal and other key administrators who have the authority to establish schoolwide priorities and devote the necessary resources to carrying them out. But a top-down directive to "do RTI" is not going to be successful. RTI is not a program that you can "do." There is no single switch you can turn on to make Tier 1 instruction happen. This is a systemic initiative that requires shared leadership among key personnel who have deep knowledge of and expertise in these components of the three-tiered model (Tackett, Roberts, Baker & Scammaca, 2009):

- The structure, policies, and procedures of RTI.
- Research, resources, and strategies for adolescent literacy.
- Ways of carrying out literacy instruction in a framework that interweaves regular and special education.

As the components above imply, this work crosses over the traditional boundaries separating academic departments in secondary schools. Therefore, we recommend establishing a literacy or RTI team to oversee the implementation of tiered literacy instruction. This team will foster coordination among content areas, support services, and other pertinent individuals or departments. Sharing the leadership responsibilities will increase the chances of gaining "buy-in" from across the school. In addition, having more people involved in and knowledgeable about the initiative will increase the likelihood that the strategies and processes will be implemented. Let's take a closer look at the structure and functioning of this group.

One of the first decisions to make involves who should be on the team. This can be a difficult decision, because people attach many feelings to invited-membership committees, particularly those with "leadership" as part of the title or function. The schools in which we have worked are tempted to put anyone and everyone who will be involved in implementing RTI onto the literacy leadership team. This may make the decision easier, but it will make management of the team much harder. A group larger than 5–8 people will not function as well. Imagine trying to set up tables in your school library for 20 people to sit around. Will they even be able to see each other? How many of them can reasonably participate in the discussion without causing the meeting to last 3 hours or more? Will participants feel free to share their ideas and opinions, or will they be discouraged about participating in such a large group? Ultimately, the people you might have thought were so important to include will actually disengage themselves and may even carry negative feelings about the group back to their colleagues.

It is much better to be purposeful about selecting the right group to direct the work. Certainly the principal will have to be involved, but not every administrator needs to be a member. If there is an academic dean or director of curriculum and instruction at the school, that person should participate. If there is no administrative position comparable to this, the person most familiar with course requirements and scheduling, such as a head counselor, will usually be the most appropriate.

Also consider including the reading interventionist or reading specialist on the committee. If the school does not have a reading specialist, then perhaps the ELAR department head might be included. Because RTI involves the intersection of regular and special education, it is important to include the special education department head, coordinator, or lead teacher as well.

That already makes four members: principal, academic dean/course and scheduling expert, reading specialist/ELAR department chair, and special education chair. To whom should the other one to four spots be offered? In our work at Tier 1, we have found that having a math and/or science expert on the literacy leadership team is very influential in achieving buy-in for the cross-curricular literacy work. (This issue is addressed below.) The math or science contributor does not have to be the department chair; rather, it may be better to select the individual who can contribute the most to the work of the group, even if that individual has negative feelings about RTI. Hearing and constructively discussing all points of view will be important to the collaborative process.

It may also be helpful to have a representative of the school's gifted and talented (GT), advanced placement (AP), or International Baccalaureate (IB) program on the team. RTI involves meeting the needs of students at all ability levels. There should be no question that Tier 1 instruction is intended to present the appropriate amount of rigor to students who are excelling, as well as students who are performing at an average level and students who are struggling to meet minimum expectations. A team member who is associated with the "advanced" courses will help you address any concerns about lowering the standards.

The remaining positions on the literacy leadership team should be filled by individuals who provide support services. Although it is important not to make the team unmanageably large, you will want to ensure that all students are represented. Therefore, you may want to include a teacher of English as a second language (ESL) or a bilingual teacher. If you have an Advancement Via Individual Determination (AVID), Gaining Early Awareness and Readiness for Undergraduate Programs (GEAR UP), or other college readiness program, then you may want to include the program's coordinator or a key teacher. Alternatively, a paraprofessional may be included if ancillary staff members are involved in the interventions.

Figure 2.3 provides sample RTI literacy leadership team configurations for different school types. Although these are not the only possibilities for forming your team, the examples allow you to see how different stakeholders might be represented and which are consistently included across contexts.

Large middle/high school: 8 members	Medium-Sized middle/high school: 6 members	Small middle/high school: 5 members
• Principal • Academic dean • Reading specialist/literacy coach • Special ed. dept. chair • Math/science teacher • AP/IB coordinator • ESL teacher • AVID coordinator or paraprofessional	• Principal • Head counselor • ELAR dept. chair • Special ed. coordinator • Math/science teacher (who also teaches GT) • ESL teacher or paraprofessional	• Principal • Counselor • ELAR teacher • Special ed. teacher • Math/science teacher (who also teaches GT)

FIGURE 2.3. Sample RTI literacy leadership team configurations.

Stop and Think

How are the leadership team configurations suggested in Figure 2.3 unique to implementing RTI for reading at the secondary level? How are they similar to leadership team configurations at the elementary level? How can you explain this to administrators, faculty, or other staff members?

Once the RTI literacy leadership team is formed, its work might begin with these issues:

• *What are our goals, and how might we know if we have accomplished them?* A possible answer is: Our goals are to identify students with reading difficulties as early as possible, establish supplemental Tier 2 and Tier 3 interventions to support their learning needs, and monitor their progress to determine our success. We also intend to use the information from the progress monitoring at Tiers 2 and 3 to facilitate identification of students with special needs.

• *Do we have adequate schoolwide support for implementation, and if not, how might we obtain it?* A possible answer is this: We have adequate support from our school building's leaders, but the majority of teachers are unaware of what RTI is and are unsure of what the expectations for them would be. Following is a sequence of activities we need to implement to assure school-level support: (1) Principal makes announcement of RTI initiative at faculty meeting and indicates strong support with a full day of professional development on RTI in 1 month; (2) RTI professional development is scheduled, with a dynamic and informative speaker; (3) content-area lead teachers meet with their content-area teams to establish the need for RTI and to prepare key teachers for the professional development; and (4) procedures for following up on professional development and implementing key practices are established.

To help keep the focus throughout the school on effective instructional practices, your literacy leadership team can try some of the following ideas:

- Make effective instruction a part of the instructional conversation by:
  o Providing the faculty with frequent updates on the progress made in implementing effective instruction within the RTI framework.
  o Fostering discussion among colleagues about the use of effective practices.
  o Asking students about their application of effective strategies in content-area classes.
- Support implementation by modeling or demonstrating effective practices in colleagues' classrooms and collaboratively planning lessons that will incorporate research-based instruction.
- Commit the necessary resources, such as planning time, professional development, supplemental materials, and assessments.

More information, examples, and tools for these suggestions are provided throughout this book.

Throughout this chapter, we have mentioned different people involved in strengthening and maintaining the core curriculum. We have created Table 2.4 to highlight the roles and responsibilities of different personnel in implementing Tier 1 of RTI for literacy. As with the features of effective instruction, this table will recur later in the book as new information is added. Districts and schools assign different titles to the various positions, based on certification/licensure requirements or local custom. Therefore, we suggest that you attend to the responsibilities assumed by the individuals (listed down the far left column), rather than to the particular titles (listed in the column heads). The following is a key to the symbols (this key is repeated in the table footnote):

> ***The identified individual has primary responsibility for the task.
> **The task is an important part of the work for the individual, but he or she has secondary responsibility for completing it.
> *This is the most common symbol in the table. These individuals share a supportive responsibility for the task.

Please note that some of the individuals in the table will fall into two categories: their primary contractual role (e.g., special education teacher) and the role they play on the RTI literacy leadership team. The symbols indicate the responsibilities for each specific role. For example, a special education teacher only serves a supportive role in communicating expectations for the schoolwide approach to literacy. However, a particular special education teacher may have slightly more involvement with that task if he or she is carrying out duties relative to membership on the RTI literacy leadership team.

The information in this chapter is intended to give you guidance in establishing Tier 1, the foundation for a schoolwide approach to literacy instruction and support. In the next two chapters, we look more specifically at the components of the reading intervention tiers. We revisit some of the topics raised here, such as effective instruction and the roles and responsibilities of various faculty and staff members, as they relate to Tiers 2 and 3. Before you move on, take a moment to reflect on the information you have read so far and check your understanding of the content.

REFLECTION QUESTIONS

1. What are the goals of Tier 1, and how does this concept differ between the elementary and secondary levels?

2. What indicators can a school use to judge whether it needs to strengthen its Tier 1 program?

TABLE 2.4. Roles and Responsibilities

	General education teachers	Special education teachers	Literacy/ instructional coaches	Reading interventionists	Administrators	Literacy/RTI leadership team
Tier 1						
Communicate expectations for schoolwide approach to literacy	*	*	**	*	***	**
Plan professional development in literacy strategies	*	*	**	*	**	***
Implement cross-curricular literacy strategies	***	***	**	**	*	*
Implement effective instruction	***	***	**	***	*	*
Administer and interpret screening assessments	***	***	***	**	*	**
Select instructional materials/ resources to support literacy across the curriculum	**	**	***	*	*	***
Monitor the core literacy program (for coaching, feedback, modeling, co-teaching, etc.)	*	*	***	*	***	***
Observe fidelity of Tier 1 implementation	*	*	***	*	***	***
Communicate with parents regarding Tier 1 components, including screening assessments	**	**	**	*	***	**
Ensure funding for Tier 1 materials and professional development	*	*	*	*	***	**

Note. ***The identified individual has primary responsibility for the task.
**The task is an important part of the work for the individual, but he or she has secondary responsibility for completing it.
*This is the most common symbol in the table. These individuals share a supportive responsibility for the task.

3. What are some signs that your school may need to focus on creating an environment more conducive to learning?

4. Considering the size and population of your school, who would you choose to include in your RTI literacy leadership team, and why?

5. What are some benefits of providing small-group instruction, even in the Tier 1 classes?

6. Can you think of a common lesson taught by you or a colleague, and list a few ways you might be able to differentiate that lesson for learners at different levels?

7. What are some questions you can ask yourself to ensure that you are being a good consumer of programs and available research?

8. Can you think of a strategy or skill that can be implemented across content areas (e.g., two-column note taking), even if it might need to be implemented differently?

9. Why is using state assessment data an effective/efficient way to screen students?

10. Use the professional development checklist on pages 51–53 to rate the faculty in your school. Where might you have the most professional development needs?

CHAPTER 3

Step 2

Establishing Interventions in Reading

In Chapter 2, Tier 1 instruction at the secondary level has been presented as an essential element of enhancing academic vocabulary and understanding content. However, let's face it: We would be very optimistic to think that every middle and high school student will experience success with the benefit of strong academic core instruction alone. If you have spent any time in a middle or high school classroom lately, it will come as no surprise that some students "slip through the cracks." Some were not provided sufficiently intensive interventions in elementary grades, or were provided interventions but continue to fall behind.

Due to pressures at the district, state, and national levels, many administrators and teachers are concerned that students' failing scores on a mandated assessment will be considered their fault. You can spend precious time trying to explain why students in your school have low literacy skills, but effective teachers and leaders say, "We provide high-quality instruction for all students, and we will design the most effective instruction and programs we can to meet their needs and prepare them for postsecondary learning." After all, we all know that whatever the cause, students who are not making adequate progress in Tier 1 alone, or who enter the secondary grades severely behind in the skills they need to learn from and comprehend content-area texts, may require additional support. More strategic literacy intervention, provided as a supplement to the core curriculum, may be necessary to accelerate some students' progress and ensure that they do not fall even further behind (Griffiths, Parson, Burns, VanDerHeyden, & Tilly, 2007).

 Stop and Think

> *Recall some of the differences between the structure of RTI at the elementary and secondary levels. Because students in middle and high school take different courses throughout the day, the different definition of core instruction has been discussed in Chapter 1. Who is involved in providing effective instruction at Tier 1? As you read this chapter, think about how you would answer the following questions: If students require an intervention, when would we deliver it in the upper grades, and what other class would it replace? Would students earn credits for this course, and, if so, what role would it have in a student's overall "graduation plan"?*

(i) INTERVENTION SUPPLEMENTS BUT DOES NOT SUPPLANT TIER 1

Did you notice the phrase "provided as a supplement" in the text paragraph above? That wording is intentional, because a common misunderstanding about Tiers 2 and 3 is that students enrolled in intervention stop participating in general education. For example, students with reading problems who are provided with a Tier 2 intervention continue to participate in core ELAR courses. Intervention needs to be provided *in addition to* Tier 1. Consider the following illustrations of this:

1. Student A is enrolled in the regular ELAR course during Period 2 of the day for 50 minutes. During Periods 4 and 5, she attends the Tier 3 class for a combined 100-minute dose of supplemental instruction.
2. At another campus, Student B attends the regular ELAR course during Period 6 for 45 minutes. In addition, he is enrolled in a 45-minute Tier 2 intervention during the campuswide Strengthen Our School time. All students participate in either an academic intervention or an academic enrichment course during this extra period of the day.
3. At a third school, Student C is enrolled in a reading intervention elective for 50 minutes during Period 1. This is a supplement to the regular ELAR course he attends for 50 minutes during Period 3.

The best possible option would be to offer the maximum amount of intervention possible, as in Student A's case. Students who make it into middle and high school with persistent reading difficulties need as much concentrated time as possible to catch up with their peers before their years in school run out. However, providing a double period of intervention may seem like an unreachable dream, given your school's limited time and resources. Let us consider this the ideal situation for now and concentrate on how to get at least one additional intervention class into the schedule—more similar to the options for Students B and C.

 *Stop and Think*

Is your school most like the scenario for Student A, B, or C? What barriers have to be overcome to offer the ideal intervention (Student A's situation)?

WHAT ABOUT FITTING IN ALL THE CREDITS I NEED?

You may be wondering how to fit an extra class for supplemental intervention into a student's schedule, when there are so many required courses and so little time in the day and year to earn those credits. Unfortunately, the core curriculum and minimum graduation requirements often do not leave much room for accommodating interventions (Tier 2 or 3), so the intervention class may need to take the place of one or two electives. This is always a difficult choice to make, particularly for students who have few classes they actually look forward to attending, but sometimes it must be done. As a general rule of thumb, the intervention setting (1) supplements core academic classes in general education, and (2) takes precedence over optional electives. Box 3.1 sets forth the options for intervention course credit for students with reading problems.

BOX 3.1. OPTIONS FOR INTERVENTION COURSE CREDIT FOR STUDENTS WITH READING DIFFICULTIES

Course type	Requirements
Reading intervention	The state department of education distinguishes the course from the core ELAR course.
Elective	The class takes the place of another elective, such as study skills/test preparation, fine arts, or career and technology.
Core ELAR	The student is enrolled in special education, and the IEP team or state department of education authorizes a "resource" or "pull-out" class, depending on the severity of the reading difficulty.
Core ELAR	The state department of education allows for blocked classes to address both intervention and core requirements in an extended period.

In Appendices A–C, we provide sample master and bell schedules to show different ways of working intervention classes into the school day. The literacy leadership team will play an important role in gaining support for whichever option is deemed most feasible for your school. Present the plan to teachers, parents, and students in a way that all stakeholders will be fully informed and realize the benefits from participating in the intervention.

 Stop and Think

> *Can your school reallocate time and other resources to accommodate not just one but two intervention classes, as many elementary schools are able to provide? In the event that this is not feasible, what alternatives do you have to ensure that students will still receive the instruction they need to close the gap?*

TIERS 2 AND 3 AT THE SECONDARY LEVEL: ARE THEY REALISTIC?

Part of the design of the intervention classes depends on the number of tiers in the RTI model. This issue has raised many questions in secondary schools. As we have discussed in previous chapters, RTI has been primarily designed for and implemented in elementary settings; fewer models are available for secondary settings. For this reason, using increasingly intensive tiers of intervention is perceived as more appropriate for elementary than for secondary settings. Typically, Tiers 2 and 3 are represented as follows:

- Tier 2, or strategic intervention, for students who are having some difficulty keeping up in Tier 1 alone.
- Tier 3, or intensive intervention, for students who have not made adequate progress in the Tier 1 + Tier 2 combination of instruction.
- In some multi-tiered models, another separate tier for special education.

This structure has established Tier 2 as a gateway through which students have to pass before moving to the most individualized instruction in Tier 3.

 Stop and Think

> *What challenges come to mind when you think of implementing this model (i.e., moving through Tier 2 as a gateway to Tier 3) in the secondary setting?*

Like many other secondary administrators and teachers, you are probably thinking something like this: "That's great, but elementary students do not have to earn specific credits, can be more easily pulled out of a core class for intervention, and have access to ancillary personnel already in the school who are able to teach interventions." It does *seem* a lot more feasible to implement a three-tiered framework in the elementary grades than at the secondary level. So let's address two important questions about the design of RTI in secondary schools:

1. Is it necessary to have two different levels of intervention?
2. If so, is it necessary for adolescents to pass through Tier 2 first?

We think that it may be constructive for some secondary schools to use two levels of intervention (Torgesen, Houston, & Rissman, 2007). These schools may use a lower-intensity "booster class" for students who have barely failed the state test or are "on the bubble." This Tier 2 class replaces the usual test remediation and offers students an opportunity to improve their literacy skills in ways that will transfer better to content-area learning. Remember that Tier 2 is offered as a supplement to Tier 1; moreover, it provides a different curriculum tailored to students' needs, rather than simply reteaching the same curriculum of the Tier 1 class.

For schools that use these multi-tiered interventions, students who are more seriously behind in reading are prioritized for placement in Tier 3, which offers an even smaller class size with even more intensive intervention. These students often are still developing decoding or word-reading skills, so their needs are quite different from (and more significant than) those of students who are closer to meeting grade-level standards. Adolescents with more severe reading problems read laboriously—if they are reading at all. Teachers have described it to us as a "painful experience" that they want desperately to stop. Therefore, we are more certain that these students must have intensive instruction. We recommend placing any adolescent who is seriously behind in reading *directly* into a Tier 3 class, without requiring Tier 2 interventions first (Lang et al., 2009).

 Stop and Think

> *Can you think of any reason why you would* not *directly move students in need of a more intensive Tier 3 intervention into a Tier 3 class? What would be required to provide appropriate instruction to adolescents who are severely behind their typically developing peers in a lower-intensity setting?*

Usually, we do not encounter administrators or teachers in secondary schools who disagree with this approach of having different course options to meet different students' needs. Rather, some secondary-level personnel just do not see how providing multiple tiers is possible. You may share their feelings of frustration over not having the resources to provide one, much less two, distinct levels of intervention. We consider this a situation in which you must perform triage. Using results from your state reading assessment and any other available data, identify the students who are least likely to succeed without intensive assistance, and place them in an intervention class not designated by tier.

Given the logistical issues in secondary schools, as well as research indicating that adolescents who are significantly behind their peers in reading will need intensive, long-lasting interventions (Lang et al., 2009), we think that there are reasonable arguments for either one or two levels of intervention. If there is one level of intervention, it should be a more intensive intervention (Tier 3). If there are two levels of intervention, then both a secondary and a tertiary intervention should be implemented (Tier 2 and Tier 3). For most schools, there is value in providing two levels of intervention. The remainder of this chapter describes both Tiers 2 and 3. If you know that you will have only one type of intervention class, we recommend paying closer attention to the information on Tier 3.

In general, intervention classes at the secondary level are intended to do the following:

- Provide an appropriate, and often "safe," environment for older students to benefit from supplemental instruction in their areas of need.
- Accelerate these students' progress so that they are able to keep up with their Tier 1 content-area classes.
- Close the gap between the literacy performance of the students who are struggling with reading and that of their peers.

These features should be present, regardless of the number of tiers your school is able to implement. However, there are added benefits of providing separate Tier 2 and Tier 3 interventions. As we have indicated, offering one class for students who are close to meeting grade-level standards and one for those who have more serious reading problems will allow you to do these things:

- Individualize the supplemental instruction as much as possible.
- Appropriately adjust the intensity of intervention for students of different educational backgrounds and abilities.

As we have described, even if you are able to create two tiers of intervention, it is not necessary for students to progress in a linear fashion through Tier 2 into or out of Tier 3. *In other words, the numbers designating the tiers should not be treated as sequential steps to follow. Rather, you should consider them only as indicators of the level of intensity.* This is one of the major differences between the way a three-tiered model functions in secondary versus elementary schools.

Tables 3.1–3.4 provide additional information to enable you to compare and contrast elementary with secondary intervention classes. As you review them, notice as well the differences that are apparent between the structure and components of Tier 2 and Tier 3.

TABLE 3.1. Elementary Tier 2 Strategic Intervention

Focus

For students who have been identified with marked reading difficulties, and who have not responded to Tier 1 efforts

Curriculum

Specialized scientifically based reading curriculum (or currucula) emphasizing the five critical elements of beginning reading

Grouping

Homogeneous small-group instruction (1:5)

Time

25–30 minutes a day, in addition to 90-minute core instruction

Assessment

Weekly progress monitoring on target skills to ensure adequate progress and learning

Interventionist

Research-provided interventionist, reading specialist, or classroom teacher

Setting

Appropriate setting outside classroom

Note. Adapted with permission from the University of Texas Center for Reading and Language Arts. (2005). *3-tier reading model: Reducing reading difficulties for kindergarten through third grade students.* Austin, TX: Author.

TABLE 3.2. Secondary Tier 2 Strategic Intervention

Focus

For students who have been identified with marked reading difficulties, and who have not responded to Tier 1 efforts

Curriculum

Reading classes or small-group instruction designed to accelerate the reading growth of students with reading difficulties; this usually includes scientifically based program(s) emphasizing multisyllabic word recognition, fluency, vocabulary, and reading comprehension instruction

Grouping

Homogeneous instruction provided within class sizes of 10–16 (typically)

Time

30–50 minutes per day for two semesters

Assessment

Diagnostic assessment to determine the focus and pacing of instruction; progress monitoring with informal CBMs on target skills to ensure adequate progress and learning (see Chapter 4 for more information) every 2–4 weeks; formal progress monitoring about every 6 weeks

Interventionist

Intervention provided by personnel determined by the school (usually a reading teacher or other interventionist)

Setting

Appropriate setting designated by the school (usually the reading class or supplemental tutoring)

Note. Adapted with permission from the University of Texas Center for Reading and Language Arts. (2005). *3-tier reading model: Reducing reading difficulties for kindergarten through third grade students.* Austin, TX: Author.

TABLE 3.3. Elementary Tier 3 Intensive Intervention

Focus

For students who have been identified with marked reading difficulties, and who have not responded to Tier 1 and Tier 2 efforts

Curriculum

Individualized and responsive intervention emphasizing the critical elements of reading for students with reading difficulties/disabilities

Grouping

Homogeneous small-group instruction (1:3)

Time

50 minutes a day, in addition to 90-minute core instruction

Assessment

Weekly progress monitoring on target skills to ensure adequate progress and learning

Interventionist

Research-provided reading specialist, or classroom teacher

Setting

Appropriate setting outside classroom

Note. Adapted with permission from the University of Texas Center for Reading and Language Arts. (2005). *3-tier reading model: Reducing reading difficulties for kindergarten through third grade students.* Austin, TX: Author.

TABLE 3.4. Secondary Tier 3 Intensive Intervention

Focus

For students with severe and persistent reading difficulties who do not make sufficient progress in Tier 2, or who the school determines are so significantly behind that they initially require more intensive intervention than Tier 2 can provide

Curriculum

Specifically designed and customized reading instruction delivered in small groups or individually to students. Typically includes very individualized instruction in phonemic awareness, decoding, fluency, vocabulary, and comprehension; scientifically based reading program(s) emphasizing individual needs

Grouping

Homogeneous small-group instruction (no more than 4–5 students)

Time

50–60 minutes every day for one or more school years

Assessment

Diagnostic assessment to determine the focus and pacing of instruction; progress monitoring with informal CBMs on target skills to ensure adequate progress and learning (see Chapter 4 for more information) every other week; formal progress monitoring about every 4 weeks

Interventionist

Intensive intervention provided by personnel determined by the school (usually a reading teacher or other trained interventionist)

Setting

Appropriate setting designated by the school

Note. Adapted with permission from the University of Texas Center for Reading and Language Arts. (2005). *3-tier reading model: Reducing reading difficulties for kindergarten through third grade students.* Austin, TX: Author.

HOW DOES TIER 3 DIFFER FROM TIER 2?

If your school is able to offer Tier 2 and Tier 3 classes, you need to make a clear distinction between them. You already know that Tier 3 must be more rigorous and intense than Tier 2 if you are to accelerate students' progress toward meeting grade-level standards (see Figure 3.1 for indicators that can be used to identify students in need of Tier 2). But how do we define *intensity*? Many teachers think that it is only a matter of group or class size: You increase intensity by decreasing the group size. Although this is one aspect to consider, it is not necessarily the most important indicator.

 Stop and Think

> *Review the information in Table 3.2, Table 3.4, and Figure 3.1. Why is it necessary to change the organizational structure and curricular plan of the intervention class from Tier 2 to Tier 3? If your school does not provide two tiers of intervention, what impact will this have on the way you provide a single intervention tier?*

Having fewer students in the room at a time, in and of itself, does not create intensive instruction. The teacher providing the intervention must be skilled at using assessment data to group the students appropriately and plan for individualized instruction. Remember that students identified for Tier 3 intervention usually lack many of the skills that are typically acquired in the lower grades, such as beginning word study or decoding skills, as well as reading comprehension (at least with respect to retelling of the main idea and key ideas in the text). Their interventions must be specifically targeted to their individual needs, and the students must spend the maximum amount of engaged time on task. This requires the intervention teacher to be very knowledgeable about these things:

Reading component	Identifying student characteristic for Tier 3 intervention
Word reading	Students with low word-reading skills (two grade levels or more behind peers)
Fluency	Students whose reading is slow and laborious* and who do not sound as though they are reading for meaning
Comprehension	Students whose understanding of text is significantly below peers, according to state-level reading tests or other reliable and valid indicators

*"Slow and laborious" might be defined by calculations of reading rate and accuracy. Reading fewer than 90 words correct per minute with less than 90% accuracy (more than 1 error per 10 words) in grade-level text can be considered slow and laborious (Meadows Center for Preventing Educational Risk, 2009).

FIGURE 3.1. How to determine whether Tier 3 intervention is suitable for students.

- The components of reading
- Effective interventions for identified skill areas
- Multigroup instruction
- Quick pacing of instruction

More information and suggestions on group sizes, assessments, lesson planning, and teacher qualifications are provided in this chapter. We mention these features here as ways to distinguish Tier 2 from Tier 3 interventions. A brief example of how lesson components might be redefined at increasing levels of intensity can be found in Figure 3.2.

Tier 1

Dragonwings by Laurence Yep (1977)
- Vocabulary
  - ○ *scrappy, petty, prudent, gracious, sly, skeptical, smug, reckoning, fastidious, spiteful*
  - ○ Semantic feature analysis
- Comprehension
  - ○ Multiple chapters (average 30 pages per assignment)
  - ○ Compose a summary for the entire reading

Tier 2

Dragonwings by Laurence Yep (1977)
- Vocabulary
  - ○ *scrappy, petty, prudent, gracious, sly, skeptical, smug, reckoning, fastidious, spiteful*
  - ○ Semantic feature analysis
  - ○ Spelling rules: doubling, /k/ sound, *-cious*
- Comprehension
  - ○ Partner reading (5-minute turns)
  - ○ Self-generated questions (one per round)
- Progress monitoring
  - ○ Multisyllable word identification with terms from novel × 2 weeks

Tier 3

Dragonwings by Laurence Yep (1977)
- Vocabulary
  - ○ Identifying syllable types with reduced list
    - ■ Closed, open, silent *e*
    - ■ *scrappy, petty, prudent, smug, spiteful*
  - ○ Semantic feature analysis
- Comprehension
  - ○ Echo reading by paragraph
  - ○ Repeated reading with partners (2-minute turns)
  - ○ Self-generated questions (one per round)
- Progress monitoring
  - ○ Multisyllable word identification and fluency (with novel) × 1 week

FIGURE 3.2. Lesson components redefined at three different levels of intensity.

Note that it may be necessary to work with material more suitable to the ability levels and interests of the students in different tiers. The example in Figure 3.2 is intended to illustrate what "more intensive" instruction might look like in a comparative fashion, assuming that the text is at an appropriately challenging level for each tier. Our use of a single novel is not intended to suggest that students should all be reading identical material, regardless of their placement in intervention. Because these students are simultaneously enrolled in Tier 1 and either Tier 2 or Tier 3, it may be particularly inappropriate to repeat content in multiple classes during the day. To make the best use of Figure 3.2, focus on the target areas of instruction, amount of text covered in a lesson, and types of reading support planned for more or less intensive classes.

When you are choosing text for a Tier 2 and/or Tier 3 class, it may be beneficial to consider what content is being taught in the students' content-area classes, and then to align the text with those content topics. Some districts use curriculum "bundles" across all content areas in their schools. For example, one high school science curriculum bundle unit might be on viruses and provide the key ideas, guiding questions, state standards, examples, and resources teachers should use for planning instruction. To support the content that students are learning in their science class, the Tier 2 and/or Tier 3 reading intervention class can use supplementary text(s) about viruses. This not only supports the content the students are expected to learn, but also provides a structured opportunity for them to practice applying the skills they are learning to the actual academic demands. This may help increase the likelihood that students will use reading strategies to support their learning outside the intervention class; it may also enhance their motivation if they perceive that they are better prepared to access content-area curriculum.

Another important difference between Tiers 2 and 3 involves the numbers of students who are given these services: Increasingly fewer students are provided with services as the interventions become more intensive. In Chapters 1 and 2, we have discussed how 80% of the student body would ideally have their literacy needs met through enhanced Tier 1 instruction. Using this 80% standard for Tier 1, we would expect that approximately 15% of students would require the targeted assistance in Tier 2, and 5–10% of students would require customized supplemental support for even greater durations in Tier 3 (Fletcher & Vaughn, 2009; Reschly, 2003).

As explained in Chapter 2, these figures can be misleading in some school contexts. However, it is generally accepted that fewer adolescents should exhibit the most severe reading difficulties. That is not to say that the problems experienced by students in Tier 2 are "minor." Quite the contrary: The reading difficulties are serious enough that they have persisted into middle and high school, have resulted in academic failure, and will continue to put the affected students further and further behind their peers. We simply make the distinction between those who have difficulties with skills typically considered "foundational" (e.g., the decoding and word identification skills usually mastered by grade 3) and those that are more commonly experienced by adolescents (e.g., multisyllable word identification, vocabulary, and comprehension). To help you understand Tier 2 better, let us take a closer look at the focus and components of this level of intervention.

HOW DOES TIER 2 DIFFER FROM A STUDY SKILLS CLASS?

(i) Tier 2 Is Not for Study Skills

One common mistake schools make when implementing a three-tiered RTI model is confusing Tier 2 with a study skills class. Let's be clear: We understand the importance of helping students with organizational skills, test-taking skills, and the like. However, these can be handled as part of the enhanced core instruction provided at Tier 1, because they are designed to help students figure out procedures for different academic tasks, manage their workloads, and access course content. They are often the modifications or accommodations for a given assignment or test; they enable students to demonstrate what they actually know or can do.

Tier 2 is designed to accelerate students' development of the literacy skills needed for overall academic success. The intervention support provided includes evidence-based curriculum, strategies, and procedures to *supplement* Tier 1 effective instruction and differentiation, but also to fill in any gaps or to teach fundamental skills students may be missing.

We have created Figure 3.3 as a way for you to see at a glance what a Tier 2 class is supposed to be and what it is not.

So if students are not enrolled in a Tier 2 class to get help with homework and class assignments or to practice test-taking skills, what does this instruction focus on? The instructional focus is on the literacy skills and strategies identified through diagnostic assessment as the root cause of students' reading difficulties. These skills are assumed to interfere with the students' ability to understand and

What Tier 2 *is*	What Tier 2 *is not*
A class for delivering instruction in literacy skills students need to succeed in Tier 1 content-area classes	A study skills class
A class that requires a literacy specialist	A homework club
A class that requires specific research based materials and practices	A test-taking preparation class
A class with a carefully designed curriculum	A center at the school for delivering components of a student's IEP, such as extended time or reading directions aloud

FIGURE 3.3. Defining Tier 2.

learn from their content area texts. It may be helpful to use text from students' content-area classes during strategy instruction. The goal in using authentic texts or making a connection to a core academic course's content is not to help students to complete assignments, but to provide meaningful opportunities for the students to demonstrate their use of literacy strategies with the different texts. The ability to transfer skills to new material or a variety of text types is considered a reliable indicator of global gains in student learning (Ardoin, 2006).

We are frequently asked by teachers and administrators whether a particular practice being used would be classified as differentiated instruction in Tier 1, as study skills, or as Tier 2 intervention. Sometimes an example of the tiers operating in concert helps to clarify these distinctions. Please read Box 3.2 for an illustration of how a Tier 2 interventionist might coordinate efforts with those of a Tier 1 content-area teacher. Notice how Ms. Watkins prioritized the use of the literacy strategy, not the learning of the content itself. She had her own assignment related to students' reading comprehension skill needs, but she also planned to reinforce what they were learning in the content-area class.

BOX 3.2. AN EXAMPLE OF HOW TIER 2 DIFFERS FROM BUT COMPLEMENTS ENHANCED TIER 1

Ms. Watkins was a Tier 2 interventionist who had been teaching the students in her class to monitor their comprehension in informational texts by inferring the main ideas of paragraphs. The students had mastered the basic steps with passages she carefully selected for these lessons, but she wanted to know how well they could apply the strategy when reading material they were more likely to encounter in their Tier 1 classes. Ms. Watkins used this information to determine how to adjust her instruction for the main-idea strategy, as well as to prepare for other lessons on monitoring comprehension.

Ms. Watkins asked Mr. Pons, the Tier 1 science teacher for several of her students, to select an excerpt from a current unit that she could use to demonstrate the strategy for inferring the main idea. Mr. Pons provided a page from the science textbook and told the interventionist what vocabulary words and concepts he had been teaching. He also offered Ms. Watkins a graphic organizer the students were using to compare and contrast the features of related terms and concepts in the chapter. Ms. Watkins planned to have copies of this organizer available as a reference for her students while they were reading the excerpt.

The next day, Ms. Watkins began her lesson by explicitly telling her students why they would be using text from a science class to monitor their comprehension:

"Today we are going to use a new text to practice the main-idea strategy we have been learning to use to monitor our comprehension. The text comes directly from your science textbook. The reason I chose to use this is not necessarily to help you with your homework this week, but to show you that the strategy we learned in this class can also be used to help you in your other classes. Remember that the purpose of using the main-idea strategy is to check how well you understand what you are reading. Watch how I apply this strategy to the first paragraph in your science text, and then you'll have a chance to try it."

Ms. Watkins explained why she was using the science text, so she did not leave it up to chance that her students would figure out they could use strategies in one class to support their learning in another. In other words, she realized that her students might not generalize the use of strategies and instructional principles they were learning in one setting to another setting. Ms. Watkins knew it was helpful for teachers to demonstrate how the practices their students were learning in their reading class could be used in social studies and science.

To close the lesson that day, she modeled for her students how the main-idea strategy could be applied within the science text, demonstrating clearly the aspects of the main-idea practice that would need to be adjusted for the the science text. Then she provided them with opportunities to practice the strategy in the science text, providing them with feedback as they proceeded. She also asked students to discuss how they might be able to apply the strategy to monitor their comprehension in other classes. She used the information to plan additional practice with texts from other courses and to select the next comprehension-monitoring skill to teach.

Other elements of Tier 2 instruction that will help you distinguish it from a more traditional study skills class include the teacher's expertise and the evidence base for the materials used. Unlike a teacher of a study skills or test preparation class, a literacy interventionist should be:

- Specially prepared to address the needs of adolescents who struggle with reading and writing.
- Skilled at motivating and fostering the reading engagement of adolescents with a history of academic failure.
- Knowledgeable about ways to individualize and intensify instruction by incorporating features of effective instruction in every lesson.

Reading interventionist candidates should be evaluated on their advanced training in scientifically based literacy instruction for word identification, fluency, vocabulary, narrative and informational text comprehension, and writing. Candidates should demonstrate that they participate in ongoing professional development in literacy instruction and effective practices for adolescents with low motivation and low achievement. We provide more information about the features of effective instruction and motivation in Tiers 2 and 3 in Chapter 4. Meanwhile, Box 3.3 provides further guidance for selecting a reading intervention teacher.

BOX 3.3. SELECTING A READING INTERVENTION TEACHER

Who can serve as a reading intervention teacher?

- A certified reading specialist or master reading teacher
- A special education teacher with special training in literacy*
- An ELAR teacher in general education who has special training in literacy with an emphasis on helping struggling readers*

What interview questions would help evaluate candidates?

1. (General) "This position involves teaching an intensive, explicit reading intervention program to adolescent struggling readers. What in your background prepares you for success in this position? Have you ever taught reading? What was the nature of instruction and your experience?"
2. (General) "What do you find most challenging about teaching reading at the secondary level?"
3. (General) "What do you consider your strengths, and how would they lend themselves to this type of teaching position?"
4. (Behavior management/engagement) "You give students directions for a reading activity in your class. One student doesn't understand the task and becomes distracted with something totally unrelated. What would you do?"
5. (Behavior management/engagement) "If hired for this position, you would be working with students who have a history of difficulty in reading, and perhaps inappropriate behavior as well. What would you do to motivate students who have not had much success in the past, especially if you were limited in giving out tangible incentives?"
6. (Assessment/evaluation) "Do you have any experience with assessing students, either formally or informally? Tell me about that."
7. (Differentiation) "One challenge of this position will be differentiating instruction for students with different skill levels. Have you been successful in the past with doing this? How would you support students who are functioning at different levels?"
8. (Assessment/evaluation) "How would you evaluate your teaching? In other words, how would you know you were being effective as a teacher?"
9. (Training) "What kinds of things have you done to teach word study/phonics, vocabulary, fluency, and comprehension in the past? What professional development have you had in those areas?"
10. (Training) "What knowledge do you have about the most recent research that focuses on reading instruction for secondary students? Where have you obtained your knowledge of the research? What do you know about response to intervention (RTI)?"

---

*Professional development requirements are addressed in Chapter 4.

Stop and Think

> *Are the requirements for serving as a reading interventist at the secondary level different from what would be required of an elementary teacher? If someone had experience working as a reading interventionist in an elementary school, would you consider him or her as a candidate for a position at the middle or high school level? Which interview questions would help you determine if that individual were prepared to work with adolescents? Who at your school would be prepared to evaluate candidates' responses to the suggested interview questions? If you sought guidance from someone who evaluated candidates for elementary school positions, what would you have to consider in applying that guidance to middle or high school?*

The last feature distinguishing Tier 2 from traditional study skills involves the evidence base of the materials used. We are sure you agree that adolescents who are exhibiting difficulty with fundamental literacy skills need to be provided with the best curriculum and instruction that research has to offer if progress is to be made in closing the gap between their performance and that of typically achieving peers. There is less room for trial and error, because time is running out for these students. You can find more detailed criteria for determining the appropriateness of literacy programs or curricular materials in Chapter 4, as well as websites for additional guidance in identifying curricular materials in Appendix F. We mention this here to emphasize the importance of the course content and instructional practices used in intervention classes.

WHAT IS THE IDEAL GROUP SIZE FOR A TIER 2 CLASS? A TIER 3 CLASS?

We use the term *group size* to refer to the number of students enrolled in a single Tier 2 or Tier 3 class. You might think of it more as your class size. With an effective teacher, a smaller class provides each student with more opportunities to participate actively in a lesson and receive teacher feedback. Teachers with larger class sizes often complain that they "cannot be everywhere at once." This is particularly true when teachers are providing interventions and attempting to meet the serious needs compacted into an intervention class.

This is why many researchers interpret the research as indicating that smaller group sizes may produce greater effects on student outcomes (Elbaum, Vaughn, Hughes, & Moody, 2000). So, as you move up the levels of instructional intensity in a three-tiered RTI model, you would expect Tier 2 to be smaller than Tier 1 classes, and Tier 3 to be smaller than Tier 2 classes. But what is a "small" class? For illustrative purposes, let us assume the following to be a typical configuration for middle or high school classes:

- Tier 1: 25–30 students
- Tier 2: 10–12 students
- Tier 3: Approximately 6 students

 *Intervention Group Sizes**

A multiyear study of Tier 2 interventions in grades 7 and 8 contrasted group sizes of approximately 10–12 students with group sizes of approximately 6 students (Vaughn, Wanzek, et al., 2010). Classes of both sizes provided the same standardized intervention (emphasizing word study, vocabulary development, fluency, and comprehension) for 50 minutes daily. Findings suggested that helping students who have reading difficulties to make significant gains in reading ability requires more comprehensive and extensive intervention than can be accomplished in well-designed classes with larger groups of students (e.g., 10 or more). Rather, it may involve longer periods of time in intervention (e.g., 90 minutes per day) and smaller group sizes.

---

*This symbol ✎ will alert you to closer examinations of research findings from scientific studies of RTI at the secondary level.

More research needs to be conducted to confirm the ideal group size for intervention classes in secondary schools. As we have mentioned earlier in this chapter, group size alone is not the determinant of intervention intensity; nor is it the sole determinant of intervention quality. Factors such as the quality of the teacher preparation, materials, and resources can influence the outcomes, as can affective and social factors such as group dynamics and behavior.

We also want to point out that in some circumstances, extremely small group sizes or narrowly defined homogeneous groups at the secondary level might actually make instruction too restrictive. What if you taught an intervention class with two adolescents who were still learning their syllable types? Who could serve as an appropriate peer model of using syllable knowledge to recognize an unfamiliar word in a text? Imagine working on building comprehension knowledge about complex text if neither of the students can model how to make inferences and or discuss text.

When you think about group size in these ways, you can imagine that there are opportunities for partnering students that require having four or more students.

 Partnering with Small Group Sizes

A recently conducted study of 9th through 12th graders with significant reading disabilities implemented a fluency intervention that relied on pairing a slightly higher-level reader with a lower-ability reader (Wexler, Vaughn, Roberts, & Denton, 2010). This was done to increase the modeling of fluent reading and the frequency of feedback. Peers were taught to track each other's reading and to provide

correction when a partner made an error. Even with class sizes of 10–12 students, the pairings were difficult to make because a majority of the students were very low-level readers. There were simply too few higher-level readers available to serve as appropriate modeling and feedback partners. This compromised the delivery of the intervention and, ultimately, its effectiveness.

 Stop and Think

If you don't have access to higher-level readers who can serve as models for lower-level readers, what/who else could serve as a model of good reading? Could you incorporate some sort of technology or audio recording into instruction to provide a model of good reading?

Obviously, many factors need to be considered when determining the appropriate class size for Tiers 2 and 3, including these:

- The nature of the intervention.
- The logistics required to implement the intervention with fidelity.
- The instructional and contextual factors that will contribute to positive outcomes.

So how are you to establish the right group size? The best guidance we can offer at this time is to make the intervention class as small as possible, while still maintaining some flexibility for within-class grouping. Admittedly, it can be challenging for schools to offer and staff multiple intervention classes of reduced sizes if the district has a limited budget or limited access to highly qualified reading teachers. In that case, you may need to plan for larger classes, but we want to emphasize that this places greater demands on the interventionist's skill at differentiating instruction within each class.

Keep in mind that the goal of intervention is to provide targeted, individualized instruction in an intense manner. Having class sizes of greater than 12 students is not contrary to this goal in all circumstances. As you have read in the second research note on partnering on page 81, it may be easier to implement interventions in larger groups if the needs of the students in the class are similar, although not uniform. Some changes to suit your local context or conditions may be acceptable, but it is important that you adhere to the basic principles of RTI. These limitations are discussed in Chapter 5 as "non-negotiables."

WHAT IS THE ROLE OF ASSESSMENT IN PLACING STUDENTS INTO THE TIERS?

It is probably no surprise to you that assessment plays a crucial role in determining which students go to which tier initially, as well as how they subsequently move between or exit the intervention tiers. What tends to be less apparent to secondary schools is *which* assessment data should be used and *how*.

 Stop and Think

> *Do you already have data that are easily accessible in your district to make these decisions? Could using these accessible data prevent unnecessary testing and save both resources and instructional time?*

As we have described in Chapter 2, your annual state-mandated reading test is an efficient screening tool or a means of identifying students who do not appear to be meeting or maintaining performance targets. You already have access to the data from this testing, so the literacy leadership team only needs to determine how it should be interpreted for placing students who failed the test into Tier 2 or Tier 3 classes. Let's look at two different options for doing this.

Option 1 for Placement Decisions: Percentile Ranks

Some state assessments report individual results in percentile ranks, which can be inferred from standard scores in a normal distribution. The "normal range" may be determined by your school or district. For districts that do not have a definition, it is reasonable to consider performance above the 35th percentile as in the normal range. This is a good starting point for considering which students might be in need of intervention. For example, the Washington Assessment of Student Learning (WASL; State of Washington Office of Superintendent of Public Instruction, 2009) provides percentile ranks that could be used to establish ranges for placement in the different tiers. A school in Washington State might consider any students with scores above the 35th percentile on the WASL to be in Tier 1 only, with no need for diagnostic testing. This more conservative interpretation of a passing score would allow for students "on the bubble," or barely within the normal range, to be included in diagnostic testing that might better inform instructional decisions.

With two levels of intervention, students with scores between the 16th and 35th percentiles would be placed in a Tier 2 class, in addition to the Tier 1 ELAR course. Those with scores below the 16th percentile would be considered to be approximately three grade levels behind their peers, and therefore to be in need of Tier 3 support. Like the Tier 2 class, the Tier 3 class would be provided as a supplement to the Tier 1 ELAR course. See Figure 3.4 for the decision tree that would be used with the percentile rank option for placement.

Option 2 for Placement Decisions: Cut Scores

The other option for interpreting state assessment results to make placement decisions is to use a cut score. For example, if a scale score of 146 (Achievement Level

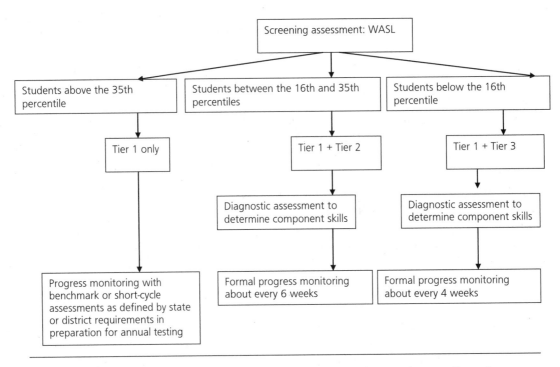

FIGURE 3.4. Direct placement into Tier 2 or Tier 3 with the use of percentile ranks.

III) is considered the passing standard on the End-of-Course (EOC) Test administered to freshmen in several states, a school might consider any ninth grader with a scale score above 148 on the EOC to be in Tier 1 only, with no need for diagnostic testing. As in the percentile rank scenario, this more conservative interpretation of a passing score would allow for students "on the bubble," or barely passing (146 ± [1 standard error of measurement × 2 standard deviations]), to be included in diagnostic testing.

Again, if there are two levels of intervention, students with EOC scores between 138 and 148 (Achievement Level II) would be placed in a Tier 2 class, in addition to the Tier 1 ELAR course. Those with scores less than or equal to 137 (Achievement Level I) would be considered to show little or no evidence of the reading skills required to comprehend grade-level text, and therefore to be in need of Tier 3 support. Like the Tier 2 class, the Tier 3 class would be provided as a supplement to the Tier 1 ELAR course. See Figure 3.5 for the decision tree with the cut score data replacing the percentile ranks.

Figures 3.4 and 3.5 serve as good reminders that secondary students do not progress through Tier 2 first before advancing to Tier 3, as you might see in an elementary RTI model (see Figure 3.6). Rather, when you already know that a middle or high school student is experiencing severe difficulties, you can place him or her immediately into the most intensive intervention. The concern with skipping Tier 2 at lower grade levels is that a younger student is more likely to

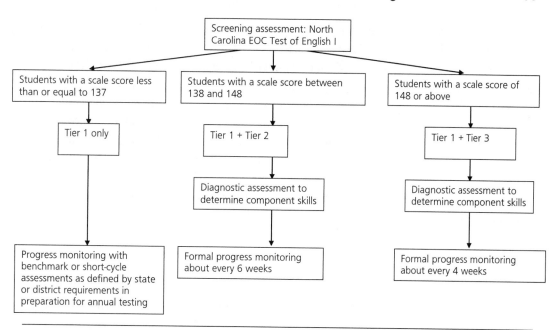

FIGURE 3.5. Direct placement into Tier 2 or Tier 3 with the use of cut scores.

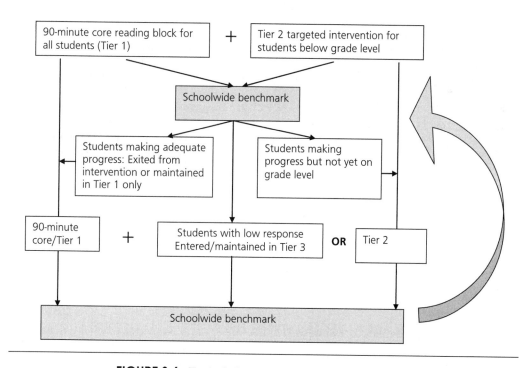

FIGURE 3.6. Typical elementary movement among tiers.

be a *false positive* than an adolescent is. In this context, a *false positive* is a student who performed poorly on the screening assessment but actually does not need supplemental support. At the secondary level, we are more confident that this is not the case.

However, there are occasions when a secondary student may be placed inappropriately. Do not let this alarm you about a scheduling disaster; movement among the tiers at the secondary level is much less dynamic than what is depicted in Figure 3.6 for elementary schools. It is more likely that adolescent students will remain in their intervention classes for a year or more (Lang et al., 2009). Table 3.5 offers suggestions for when a student may need to be moved among the tiers, and for how this should be accomplished if midsemester scheduling options

TABLE 3.5. When to Move Middle and High School Students from One Tier to Another

Situation	Placement change needed	Priority
Student is in Tier 1, but interim benchmark and teacher observation data indicate that he or she is no longer meeting grade-level standards.	Move to Tier 2 at end of quarter or semester.	High: Make the change as soon as possible.
Student is in Tier 2, but interim progress-monitoring data and teacher observation data indicate that he or she is consistently meeting grade-level standards.	Move to other class (e.g., elective) at end of semester or year.	Low: Move when it will cause the least disruption.[a] May need support during transition. Important to pay attention to progress-monitoring data in Tier 1 to determine whether student is "slipping."
Student is in Tier 2 but has not made adequate progress after a year, and data indicate that he or she has word-level deficits.	Move to Tier 3 before start of next semester/ school year.	Medium: Move is likely to coincide with a logical break, but should be made soon.
Student is in Tier 3, but interim progress-monitoring data and teacher observation data indicate that he or she is not seriously behind grade-level peers or in need of word-level instruction.	Move to Tier 2 at end of semester. If student continues to make progress, reevaluate placement again.	Medium: Move is likely to coincide with a logical break, but should be made soon.
Student is in Tier 3, has made consistent progress over the past year, and is ready for reduced support.	Move to Tier 2 before start of next semester/ school year.	Low: Move when it will cause the least disruption.[a]

[a] The reference to causing "the least disruption" is not intended to suggest that students are scheduled into the tiers for the convenience of the school. Rather, it is an acknowledgment that midsemester schedule changes can be very difficult to make in some middle and high schools and can create problems for students' credits.

are limited due to the awarding of credits and/or the availability of appropriate courses.

 Stop and Think

> *Are the situations described in Table 3.5 unique to secondary schools? How might they be similar to or different from those that arise at the elementary level? Are there other scenarios of "inappropriate placement" that might occur at your school?*

So what happens after you place students into the appropriate intervention class? The next step is to administer diagnostic assessments to identify the particular literacy skills in which each student needs targeted intervention. Some teachers ask whether it is sufficient to look at the state standards for the items the student missed on the assessment to determine what instruction is needed. Because state reading tests are primarily measures of comprehension, this type of analysis would provide good information for instruction in comprehension skills. However, most results do not indicate whether the student also has a problem with word identification and/or fluency. Diagnostic assessments should be used for more accurately determining the component(s) of reading that are causing the problem.

More information on selecting diagnostic assessments is provided later in this chapter. In addition, other assessment resources can be found in Appendix F. Regardless of which measure(s) you use, there are two approaches you can take to identify the target skills for intervention.

Assessment Sequence Option 1: Bottom-Up

One possibility for using diagnostic assessments with students who have failed the state reading test might be called the "bottom-up" approach. In this method, you would begin by administering an assessment for the most foundational component of reading, and continue administering assessments of progressively more sophisticated skills until the student is no longer able to "test out" of a skill. For example, you might sequence your diagnostic evaluation to begin with a phonemic awareness assessment, followed by phonics/word recognition, fluency, vocabulary, and finally a more detailed comprehension assessment. If the student performs well on tests of phoneme segmentation and word recognition accuracy, but then demonstrates difficulty reading connected text fluently, you would discontinue testing with fluency and start the intervention with that skill. This approach is most practical where computer-adapted assessments are available, such as the Florida Assessment for Instruction in Reading (FAIR; Florida Department of Education, 2009–2010). Otherwise, testing students in foundational skills requires a series of measures administered individually, which can be quite time-consuming. Computer-adapted assessments can more efficiently provide such comprehensive data on a greater number of students.

Assessment Sequence Option 2: Top-Down

The second order for administering diagnostic assessments to students who fail the state reading assessment would follow a "top-down" approach. In this method, you would assume that the student has adequate foundational skills but is struggling to make meaning from text. You would therefore sequence your diagnostic evaluation to begin with the critical components of comprehension and only assess foundational skills (e.g., word recognition) if the higher-level skills could not be ruled out as contributing factors.

For example, you might administer a test of vocabulary as a first step in determining the student's area of reading difficulty, and add a diagnostic assessment for fluency or word identification if your intervention for vocabulary did not improve his or her performance. Alternatively, you might include the fluency assessment if the student was not able to complete the vocabulary assessment within the time limit, or you might include the word identification assessment if you knew from his or her educational history that a previous intervention in word parts did not improve performance. To understand this approach better, read Box 3.4 for an illustration of the top-down option.

 Stop and Think

>   *The top-down assessment sequence is not used in lower elementary grades, in part because it is very difficult to assess students' comprehension accurately until about third grade. Younger students are still developing foundational skills, whereas only a small percentage of adolescents should still be struggling with phonemic awareness and the alphabetic principle (Roberts, Torgesen, Boardman, & Scammacca, 2008).*

BOX 3.4. Top-Down Assessment Scenario

Theresa Smith has failed the state reading test, and her teacher, Mr. Jones, determines that Theresa is not comprehending text for some reason. She is not an ELL, and therefore Mr. Jones hypothesizes that language/vocabulary is not a barrier for her. He decides to administer a fluency assessment because he knows that fluency (the ability to read with speed, accuracy, and prosody/expression) is necessary to free up cognitive energy and allow Theresa to focus on decoding the text. The two kinds of fluency Mr. Jones can assess are Theresa's silent reading fluency and her oral reading fluency.

Silent reading fluency is difficult to assess, because it is hard to monitor what a student is actually reading; however, secondary students need silent reading fluency in order to get through large quantities of upper-level content area text. Several measures of silent reading fluency are available to Mr. Jones. For example, the Test of Silent Contextual Reading Fluency (TOSCRF; Hammill, Wiederholt, & Allen, 2006) is one commonly administered silent reading fluency assessment available in the school district. In this measure, the student is given printed lines of letters/words strung together with no spaces between them (e.g., *ayellowbirdwithbluewings*) and asked to insert a slash mark at every appropriate point in the letter string in order to make words in a sentence. Scores are based on the number of correctly completed sentences in 3 minutes.

Another type of fluency Mr. Jones considers assessing is Theresa's oral reading fluency. He can easily determine this by listening to Theresa read brief passages aloud for 1 minute and recording the number of words she reads and the number of errors she makes. By subtracting the number of incorrectly read words from the total number of words she read, Mr. Jones can determine her words read correctly per minute (WCPM). This can be especially helpful in finding Theresa's instructional reading level for the intervention lessons Mr. Jones will plan. He also knows that very low fluency at the secondary level can indicate serious reading problems, although this relationship decreases as students get into the upper grades and are faced with reading difficult text. If Theresa has a low oral reading fluency score, she may need fluency and decoding practice.

Mr. Jones administers an oral reading fluency measure to Theresa and determines that her oral reading fluency is about 70 WCPM, which is a very low score for a high school student. In his training, Mr. Jones learned that students with oral reading fluency rates below the 50th percentile should be given additional word-reading measures. Therefore, he is concerned that Theresa is also deficient in her ability to decode words accurately. He wants to administer a diagnostic decoding tool to know for certain whether Theresa's intervention will need to include instruction in word recognition. Although the district-adopted program for word recognition has a built-in assessment system, Mr. Jones knows it is a good idea to give a standardized measure of word reading to confirm whether decoding is indeed an issue and to help target the specific word recognition/decoding skills he will need to address. He decides to administer the Test of Word Reading Efficiency (TOWRE; Torgesen, Wagner, & Rashotte, 1999) to Theresa, and determines that she is deficient in this skill.

 ### Stop and Think

Are there other situations that would be appropriate for each of these assessment procedures (top-down and bottom-up)? Does one approach make more sense to you to use in the secondary (vs. elementary) context? Is there one approach that is efficient but effective at diagnosing the reading intervention needs of adolescents?

By now, you may be wishing that we would just tell you whether the top-down or bottom-up approach is better and give you a list of the assessments to use in the proper order. We wish we could provide you an easy solution but, as for many issues in education, the answer is "It depends." Logistical issues, such as the length of time different assessments take to administer or the costs associated with procuring and maintaining them, may partly determine your selection of an approach or a particular test. Some assessments can be given in a group format or on a computer, but others will require one-on-one time with a tester. Your literacy leadership team will need to consider the extent to which the school can balance the required resources with the ability to gather the necessary information on each student. Whether you are following the bottom-up or top-down approach, the goals are the same—to understand the student's instructional needs, and to determine an instructional plan to facilitate text access and understanding.

Notice in the decision trees shown in Figures 3.4 and 3.5 that all students participate in some form of progress monitoring. Given the assumption that the skill needs are different in the two tiers, you may need different tools or assessment measures to ensure effective instructional decisions. We expect Tier 3 interventions to be highly individualized, so instruction needs to be adjusted more often to accelerate students' growth. This cannot happen if teachers do not have data about students' progress at regular intervals.

SELECTING DIAGNOSTIC
AND PROGRESS-MONITORING ASSESSMENTS

So far, we have described three different types of assessments used within an RTI framework:

1. *Screening assessment:* The use of a universal tool to determine whether any students are at risk for learning problems. With secondary students, it is likely that adequate data exist from state-level standardized tests for these tests to serve as universal screeners for identifying reading difficulties.
2. *Diagnostic assessment:* More specific assessment of a student's individual strengths and weaknesses, to determine the intensity and component skills of the intervention.
3. *Progress-monitoring assessment:* Frequent and ongoing measurement of student knowledge and skills, to evaluate the effectiveness of the instruction. While screening and diagnostic measures tend to have high levels of reliability and validity, progress monitoring may be carried out with CBMs (see Chapter 2).

You already know that your state assessment can be the universal screener that allows you to identify whether students need Tier 2 or Tier 3. The value of a reliable and valid state-level assessment is that it avoids adding unnecessary testing for students.

There are few valid and reliable diagnostic tests available for use at the secondary level. It can be tempting to adopt measures developed for elementary students that provide results in the skills or components of reading and writing needed to plan instruction for your middle and high school students. But if the assessments have not been developed or researched for use with adolescents, the results need to be interpreted with caution.

We realize, however, that assessments that have been normed and used with elementary students may be the only tools you have available. For any instrument you use, we advise you to give careful consideration to its psychometric properties, the sample on which it was normed, and its intended use. The checklist below will help you determine whether a diagnostic instrument is appropriate.

Considerations for selecting diagnostic assessments	Yes	No
1. Was the assessment normed with students of the age group for which it will be used?		
2. Was the assessment normed with students whose language, ethnic, and cultural backgrounds are similar to those of the students for whom it will be used?		
3. Is the assessment based on scientific research published in peer-reviewed journals?		
4. Do the publishers provide information on each portion of the assessment's established reliability and validity?		
5. Does the assessment provide separate results for the specific skill areas of: • Word identification? • Oral reading fluency? • Silent reading fluency? • Vocabulary? • Narrative text comprehension? • Informational text comprehension? • Writing?		
6. Are there sufficient explanations of the standardized administration procedures for each portion of the test?		
7. Is there guidance in the manual on how to interpret the results and make instructional decisions?		
8. Is training on the administration and interpretation of the assessment provided as part of the package/license?		
9. Is a mechanism for organizing the data at the classroom and school levels included with the assessment?		
10. Does the manual sufficiently explain how much time must lapse between test administrations?		

 Stop and Think

In what ways are the considerations for selecting an assessment to use with adolescents similar to or different from those for selecting an assessment to use with lower

elementary students? Do you know how to locate information on the reliability and validity of instruments? Are there other questions you might need to ask about the appropriateness of an assessment for use with your students?

Remember that different instruments may be needed to measure different skills. An assessment that provides valid and reliable results in the domain of fluency, for example, may not be appropriate to measure students' word identification skills. Use all available information to design an appropriate intervention plan for each student, and continue to gather data on students' progress.

There are also relatively few progress-monitoring instruments for secondary students. However, they present a slightly different set of considerations. To be useful, progress-monitoring assessments must be time-efficient and cost-effective. This is because they are administered more often than diagnostic assessments. If progress-monitoring instruments are too expensive or take too long to administer, the data may be acquired at the expense of valuable instructional time. Resources that summarize screening and diagnostic assessments can be found in Appendix F.

Although group-administered assessments can seem more efficient, we have experienced behavior issues when attempting to test very large groups of intervention students at a time. The distractions these issues cause in a testing environment may compromise results. If you use group-administered assessments, be sure to schedule enough adult monitors to:

- Persuade students to take the testing seriously.
- Enforce the proper testing procedures (otherwise, the results would be invalidated).

Similar to the checklist we have provided above for diagnostic assessments, we offer a set of guiding questions to help your literacy leadership team determine whether a progress-monitoring instrument is appropriate.

Considerations for selecting progress-monitoring assessments	Yes	No
1. Was the assessment normed with students of the age group for which it will be used?		
2. Was the assessment normed with students whose language, ethnic, and cultural backgrounds are similar to those of the students for whom it will be used?		
3. Is the assessment based on scientific research published in peer-reviewed journals?		
4. Do the publishers provide information on the assessment's established reliability and validity?		
5. Does the assessment have predictive validity for the annual state assessment?		

6. Is there sufficient explanation of the standardized administration procedures, including:
  • Whether it must be administered to groups or individuals?
  • How much time the administration takes?
  • How much time it takes to score each student's test?
  • Who can administer the test?		

7. Is there guidance in the manual on how to interpret the results and make instructional decisions?		
8. Is training on the administration and interpretation of the assessment provided as part of the package/license?		
9. Is a mechanism for organizing the data at the classroom and school levels included with the assessment?		
10. Does the manual sufficiently explain how frequently the assessment can be administered during a school year?		

STOP *Stop and Think*

As students get older, available assessment instruments are not as likely to detect small changes in reading performance. Moreover, we do not expect older students with serious reading difficulties to make extremely rapid progress in very short amounts of time. Therefore, you will notice in the information we provide throughout this book that progress monitoring is conducted much less frequently on the secondary level than it is in elementary grades. However, CBMs can be used as proximal measures to make instructional decisions more frequently, as we discuss in Chapter 4.

If you look back to the section on assessments in Chapter 2, you will see that we account for having all students in all tiers participate in some form of progress monitoring. Secondary schools may elect to use the state assessment and associated benchmarks (also referred to as *short-cycle assessments*) to monitor progress at the Tier 1 level, as well as for entry and exit decisions at the Tiers 2 and 3 levels.

ⓘ USE AND REPORT STANDARD SCORES, NOT GRADE-EQUIVALENT SCORES

When the literacy leadership team is devising the assessment system, we believe that it is crucial to plan professional development about the tests. Teachers need to be knowledgeable about what assessment options are available to them and what information each measure can or cannot provide. Training in the use and interpretation of assessments will also help teachers evaluate a student's progress and explain it in the most appropriate way. For example, it is a common mistake to use grade equivalent scores to describe and track a student's reading ability. Although this is a seemingly simple means of evaluating whether a student is on par with his or her peers, grade equivalent scores are statistically unstable and therefore not suitable for tracking progress over time or comparing performance from year to year. A more reliable and valid way to explain student progress is with percentiles or standard scores.

DIFFERENTIATION OF INSTRUCTION

We have spent a good portion of this chapter outlining the ideal situation: providing two tiers of intervention support and directly placing all students who fail the state assessment into the appropriate tier. We know that this may be impossible for some schools. You may consider your school lucky to be able to provide one tier of intervention.

Let's return to our estimates of the numbers of students who would need intervention in an average school operating within an RTI framework. If you can meet the needs of 80% of the students with enhanced Tier 1, this means that approximately 20% of students will require supplemental support (Fletcher & Vaughn, 2009; Reschly, 2003). To serve as many students as possible with the resources you have available, adjust the group size recommendations provided earlier according to the comparison below:

Standard three-tiered model	One level of intervention
• Tier 1: 25–30 students	• Tier 1: 25–30 students
• Tier 2: 10–12 students	• Tiers 2–3: 10 students
• Tier 3: approximately 6 students	

Within this single form of intervention class, the teacher may need to differentiate instruction on the basis of students' needs. This involves multigroup instruction, which tends to be unfamiliar to middle and high school teachers. So you are probably wondering how to go about differentiating groups. This can be particularly challenging when you do not have support from a teaching assistant. It may be more helpful if we use a specific example to explain the steps.

The interventionist at Hillcrest High School, Mr. Jardin, reviewed the results of the state reading test for the 10 sophomores in his intervention class. At this grade, students must obtain a scale score of 2100 or better to be considered passing. However, Hillcrest considers students whose scale score is 2150 and below at risk for reading failure, given the 50-point confidence interval. The students in Mr. Jardin's class represented a spread of scale scores from 1702 to 2135.

After administering diagnostic assessments to the students, Mr. Jardin knew he would need to divide the students into more homogeneous groups to meet their specific needs as indicated by the test results. Given his class size and the kinds of instructional practices he identified to meet students' needs, Mr. Jardin decided to form two groups. Group 1 would be a group of students with relatively average word-reading ability who had more needs in the area of vocabulary and comprehension. Group 2 would consist of students with needs not only in the area of vocabulary and comprehension, but also in the area of basic word-reading and decoding skills. The chart below shows the available assessment data on Mr. Jardin's students.

	WJ III* Word Attack	WJ III* Letter Word ID	WJ III* Passage Comprehension	GRADE** Reading Comprehension	TOWRE Sight Word Efficiency	TOWRE Phonemic Decoding Efficiency	State Reading Test
Group 1							
Student 1	**115**	93	86	89	94	102	2019
Student 2	**95**	90	74	78	91	86	1947
Student 3	**99**	97	90	92	98	97	2000
Student 4	**123**	109	92	94	107	110	2135
Student 5	**97**	90	87	87	97	86	1994
Group 2							
Student 6	**88**	83	90	72	89	84	1750
Student 7	**81**	78	82	92	89	80	1822
Student 8	**71**	64	56	83	71	72	1735
Student 9	**88**	82	83	92	85	97	1831
Student 10	**67**	52	53	76	56	59	1702

*WJ III, Woodcock–Johnson III. **GRADE, Group Reading Assessment and Diagnostic Evaluation.

To divide these students into the two groups, Mr. Jardin looked at the students' WJ III Word Attack scores (given above in boldface), which are indicative of word-reading ability. Using the interpretation guidance provided with the WJ III, he considered students who scored 95 or above on this measure to be average word readers, while those who scored below 95 needed more direct word study instruction. With this standard, Mr. Jardin was able to form two groups of five students each, as shown in the data table.

Once you have determined your smaller groups within the class, you are ready to plan approximately how much time each week you will devote to the different reading components or skills. Careful planning will ensure that you address all components, even though you have groups with different primary focus areas. To get you started, we have made an example of how Mr. Jardin might apportion a week's worth of class time to the skill areas his two groups of students need:

Group 1: 50-minute periods (250 minutes weekly)

- Vocabulary/morphology: 35–45 minutes
- Comprehension/text reading: 170–180 minutes
- Attitude/motivation: 15–25 minutes

Group 2: 50-minute periods (250 minutes weekly)
- Word study/text reading: 100–110 minutes
- Vocabulary/morphology: 35–45 minutes
- Comprehension/text reading: 70–80 minutes
- Attitude/motivation: 15–25 minutes

The final stage of planning for multigroup instruction is to develop the actual lesson plans. Because the two groups of students in the Mr. Jardin example had some common needs (e.g., vocabulary or attitude and motivation), he could design part of the lesson activities around whole-group instruction for meeting all students' needs. For example, he might determine that all students would benefit from learning an "inference strategy," and he could teach and practice with the entire group, but would then differentiate the text and time devoted to practicing the strategy between groups.

To connect this with the information on effective instruction reviewed in Chapter 2, the "I do" stage of instruction could be delivered to the entire class. Then some students would need extra practice or support in the "We do" phase before moving on to the "You do" phase. To see a sample lesson plan that combines whole-group and small-group instruction, see Box 3.5.

 Stop and Think

The sample plans in Box 3.5 are based on 50-minute intervention class periods. They may need to be adjusted for other class durations or alternative schedules. See Appendices A–C for sample master and bell schedules in middle, junior high, and high schools of different sizes. The descriptions are suggestions for what might take place, but the actual instruction you plan must be tailored to the needs of your own students as identified in diagnostic testing. You will notice, for example, that not all students receive instruction in word study. By dividing the class into smaller groups, you can target those skills that students need to develop and not waste instructional time on those skills that students have already mastered. Also keep in mind that any strategy included in the lesson plan must be taught to students, using the effective instructional techniques described in Chapters 2 and 4 of this book.

(The Reflection Questions for Chapter 3 appear on page 100)

BOX 3.5. SAMPLE LESSON PLAN FOR TWO-GROUP INSTRUCTION

Week X Sample

Monday	Tuesday	Wednesday	Thursday	Friday
Vocab./morphology (*10 min.*) *Whole group* • Text: Expository passage related to novel. • Intro. key words. • Examples/nonexamples; tell Tier 3 words.	**Vocab./morphology** (*10 min.*) *Whole group* • Intro./model a vocabulary graphic organizer that includes the definition of a word, the characteristics of the word that help a student understand it, and examples and nonexamples of the word. • Use words from Day 1 with which students have struggled (complete one as a model and have students complete one by themselves)	**Comp./text reading** (*25 min.*) *Whole group* • Partner reading: Each pair generates the main idea of a passage and logs the words with which partners struggled. • Pairs share and come up with main idea of whole passage.	**Vocab./morphology** (*10 min.*) *Whole group* • Review vocabulary map model.	**Vocab./morphology** (*15 min.*) *Whole group* • Morphology work: Sort word parts (incorporate clunk cards).
Comp./text reading (*35 min.*) *Whole group* • Intro. passage: Chapter 4. • Read passage. • Intro. strategy: Generating the main idea (weave in questioning and words with which students struggle).	**Comp./text reading** (*35 min.*) *Group 1 only, independently* • Read again and keep log of difficult words. • Generating the main idea (weave in questioning).	**Comp./text reading** (*20 min.*) *Group 1 only* • New passage and repeat above.	**Comp./text reading** (*20 min.*) *Whole group* • Chapters 5 and 6: Main idea of whole passage.	**Comp./text reading** (*30 min.*) *Group 1 only* • Read expository text related to novel and log difficult words.
	Word study/ text reading (*35 min.*) *Group 2 only, with teacher* • Word study technique: Syllable division. • Word study technique in sentences. • Word study technique in paragraphs. • Read whole passage.	**Word study/ text reading** (*20 min.*) *Group 2 only, with teacher* • Word study practice: Syllable division.	**Comp./text reading** (*15 min.*) *Group 1 only* • Generate questions for chapters.	**Word study/ fluency** (*30 min.*) *Group 1 only, with teacher* • Fluency progress monitoring
			Word study/ text reading (*15 min.*) *Group 2 only, with teacher* • Review syllable types.	
Attitude/motivation (*5 min.*) *Whole group*	**Attitude/motivation** (*5 min.*) *Whole group*	**Attitude/motivation** (*5 min.*) *Whole group*	**Attitude/motivation** (*5 min.*) *Whole group*	**Attitude/motivation** (*5 min.*) *Whole group*

Week Y Sample

Monday	Tuesday	Wednesday	Thursday	Friday
Vocab./morphology (10 min.) *Whole group* • Text: Novel. • Intro. key words. • Examples/nonexamples; tell Tier 3 words.	**Vocab./morphology** (5 min.) *Whole group* • Review words from Monday. • Review difficult words.	**Vocab./morphology** (15 min.) *Whole group* • Model the vocabulary graphic organizer, using words with which students have struggled.	**CBM** (15 min.) *Whole group* • Generate the main idea of a paragraph. • Who, what, when, where questions. • Review difficult words from logs. • Word study concepts: Morphology or syllabication.	**Vocab./morphology** (15 min.) *Whole group* • Morphemic analysis with difficult words from log.
Comp./text reading (35 min.) *Whole group* • Review generating the main idea. • Read Chapter 7 (partner reading). • Generate main idea with partners and share. • Log difficult words.	**Comp./text reading** (40 min.) *Whole group* • Read Chapter 8 and have partners generate the main idea. • Log difficult words. • Generate main idea and questions.	**Comp./text reading** (30 min.) *Group 1 only* • Give supplemental related expository text and do same routine as Tuesday. **Word study/text reading** (30 min.) *Group 2 only* • Word study concept: Syllabication. • Word study concept in sentences. • Word study concept in paragraphs.	**Comp./text reading** (35 min.) *Group 1 only* • Read Chapter 9 and have partners generate a main idea at end of each paragraph. **Word study/text reading** (35 min.) *Group 2 only, with teacher* • Read Chapter 9	**Comp./text reading** (15 min.) *Group 1 only* • Game: "Would a ___ be a ___?", using difficult words from log. **Word study/text reading** (15 min.) *Group 2 only, with teacher* • Directions/modeling for independent word study activity. **Comp./text reading** (15 min.) *Group 1, with teacher* • Review game. **Word study/text reading** (15 min.) *Group 2 only, independently* • Word part sorts.
Attitude/motivation (5 min.) *Whole group*	**Attitude/motivation** (5 min.) *Whole group*	**Attitude/motivation** (5 min.) *Whole group*	**Attitude/motivation** (5 min.) *Whole group*	**Attitude/motivation** (5 min.) *Whole group*

Week Z Sample

Monday	Tuesday	Wednesday	Thursday	Friday
Comp./text reading *(30 min.)* *Whole group* • Model keeping new log of difficult words with first few paragraphs. • Have partners read Chapter 10 and log difficult words.	**Vocab./Morphology** *(15 min.)* *Whole group* • Model completing the vocabulary graphic organizer with difficult words logged on Monday.	**Comp./text reading** *(15 min.)* *Whole group* • Review questions generated by Group 1 on Tuesday. • Review generating *when* and *where* questions.	**Vocab./morphology** *(15 min.)* *Whole group* • Word sorts. • Breaking words into morphemes.	**Vocab./morphology** *(15 min.)* *Whole group* • Making real words with word parts.
Attitude/motivation *(20 min.)* *Whole group* • Student reward for meeting class 6-week progress goal.	**Comp./text reading** *(35 min.)* *Group 1 only* • Give supplemental related expository text. • Log difficult words in new text and identify appropriate strategy. • Also generate "when" and "where" questions. ‖ **Comp./text reading** *(35 min.)* *Group 2 only, with teacher* • Read supplemental text with students. • Review generating the main idea.	**Comp./text reading** *(30 min.)* *Group 1 only* • Read supplemental expository text, and make a quiz with self-generated questions. • Partners give each other the quiz. ‖ **Word study/text reading** *(30 min.)* *Group 2 only, with teacher* • Reteach breaking words into morphemes and rules of syllabication. ‖ **Attitude/motivation** *(5 min.)* *Whole group*	**Comp./text reading** *(35 min.)* *Group 1 only, with teacher* • Introduce *how* and *why* questions. • Practice with supplementary text. ‖ **Word study/text reading** *(35 min.)* *Group 2 only* • Breaking words into syllables. • Read text and identify words matching certain syllable types.	**Comp./text reading** *(35 min.)* *Group 1 only, with teacher* • Read Chapter 11. • Generate *how* and *why* questions in chapter. ‖ **Word study/text reading** *(35 min.)* *Group 2 only, with teacher* • Read Chapter 10 with students. • Generate main idea.

REFLECTION QUESTIONS

1. Why is it a good idea to provide Tiers 2 and 3 *in addition to* (rather than in place of) the Tier 1 core classes?

2. Consider the resources and needs of your school. Will you be able to provide two tiers of intervention or just one? How will you place students in each of those interventions and why? Describe your choices.

3. How can you distinguish Tier 2 from Tier 3?

4. Can you describe what a Tier 2 class is and what it is not?

5. What are some qualities and qualifications you might look for in a reading intervention teacher?

6. Think about the typical class sizes and struggling readers at your school. If you implemented a three-tiered model, about how many students in each class at each tier are likely?

7. What are two options to use to place students into the appropriate tiers? Explain.

8. What are some factors to consider regarding assessing students in the top-down or bottom-up procedure?

9. Why is it important to monitor progress more frequently for students in more intensive interventions?

10. Describe the overall purpose of screening, diagnostic, and progress monitoring assessments.

11. What are some factors to take into consideration in deciding which diagnostic and progress-monitoring measures to use?

CHAPTER 4

Step 3

Guidelines for Tiers 2 and 3

In Chapter 3, we have differentiated Tiers 2 and 3 to assist you with determining which tier is suitable for students with different instructional needs. Essential to effective implementation of interventions is knowing how to provide highly effective and well-specified instruction to meet these students' learning needs. This chapter expands on the features of effective instruction introduced in Chapter 2 as a means to enhancing Tier 1 instruction. Now we examine how to build on those features to enhance outcomes for students with reading difficulties.

HOW TO PROVIDE EFFECTIVE INSTRUCTION

The ultimate goal of teaching is to provide instructional practices that maximize students' learning. Although this is true for all teachers and all content areas, it is even more important for students with learning difficulties. The students who are least able to learn incidentally and independently are the ones who most need highly effective instruction.

Have you ever been in a class where the teacher knew the content really well, but the *delivery* of the content made it difficult for you or others to learn? Perhaps the teacher was just lecturing to the whole class, not requiring students to respond or to practice the skill being taught. Perhaps the teacher posed a question to the whole class, but only one student actually had the opportunity to apply knowledge in answering the question. Perhaps every student was required to move at the same pace and work on the same skill, with little room for differentiation or few means for catching students who performed below their peers.

The essential instructional practices described in Chapter 2 for Tier 1 also apply to the instruction and teaching practices for students in Tiers 2 and 3. Incorporating features of effective instruction ensures that students are provided with adequate modeling, feedback, and opportunities for practice to be successful and make progress. This is especially important for students who are struggling and need more guidance. Let's review those features we have previously introduced, before we look at additional practices needed to support students who have been identified for reading intervention. Table 4.1 is the same as Table 2.1 in Chapter 2.

Effective instruction is important in all tiers. However, students in Tiers 2 and 3 will need even more explicit and individualized feedback, attention to pacing, and opportunities to respond and practice their newly acquired strategies. To help you expand your knowledge of these practices, Table 4.2 adds several categories to the features of effective instruction listed in Tables 2.1 and 4.1.

 Stop and Think

Implementing effective instructional practices is a critical aspect of RTI. Although we have introduced the features in separate groups (and chapters), all the features are applicable in every tier. How can you help content-area teachers understand the importance of implementing effective instructional practices? Is there anything about the features that might differ in elementary versus secondary classes?

TABLE 4.1. Features of Effective Instruction for All Classes

1. *Communicate clear expectations.*

2. *Model expectations with overt demonstrations* of thoughts and actions ("I do").

3. *Break the task into small steps, and provide feedback* after each step ("We do"). Gradually increase the number of steps or the length of work completed between feedback periods.
   • Offer feedback that specifically identifies what to continue and what to change.
   • Provide many opportunities for students to discuss their developing understanding.

4. *Plan for follow-up instruction* ("You do") to include:
   • Teaching self-monitoring and fix-up strategies.
   • Supplementing background knowledge.
   • Providing real-world applications.

5. *Incorporate student engagement,* such as:
   • Offering some choice in materials, activities, and/or products.
   • Making connections to other lessons and content.

6. *Provide distributed practice.*

7. *Differentiate instruction* by:
   • Utilizing different groupings of students.
   • Making the curriculum appropriately challenging across ability levels.

TABLE 4.2. Features of Effective Instruction for Intervention Classes

8. *Adjust the pacing* of instruction.

9. Redirect off-task behavior to *maximize engaged time on task*.

10. Teach students the "big ideas" and/or key concepts that you want them to learn, and provide multiple opportunities to apply them.

11. *Provide immediate instructional feedback,* with these characteristics:
    - It is *task-specific.*
    - *It leads to self-regulated correction.*
    - It contains a clear and *explicit indication of goals.*

12. *Build students' motivation and engagement.*

13. *Use ongoing assessment.*

Tables 4.1 and 4.2 are valuable for all teachers and essential for teachers working with students who have reading difficulties. Let's examine each of the features presented in Table 4.2.

Adjusting the Pace of Instruction

In discussing class sizes in Chapter 3, we have said that having fewer students in an intervention class may increase the engaged time on task. The rationale is that with fewer students, each individual has more practice opportunities specific to his or her instructional needs.

(i) COMMON MISUNDERSTANDINGS ABOUT DIFFERENTIATION AT TIERS 2 AND 3

Although there are instructional advantages to smaller class sizes, they also present potential misunderstandings. For example, some intervention teachers may be tempted to slow the pace because the students are considered to be struggling with reading. In addition, creating these small, homogeneous groups is occasionally misinterpreted as the only differentiation the students need. On the contrary, students in Tiers 2 and 3 need effective instruction all the more if they are to make enough gains to keep up with the core curriculum in Tier 1. This means that even in small groups, pacing needs to be quick, and instruction needs to be highly individualized.

At this point, you may be wondering whether our recommendations are feasible. We want to assure you that not all features of effective instruction are complex, and that most are interwoven into a teacher's regular practices and procedures. Adjusting the pacing of instruction is one such feature of effective instruction that can be easily implemented. To adjust pacing, the teacher does the following:

1. Reviews initial practice items for accuracy, and provides immediate feedback.
2. Checks in with students during an activity, to be sure they are performing it correctly.
3. Asks students to demonstrate what they are doing by having them either:
   a. Explain the process as they accomplish the task, or
   b. Show each step to accomplish the task, as appropriate.
4. And, when necessary, assists students with performing tasks correctly.

Did you notice the substeps of item 3 above? These are very important. Checking in with students does not need to be difficult, but it does need to be thorough. It is usually not enough to simply ask students whether they understand a concept. Many adolescents who have struggled with reading for a few years are reluctant to draw extra attention to their difficulties and may not be very skilled at self-monitoring their understanding. Often students choose the response that will encourage the teacher to move on, even if what they really need is to be retaught material they may consider boring.

Therefore, our use of "checking in" extends beyond the superficial and requires that the students demonstrate what they know in some way. One way to do this is to have them demonstrate the skill to a partner. Another option is to use response cards that will enable the teacher to assess the understanding of all students at once. For example, you can fasten three cards to each student's desk: a green card that says "YES," a yellow card that says "MAYBE," and a red card that says "NO."

Then you orally pose a question that reflects the concept just taught and ask the students to hold up their answers quickly. If you are working on identifying syllable types, you may ask, "Does a closed syllable end with a vowel?" After the students show the response card of their choice, you can ask a student who answered the question correctly to explain the reasoning for the response. This will give students who did not answer correctly an immediate reteaching. It will also prevent you from basing decisions about future lessons on the response accuracy, inaccuracy, or lucky guessing of one student.

You can also adjust the type of response required to students' individual needs. Some students may have a lot of difficulty with a skill and require a response with a lower risk for error than their peers who are performing the skill at a slightly higher level. The higher a student's level of proficiency with the skill, the higher the risk for error that can be built into the response type. We offer suggestions for different responses in Table 4.3.

TABLE 4.3. Varying Response Types According to Students' Needs

Not yet proficient at the skill = response with low risk for error	Intermediate proficiency with skill = response with moderate risk for error	Advanced proficiency with skill = response with high risk for error
YES/NO/MAYBE cards	Oral response based on pattern, template, or stem	Independent oral response (no choices or templates offered)
Point to correct answer	Multiple-choice answers	Written/open response

 Stop and Think

Frequent checking in with students can take extra time (even when done quickly), but can save time in the long run. What benefits can you identify for frequently checking in with students? Are there techniques that are more appropriate for adolescents than for younger students? Can you think of other efficient ways to check on students' understanding? How do check-in procedures fit within the components of RTI as you understand them?

Checking in with students usually can be done very quickly and takes minimal instructional time. In fact, it will save time in the long run by allowing you to make much more accurate decisions about the direction and pacing of your teaching. Figure 4.1 provides additional guidelines for pacing. Remember that the goal is to accelerate the learning of adolescents who are significantly below grade-level ability in reading, so checking in with students during a lesson is linked to moving them along appropriately. To help you understand what monitoring and adjusting the pacing might look like in practice, Box 4.1 describes what is happening in a reading intervention class.

• Use a quick, manageable pace during your lesson.
• Pull "slower students" ahead at a reasonable pace by incorporating other effective instructional practices, rather than decelerating instruction overall.
• Prepare a variety of relevant and engaging lessons, so that you are ready to skip ahead if you notice that students have mastered a skill (i.e., they can independently complete or apply the skill with ease).
• Change activities frequently during the class period to reduce "downtime" and keep an appropriate amount of pressure on students to stay actively involved in the lesson.

FIGURE 4.1. Pacing of intervention instruction.

BOX 4.1. ADJUSTING THE PACE OF INSTRUCTION WITH A COMMERCIAL READING PROGRAM

Miss Lewis is using a scientifically based reading program in her class. The program has a scope and sequence with 42 lessons. When she was trained to use the program, Miss Lewis was told she must do every lesson, in order, with every student. On Lesson 12, however, she realizes that many students in her seventh-period class are increasingly off task, and Miss Lewis is spending more time redirecting them. She suspects that these students are bored because they are able to whiz through the practice examples. Miss Lewis wonders if some of the lessons are covering skills the students have already mastered, so she decides to try to review Lesson 15 with the off-task group while the other students complete an independent practice included with Lesson 12.

The small group is able to answer a majority of the questions in the review of Lesson 15 with automaticity, and the off-task behavior stops. Miss Lewis decides to finish reviewing Lesson 15 with these students, and to start them quickly on Lesson 16. She now has two homogeneous groups in her seventh-period intervention class, so she will have to stagger her instruction. She also realizes that she must carefully monitor the students who have "skipped ahead," to ensure that they do not later struggle with skills they missed in Lessons 13 and 14. If they demonstrate difficulty in a later lesson, Miss Lewis will probably need to go back to the appropriate material, adjust her pacing, and/or reteach particular concepts.

Redirecting Off-Task Behavior as Appropriate

The description of the intervention class in Box 4.1 refers to students' being off task during the lesson. As you know, this problem is not unique to students who struggle with reading. Any secondary teacher or administrator knows the importance of a supportive learning environment for making instruction smooth and efficient. We have discussed in Chapter 2 how such an environment is fostered, in part, by a PBS system. At the classroom level, PBS includes an observable plan for preventing and managing disruptive behaviors so that they do not interfere with maximizing the instructional time.

Sometimes simply ignoring students' negative attention-seeking behavior is the best approach to extinguishing it. However, we believe that the most important tool for a well-managed classroom is to maintain appropriate, fast pace instruction and to incorporate all the other features of effective instruction, such as providing multiple opportunities for students to be engaged and to receive feedback on their learning. When students are actively involved in learning and applying the specific skills they need to be successful, they will have less time even to think about misbehaving.

Teaching the "Big Ideas"

Students need to understand the fundamental principles of a unit of study in order to make sense of and remember all of the subordinate concepts (Vaughn & Bos, 2009). In reading, for example, the "big ideas" are phonemic awareness, phonics and word study, fluency, vocabulary, and comprehension. Therefore, reading courses focus on teaching these domains and giving students multiple opportunities to apply their developing knowledge or skills. Every subject area, course, and unit within a course has its own key concepts. So although you may be teaching the "big idea" of comprehension in a reading intervention class, you may be using a science text that addresses the key concept of acoustics. Students need to be taught not only the targeted comprehension strategy, but also the principle of acoustics, in order to understand the text.

When reading intervention teachers use content related to what students are learning in social studies and science, they provide opportunities for students to extend their academic vocabulary and their comprehension. Students who attend reading intervention classes may have more opportunities to apply their developing knowledge of the scientific concepts they are learning in their physical science class. In our science example, the students' goal is to acquire a deeper understanding of acoustics, so they need to practice solving real-world problems that require application of that principle and its related concepts. In reading intervention, the goal is for students to understand increasingly complex text, so they need opportunities to practice applying comprehension strategies to multiple texts of different genres and integrating their developing comprehension skills with the other "big ideas" in reading. Chapter 3 contains sample lesson plans (see Figure 3.2 and Box 3.5) and a scenario of instruction (see Box 3.2) that provide more explanation of how to accomplish this. In addition, you will find sample lessons appropriate for content area and reading intervention classes in Appendix D and additional lessons for reading intervention classes in Appendix E.

Providing Immediate Instructional Feedback

Keeping students on task and providing time for them to practice their newly learned skills is valuable as long as students are practicing the skills correctly. *Immediate, explicit feedback* and follow-up instruction are essential to make productive use of the practice opportunities. There are three important elements to effective feedback:

1. *Feedback is* task specific. When students are performing a skill correctly, saying "Good job!" does not indicate what they were doing that was "good" and contributing to their success. Rather, vague praise requires students to infer what behaviors they should continue. Instead, the positive feedback should be very spe-

cific to the task on which they are working, such as "I really like how you blended that word together after you figured out each sound."

If, on the other hand, a student makes an error, you should not be afraid to deliver corrective feedback. Contrary to the concern of many teachers, you will not hurt a student's feelings by giving him or her a correct answer or modeling a correct method—as long as you deliver it in a neutral tone. A tone of exasperation or condemnation is what demotivates students. Rather, corrective feedback should be immediate and firm, and should provide the student with the correct response and the justification for that response. For example, if a student is practicing spelling and changes the word *focus* to *focussed*, you might say:

> "I notice you are trying to apply the doubling rule before adding a suffix that starts with a vowel. When the accent is not on the final syllable with the short vowel, the consonant is not doubled. The accent on the word *focus* is on the first syllable, *fo-*, so you would not double the *-s*. The word would be spelled *f-o-c-u-s-e-d.*"

It is far more beneficial to model a correct method or response than to allow students to struggle continually through incorrect applications of skills. If you are feeling overwhelmed at the prospect of reaching each student at the exact moment he or she needs task-specific feedback, remember that peers can also support each other in this process. You might try assigning partner roles, such as Partner A and Partner B. Then you can ask students to make a response to each other: "Partner A's, tell the B's what the first sound in *shepherd* is." The Partner B's can then deliver positive or corrective feedback that reinforces both students' learning.

2. *Feedback leads students to self-regulated correction.* Being specific about what the student is doing correctly or incorrectly has the additional benefit of providing the information needed for self-monitoring future applications of the skill. It serves as a form of scaffolding that reinforces the rules and procedures students can use strategically to support their own learning. Other ways you can use feedback to help students become more self-sufficient include directing students to sources of information, telling them what options they can try to improve their understanding, and providing them with such tools as lists of steps or self-check questions.

3. *Feedback contains an explicit indication of the goals.* You should clearly and repeatedly explain the purpose of activities and the expectations for what students should know and be able to do. We have mentioned this in Chapter 2 (see also Step 1 in Figure 4.1), but it plays a role in feedback as well. Students need to be reoriented to the purpose and expectations to know how effectively they are meeting those goals. Students should be able to repeat directions in their own words to demonstrate understanding of the expectations. That way, when they are receiving task-specific feedback or self-regulating their learning, they will be able to connect each action or step with the purpose and expectations for the overall lesson.

4. *Feedback identifies what aspect of a response is correct and then scaffolds how to refine the answer for improvement.* For example, a teacher asks students, "How do you know that the Civil War was going to last for more than a few months?" A student responds that the chapter they read indicated that the Civil War would be long. The teacher acknowledges this student's use of text: "I appreciate that you remembered what you read about the Civil War and that it said it would be long." The teacher then follows with a scaffold: "However, in the figure on page 46, Lincoln's views of the war are described. What did Lincoln say that makes you think the war will take place over a long time?" Students are eager to respond thoughtfully when they realize that a teacher will acknowledge what they know and will also guide them to think or learn more about what they read.

Building Motivation and Engagement

Motivation and engagement are separate elements of effective instruction that are related to pacing and feedback. In this section, we define and illustrate the two terms, which are frequently considered synonymous.

Students who are *motivated* have a willingness to do the work well. You cannot assume, however, that they are doing any more than complying with your directions. After all, students can be motivated for many different reasons: wanting to avoid punishment, wanting to maintain eligibility for extracurricular activities, wanting to please the teacher or their parents, wanting to be left alone, and so on. As you know, fostering some form of motivation is essential for secondary students who struggle with reading. Students who are not motivated to do well in school, or who feel hopeless after years of not experiencing success, usually do not have a sense of connection to school—they "shut down" during the day. This makes it challenging to teach them and increases their difficulty in making academic gains (Kamil et al., 2008). You can motivate students in these ways:

- Offer regular encouragement and positive feedback.
- Involve the students in setting personal learning or behavioral goals.
- Keep their attention and interest with quick-paced lessons.
- Provide interesting texts to read, as well as choices among texts.
- Maintain a positive, supportive environment.

Sadly, many struggling students report that they are never praised by teachers. A high school dropout once told us:

"When I was dropping out, I was only noticed and remembered for my negative behavior or poor grades. All the negative attention drove me away from class and prevented me from seeking assistance from teachers . . . which was *not* what I needed. I was honestly desperate for some kind of positive recognition, but didn't really receive any."

This student's experience serves as a poignant reminder to us all that it is especially important to be attentive to even small accomplishments, and not to reserve our praise for those who excel. For example, you might praise students for being in their seats on time or for asking a question. You might have heard this referred to as "catching students being good." The point is not to overlook opportunities to acknowledge students in positive ways.

Motivating students to give school (and reading) another try is the first step, but to accelerate progress and sustain improvements, students need to be engaged in the work. Students who are *engaged* are deeply and meaningfully involved in processing information. You might say they are engrossed in the work to such an extent that they would continue it whether you were there to monitor them or not. Recommendations for fostering engagement (Guthrie, 2008; Kamil et al., 2008) include these:

- Teach the processes or strategies that can assist students in assuming greater responsibility for their learning.
- Explain how and when strategies are useful, as well as how to modify strategies for different tasks.
- Link performance to effort rather than ability.
- Create opportunities for choices (e.g., choices among texts, topics, sequence of activities), and teach students how to make appropriate choices.
- Give a rationale for the work or lesson, and recognize the challenges in completing it.
- Include social interaction during lessons.
- Make lessons valuable beyond the immediate class by connecting them to other lessons, courses, subject areas, and life experiences.

Implementing these recommendations is a means of planning for student success and giving students an active role in managing their learning. This involves, in part, sharing data on or indicators of their progress toward those learning goals.

What Is the Role of Ongoing Assessment?

In Chapters 2 and 3, we have addressed the selection and use of progress-monitoring measures in an RTI framework. You will recall that these assessments provide ongoing measurement of students' knowledge and skills. Data from progress monitoring are intended to help you evaluate your instruction and to provide feedback to students, so that they can monitor their own progress and set their own learning goals. Unlike diagnostic assessment, progress monitoring does not involve a lengthy battery of assessments. Rather, a few short measures capable of generating the pertinent information are acceptable.

Often you will see progress-monitoring results graphed so that the level of student performance and the rate of improvement are easily visible. Figure 4.2 contains

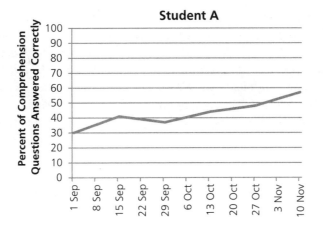

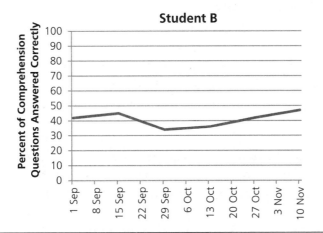

FIGURE 4.2. Progress of Student A and Student B.

two sample graphs created from student progress-monitoring data in the area of reading comprehension. Students were asked to read a series of short paragraphs and answer five comprehension questions targeting the discrimination of main ideas and details (a skill on which they had been working in their intervention class). With their percentages of correct responses at each testing point graphically displayed, can you quickly recognize which student is improving his or her comprehension at a faster rate, even though both students remain below a proficient level?

 Stop and Think

Progress monitoring in lower elementary grades usually involves administering oral reading fluency probes and tracking students' progress in the number of words they read correctly per minute. However, it is believed that the slope of students' growth in oral reading fluency decelerates in the middle grades and above, so that the line mapping their progress flattens (Fuchs, Fuchs, Hosp, & Jenkins, 2001;

Stage & Jacobsen, 2001). An oral reading fluency probe is unlikely to detect small changes in adolescents' performance over short periods of time, so you will notice that throughout this book we do not refer to using oral reading fluency as a progress monitor. This will be an area where implementation of RTI at the secondary level differs from implementation at the elementary level. When examining graphs of data or discussing progress monitoring with colleagues who teach lower grade levels, be aware that you are referring to different skills. Explain your use of CBMs, as will be described in this section.

Progress-monitoring data allow you to determine whether the instruction being delivered is appropriate. The upward trend in the percentage of comprehension questions Student A is answering correctly shows growth, indicating that he is on track to meet grade-level proficiency with this skill. You can continue using the method of strategy instruction that has contributed to his improvement and perhaps move to the next step or add another skill.

Student B, on the other hand, is not showing growth. You will notice that the student's level of performance is not dramatically different from that of Student A. However, the trend line of Student B's progress-monitoring data has a relatively flat slope. She is not profiting as much from the same strategy instruction that Student A is receiving, so she might need one of more of the following adjustments:

- Reteaching by breaking down the strategy into smaller steps.
- A tool for self-checking whether she has followed all the steps of the strategy.
- Instruction in a different method for discriminating main ideas and details.
- Practice applying the skill with passages on her independent reading level, or text she can easily decode, so that the student is not struggling to identify words while also trying to practice the strategy.
- Instruction in other reading skills that might be interfering with her ability to comprehend (e.g., word identification and/or fluency).

Overall, progress-monitoring assessments should be sensitive enough to detect improvements over short periods of time, yet quick and easy to administer and interpret. Without those key ingredients, the measures are not very practical for making instructional decisions. As we have mentioned in Chapter 3, there are not as many valid and reliable progress-monitoring instruments available for use with adolescents as there are for elementary students. Therefore, an option you might consider is using informal CBMs to collect data at regular intervals.

We have introduced CBMs in Chapter 2 as a potential means of screening students for reading difficulties when other benchmark data are unavailable. In terms of progress monitoring, an informal CBM can be thought of as a small quiz to determine whether students are making improvements in the specific skill(s) being taught. For example, diagnostic data might indicate that a student needs intervention in the area of word identification. After a week of Tier 3 instruction, the teacher may have the student read aloud a list of words containing the syllable types the student has been learning. The teacher would calculate the number of words the student read correctly in 1 minute (called the WCPM, as noted in Chapter 3, Box 3.4). WCPM data could be graphed over time to display the student's level of word identification performance and rate of improvement. Any errors the student made in reading the word list would tell the teacher in which areas the student needed instructional adaptations.

Although this type of CBM is not intended to be very complex or formal, we do not want to oversimplify these instruments. To generate the most useful information, informal CBMs need to be designed with care.

ⓘ INFORMAL CBMs FOR READING INTERVENTION ARE SPECIFIC TO IDENTIFIED SKILL AREAS

The questions and tasks on an informal CBM are created to assess no more and no less than the specific reading skill on which the student is working. For example, if you are trying to assess whether or not a student in a Tier 3 class can connect information across paragraphs, it is not necessary to have the student read several pages of text. Students in the most intensive intervention are usually those who demonstrate very slow and laborious reading. To keep the informal CBM efficient, you can have the student read two or three short paragraphs and either answer or generate a question that requires connecting information from at least two paragraphs.

Similarly, if the goal is only to monitor the student's progress in low-level inferencing, it is not necessary to add other question types to the informal CBM, such as literal-level questions about details or more complex inferential questions about causes and effects. However, if the student has been learning to answer different question types targeting different levels of thought, it would be perfectly acceptable and appropriate to include multiple question types over the two to three paragraphs. In short, when you are designing informal CBMs, consider what tasks will give you the most accurate information with the least amount of time or frustration expended in collecting it.

To help improve your ability to recognize and design informal CBMs, try this short activity. In Figure 4.3, you will find a sample informal CBM for a Tier 2 intervention class that has been working on multiple strategies to read and comprehend text independently. Take a moment to study the informal CBM and reflect on its design. When you are ready, try answering the following questions:

1. Use the CBM tasks to determine the different strategies the class has been learning. What skills is the teacher monitoring?
2. Is the teacher able to gain the needed information efficiently?

(Answers to the questions can be found at the end of this chapter.)

1. Read page 56 of *The Watsons Go to Birmingham—1963* (Curtis, 1995). As you read, record the words and/or phrases you don't understand below:

    Unfamiliar word 1: _____

    Unfamiliar word 2: _____

    Unfamiliar word 3: _____

2. Choose one of the words you didn't understand, and tell which fix-up strategy you used to figure out its meaning.

    _____

    _____

3. Write a main-idea statement for page 56.

    _____

    _____

4. Choose THREE of the following question stems. Generate one question about the information on page 56 for each of the 3 stems.

    What _____ ?

    Who _____ ?

    When _____ ?

    Where _____ ?

5. Break down the following words from the passage into their morphemes. The first one is done for you.

    Governorship: _____ govern + or + ship _____

    Fortunately: _____

    Massively: _____

    Endurance: _____

    Pleasantly: _____

    Helpfully: _____

FIGURE 4.3. Informal comprehension CBM.

After creating and administering the informal CBM (usually every 2–3 weeks in Tier 2 or every other week in Tier 3), the next step is to analyze the results. To help make instructional decisions after administering an informal CBM, we have created an informal guide for you to use (see Figure 4.4). The CBM Informational Guide is simply an organizational tool to remind you of the skills and/ or strategies you have assessed and to lead you through establishing your next steps for each student in the class. Follow these easy steps to use the guide effectively:

Weeks of: _____

Students	Strategies, skills, and/or concepts assessed				Comments
Group 1					
Group 2					
Group 3					

(cont.)

FIGURE 4.4. CBM Informational Guide.

Reflection					
What/how did I teach?					
Next steps/ instructional adaptations					

M = Mastery: They know it and can move on to a new skill or strategy.

E = Emerging: They are getting it but need more practice or follow-up instruction.

D = Deficient: They don't have it and need to be retaught with adaptations or increased intensity.

FIGURE 4.4. *(page 2 of 2)*

- *Step 1.* The first step in using the CBM Informational Guide is simply to record which strategies, skills, or concepts are being assessed on the informal CBM. These are, of course, the reading strategies and skills that have been taught and practiced since the last informal CBM was administered. Record each strategy, skill, or concept in its own cell along the top row of the guide, under the heading "Strategies, skills, and/or concepts assessed." Box 4.2 shows you a completed version of the guide as an example. You can see that the following concepts are recorded as having been assessed: identifying unfamiliar words/phrases and using fix-up strategies; generating main-idea statements; generating literal-level questions (*who, what when, where*); and word study (Group 1: breaking words into morphemes; Group 2: underlining/dividing syllables). Note that for the last concept, word study, the teacher divided the students into two groups and was assessing a different strategy in each. This means that the teacher has been differentiating instruction within the same intervention class.

- *Step 2.* The next step in using the CBM Informational Guide is to list the students in their appropriate groups. We have provided sections for up to three groups; however, you may have more or fewer groups, as the needs of your students dictate. The sample guide in Box 4.2 shows a two-group intervention class, as described in Step 1.

- *Step 3.* Next, skip down the first column to the row labeled: "What/how did I teach?" This is where you record a few quick notes about the activity or text you used when teaching each skill or concept. Take a moment to review how this row is completed in the filled-in example in Box 4.2. The information will serve as a reminder to you when reflecting on the results of the informal CBM and planning your next steps or instructional adaptations.

- *Step 4.* Now you are ready to record each student's results on the informal CBM you administered. The key at the bottom of the guide indicates the codes you will use. Record an M when CBM data indicate that the student has mastered the skill, strategy, or concept and is ready to move on to something new. Record an E when CBM data suggest that the student still seems to be emerging in his or her ability to apply the skill or strategy. Perhaps the strategy is beginning to make sense to the student, but he/she has not yet mastered all parts of it. Students designated with E's may benefit from more practice or may require follow-up instruction. Finally, record a D when CBM data indicate that the student is still deficient in his or her ability to apply the skill or strategy. This signifies that the particular concept needs to be retaught with instructional adaptations. In other words, you will need to do something different with the materials, activities, and/or delivery of your instruction, rather than just giving the student more of the same instruction. Notice how the codes are recorded in the filled-in CBM Informational Guide in Box 4.2. Under "Generating literal-level questions," the teacher has included additional information about the specific stems with which particular students had difficulty. This will be useful in the final step.

• *Step 5.* After designating the appropriate performance level (i.e., M, E, or D) for all students, look at the overall results. How did your students respond to your previous instruction? What might you plan for the students who are ready to move on? What follow-up instruction will help push the emerging students to mastery? What will it take to help the deficient students begin to make sense of the concept and experience some success with the skill or strategy? When you are planning your next steps or instructional adaptations in the final row, consider regrouping students or altering the materials, activities, or delivery of instruction in some way. For ideas of how to plan next steps, review the information recorded in the filled-in CBM Informational Guide in Box 4.2. Remember that students who are not making progress need increased intensity of instruction if they are to attain grade-level standards.

BOX 4.2. CBM INFORMATIONAL GUIDE (FILLED-IN EXAMPLE)

Weeks of: _9/10–9/21_

Students	Strategies, skills, and/or concepts assessed				Comments
	Identifying unfamiliar words/ phrases and using fix-up strategies	Generating main-idea statements	Generating literal-level questions (who, what, when, where)	Word study Group 1: Breaking words into morphemes Group 2: Underlining/ dividing syllables	
Group 1					
José	E	M	E—needs when	D	
Maribel	M	M	M	E	
George	E	M	E—needs when and where	D	
Group 2					
Cody	E	E	M	E	
Jorge	D	E	E-needs when and where	D	

Reflection					
What/how did I teach?	• Word/ phrase log (independently and together) • Vocabulary graphic organizer with student-selected words • Morphemic analysis with student-selected words	• Main-idea strategy with paragraphs and chapters (in novel and supplementary text) • Grouping: Whole group and with partners	• Integrated with main-idea strategy • Grouping: Whole group	• Sort word parts, incorporating student-selected words • Underlining syllables • Practice word study concepts in sentences and paragraphs	
Next steps/ instructional adaptations	• Review and practice comprehension fix-up strategy • Practice identifying appropriate fix-up strategy in different circumstances • Add to word log: word + fix-up strategy used • For Maribel: Increase the length of text used when applying the strategy	• Group 1 can move on to summarizing across main ideas • Group 2 needs practice with main idea strategy	• Break students into two groups so José, George, and Jorge can focus on generating when and where questions • Other students can move on to low-level inferences	• Group 1: Reteach breaking words into morphemes • Group 2: Reteach syllabication rules	

M = Mastery: They know it and can move on to a new skill or strategy.

E = Emerging: They are getting it but need more practice or follow-up instruction.

D = Deficient: They don't have it and need to be retaught with adaptations or increased intensity.

Stop and Think

The differences in the use of progress monitoring at the secondary level as compared to the elementary level are important enough to reiterate. In elementary grades, progress-monitoring measures are administered more frequently and often focus on students' oral reading fluency. For comparisons of the frequency of progress monitoring at the elementary versus secondary levels, review Tables 3.1–3.4 in Chapter 3. Be sure you understand how to develop an appropriate CBM for monitoring the progress of your adolescent students by studying pages 113–119 of this chapter, as well as Figures 4.3–4.4 and Box 4.2.

HOW DO WE MAKE INSTRUCTION MORE INTENSE?

In Chapter 3, we have looked at how instruction in each of the three tiers can be distinguished by the increasing levels of intensity. We want to return to this idea as part of reviewing your informal CBM and other progress-monitoring data indicating that students are still struggling. The reason students receive supplemental instruction in a Tier 2 or Tier 3 class is that their needs cannot be met in Tier 1 alone. These interventions are not simply a double dose of Tier 1; rather, the instruction is designed to be more intensive and individualized so that students can accelerate their progress. We offer suggestions for doing this in Table 4.4.

WHAT ARE THE ROLES OF DIFFERENT PERSONNEL?

Up to the point in this chapter, we have concentrated on a teacher's responsibilities for designing and delivering effective instruction in Tiers 2 and 3. We do not want to leave the impression that an interventionist operates alone, however. You will recall from our discussion in Chapter 2 that all members of the RTI literacy leadership team play important roles in the functioning and success of a three-tiered system. Let's return to the table on "Roles and Responsibilities" we have begun in Chapter 2 (Table 2.4 there; see Table 4.5 here).

Remember that some of the individuals in these tables will fall into two categories: their primary contractual role (e.g., special education teacher) and the role they play on the RTI literacy leadership team. The asterisks in Tables 2.4 and 4.5 indicate the responsibilities for each specific role. For example, a special education teacher only serves a supportive role in planning professional development in reading intervention strategies. However, a particular special education teacher may have primary responsibility for that task if he or she is carrying out duties relative to membership on the RTI literacy leadership team.

One of the important tasks that administrators, members of the leadership team, and literacy/intervention coaches perform is to monitor the fidelity with which the components and instructional practices of the intervention are delivered.

TABLE 4.4. Ways to Make Instruction More Intensive and Individualized

Category	Suggestions
Content and skills	• Target the domain(s) of reading (e.g., word identification, fluency, comprehension) with which the student exhibited difficulty in diagnostic testing. 　o If the student had difficulty in multiple domains, give highest priority to the most foundational content (e.g., syllable types). 　o Build from simple (e.g., single-syllable words, individual paragraphs) to complex (e.g., three or more syllables, three or more paragraphs). • Break skills down into their basic components. 　o Teach one component at a time and build up to integrated application. 　o Allow for successive approximations of the overall skill until the student achieves mastery.
Activities	• Form small groups based on instructional goals. • Gradually build from shorter tasks with more frequently interspersed feedback to longer tasks with increased self-monitoring before delivery of instructional feedback. • Adjust the type of response required (see Table 4.3).
Materials	• Allow each student to apply skills to text at an appropriately challenging level (see the descriptions of independent, frustration, and instructional levels in Chapter 1). 　o Begin with independent-level text and progress to instructional-level text. 　o Use text of different genres (i.e., narrative and informational) and organizational patterns (e.g., description, sequence, compare/contrast, problem–solution, cause–effect). • Incorporate computer-aided instruction that can be adapted to individual students' needs.
Delivery of instruction	• Follow the phases of effective instruction outlined in Table 4.1. 　o Spend the most time in "We do." 　o In all phases, offer multiple examples of skill application that show how the skill or strategy is flexibly applied in different contexts. • Adjust the pacing (see Figure 4.1).

Note. Categories are based on University of Texas Center for Reading and Language Arts (2003).

In Chapter 2, we have defined fidelity observations (see Figure 2.2) and addressed their importance in evaluating the effectiveness of the instructional program and planning the next steps of RTI implementation. The elements of the fidelity observations conducted in intervention classes are derived from the scientifically based reading research conducted in developing the adopted program, strategies, and/ or practices.

Also in Chapter 2, we have provided a fidelity observation tool that can be used across the tiers of instruction and intervention (see Figure 2.1). Another option is offered in Figure 4.5. You probably recognize the behaviors listed down the first column: They are the elements of effective instruction explained in this chapter. An observer can use the 3-point scale in Figure 4.5 (i.e., 3 = most of the time; 2 = some of the time; 1 = rarely/not at all) to rate a teacher's fidelity to these features of effective instruction. After the observation, the RTI literacy leadership team can

TABLE 4.5. Roles and Responsibilities

	General education teachers	Special education teachers	Literacy/ instructional/ intervention coaches	Reading interventionists	Administrators	Literacy/ RTI leadership team
Tier 1						
Communicate expectations for schoolwide approach to literacy	*	*	**	*	***	**
Plan professional development in literacy strategies	*	*	*	*	**	***
Implement cross-curricular literacy strategies	***	***	**	**	*	*
Implement effective instruction	***	***	**	***	*	*
Administer and interpret screening assessments	***	***	***	**	*	**
Select instructional materials/resources to support literacy across the curriculum	**	**	***	*	*	***
Monitor the core literacy program (for coaching, feedback, modeling, co-teaching, etc.)	*	*	***	*	***	***
Observe fidelity of Tier 1 implementation	*	*	***	*	***	***
Communicate with parents regarding Tier 1 components, including screening assessments	**	**	**	*	***	**
Ensure funding for Tier 1 materials and professional development	*	*	*	*	***	**
Tiers 2 and 3						
Plan professional development in reading intervention strategies	* (***for any that overlap with content-area strategies)	*	**	*	**	***
Implement reading intervention strategies	*	***	**	***	*	*
Implement effective instructional practices for intervention	*	***	**	***	*	*
Administer and interpret diagnostic and progress-monitoring assessments	*	***	**	***	*	**
Select instructional materials/resources for reading intervention	*	**	***	**	*	***
Monitor the reading interventions (for coaching, feedback, modeling, co-teaching, etc.)	*	*	***	*	***	***
Observe fidelity of Tier 2 and Tier 3 implementation (including distinctions between the levels of intensity)	*	*	***	*	***	***
Communicate with parents regarding components of Tiers 2 and 3, including assessment results and scheduling	*	**	**	***	***	**
Ensure funding for intervention materials and professional development	*	*	*	*	***	**

Note. Key to the symbols:
***The identified individual has primary responsibility for the task.
**The task is an important part of the work for the individual, but he or she has secondary responsibility for completing it.
*This is the most common symbol in the table. These individuals share a supportive responsibility for the task.

Teacher behavior	Most of the time 3	Some of the time 2	Rarely/ not at all 1	N/A
1. Teacher monitors ongoing student performance and adjusts pacing.				
a. Maintains progress-monitoring data used to make instructional decisions (e.g., has data charts, CBM Informational Guide, etc.).				
b. Uses modeling during initial instruction.				
c. Checks initial practice items for correctness and provides immediate feedback.				
d. Checks in with the students during an activity to be sure that they are performing correctly.				
e. Asks students to demonstrate what they are doing.				
f. Assists students in performing tasks correctly.				
2. Teacher redirects off-task behavior as appropriate.				
3. Teacher provides positive and corrective feedback.				
4. Teacher communicates expectations by providing clear and explicit indications of goals for assignments/ activities.				
5. Teacher selects practice items/activities to meet lesson objectives.				
6. Teacher maintains a positive and supportive learning environment.				

FIGURE 4.5. Fidelity observation tool: Features of effective intervention instruction. Based on Bryant et al. (2000).

review the behaviors marked with a 1 or 2 and plan the necessary professional development to support the teacher in strengthening his or her instruction. Keep in mind, however, that the results of one observation on one day may not provide the most complete picture of a teacher's instructional fidelity. As with monitoring the progress of students, it is best to collect data over time and across class periods, so that observers have an opportunity to see the different behaviors and program components.

Because schools may adopt different curricula, the tools in Chapter 2 and Figure 4.5 are a more generalized starting point for your fidelity observations. In addition to the components and teacher behaviors listed, you will add the specific elements of the strategies and programs being used in the intervention. During the observation, you will rate a teacher's fidelity to the steps or features the research basis has identified as integral to each strategy's or component's effectiveness. Figure 4.6 shows an example of how a comprehension strategy might be added to the observation tool. As with the features of effective instruction, the RTI literacy leadership team can review the behaviors marked with a 1 or 2 and plan the necessary professional development to support the teacher in strengthening his or her instruction in the particular curricular components.

 Stop and Think

How can the RTI team use this information to plan for more effective instruction of students or to provide professional development opportunities for reading interventionists? Is a member of your RTI team equipped to take responsibility for conducting fidelity observations? Do you have a system in place for interpreting and using fidelity observation data? How can you help explain why monitoring fidelity is a "non-negotiable" when RTI is implemented? (More information on the "nonnegotiables" can be found in Chapter 5.)

Teacher behavior	Most of the time 3	Some of the time 2	Rarely/ not at all 1	N/A
1. Generating questions				
a. Teacher introduces and models the strategy.				
b. Teacher provides guided practice in applying the strategy to text.				
c. Students independently apply strategy to text.				
d. Teacher provides students with Question cards as scaffolding.				

FIGURE 4.6. Fidelity observation tool: Comprehension instruction. Based on Bryant et al. (2000).

PROFESSIONAL DEVELOPMENT FOR READING INTERVENTIONISTS

Effective instruction is only one aspect of delivering reading intervention. In Chapter 3, we have addressed the question of who can serve as an interventionist. You may recall our emphasizing that candidates should be evaluated on their advanced training in scientifically based literacy instruction for word identification, fluency, vocabulary, narrative and informational text comprehension, and writing. These are all areas in which interventionists need ongoing professional development. The checklist below suggests critical topics for professional development within these areas. Please note that the sections are provided in the order of increasing skill development/complexity, and that for the first four categories, this order mirrors the order provided in the National Reading Panel's report (National Institute of Child Health and Human Development, 2000). Any teacher providing reading intervention should be skilled in all these areas, but not all students will receive instruction in every category. Therefore, the checklist is not to be treated as a guide to the scope and sequence for instruction.

Has the interventionist demonstrated mastery of:

	Yes	No
Word study		
1. Using the common vowel and consonant sounds appropriately in single-syllable and multisyllable words?		
2. Blending sounds to read unknown words?		
3. Segmenting sounds?		
4. Relating sounds to symbols?		
5. Identifying common syllable types?		
6. Recognizing irregular words?		
7. Breaking words into syllables?		
8. Breaking words into morphemes (prefixes, roots, suffixes)		
9. Recognizing unknown words and using efficient decoding practices to decode them?		
Fluency		
1. Reading sounds/words/sentences/paragraphs at an appropriate rate?		
2. Reading sounds/words/sentences/paragraphs with a high degree of accuracy?		
3. Reading sentences/paragraphs with proper phrasing, expression, and intonation?		
4. Using appropriate partnering activities for fluency practice?		
5. Implementing a variety of fluency practice activities (e.g., repeated reading, choral reading, cloze reading)?		
6. Writing words/sentences/paragraphs at an appropriate rate?		

Vocabulary		
1. Identifying words and/or concepts for instruction?		
2. Directly teaching new words and concepts?		
3. Teaching students to be word learners and finders, discovering known new words?		
4. Using contextual analysis to infer word meanings?		
5. Providing examples and nonexamples of word meanings and applications?		
6. Relating and contrasting words?		
7. Providing multiple exposures to words?		
8. Using a dictionary to confirm and deepen knowledge of word meanings?		
9. Encouraging word consciousness and the use of words in different contexts?		
10. Scaffolding vocabulary instruction with word-learning strategies?		
Comprehension		
1. Explicitly teaching comprehension skills such as previewing, finding the main idea, summarizing, drawing and conclusions?		
2. Activating prior knowledge and/or building background knowledge?		
3. Fostering discussion about key concepts before, during, and after reading?		
4. Teaching students to generate and answer their own questions about what they are reading?		
5. Asking questions at different levels of complexity?		
6. Supporting the learning of students at lower and higher ability levels by: • Offering alternative texts/passages to read? • Incorporating collaboration with peers? • Providing intervention and extension activities?		
7. Teaching students to recognize common text structure (description, sequencing/procedural, cause–effect, problem–solution, persuasion/position–reason, compare/contrast)?		
8. Creating and using graphic organizers for organizing and relating key information from a passage?		
9. Teaching students to think about what questions they have for the author as they read and after they read?		
10. Providing opportunities for students to discuss what they've learned from the text and how they would want to extend their learning?		
Writing		
1. Developing writing prompts provided that require students to: • Synthesize information? • Communicate ideas to a specific audience? • Demonstrate learning of subject matter concepts?		
2. Teaching prewriting (to include brainstorming, planning, and collaborating/researching)?		

3. Teaching students to draft one-paragraph responses and multiparagraph essays?		
4. Teaching students how to review a draft for writing mechanics and content?		
5. Using writing models?		
6. Fostering discussion and collaboration among students to review and revise drafts?		
7. Teaching students how to combine sentences?		
8. Teaching students how to finalize and publish a written response?		
Assessment		
1. Creating CBMs?		
2. Administering appropriate diagnostic and progress-monitoring assessments?		
3. Organizing data?		
4. Interpreting diagnostic and progress-monitoring assessment data?		
5. Planning or adapting instruction based on data?		
6. Communicating assessment results to students, parents, and other stakeholders?		

You will notice that the sections on vocabulary, comprehension, writing, and assessment have a high degree of similarity to the professional development checklist in Chapter 2 for all content-area teachers (pp. 51–53). The difference for the intervention classes (on the elements that overlap) relates to the issue of "intensity" addressed in an earlier section and Table 4.4 of this chapter.

The professional development checklist for reading interventionists can be used with individual teachers or a group of reading teachers. Along with the 1's and 2's from the fidelity observation form, the elements checked "no" would be possible topics for coaching sessions, in-class demonstrations, expert consultation, collaborative study, or formal professional development. If your school has adopted a commercial reading intervention program, additional tools and resources may be available to support teachers and improve their abilities to meet the needs of adolescents who struggle with reading.

SELECTING MATERIALS

The following checklist can be used to evaluate textbooks, programs, and other instructional materials for their appropriateness in addressing the reading intervention needs of adolescents in Tiers 2 and 3. It is unlikely that any one resource will include all the elements listed, but better texts and programs will include more of the items. The checklist can provide a quick reference to any missing components of word study, fluency, vocabulary, comprehension, and writing instruction in the materials you select. Wherever an item is checked "no" on the list, the interventionist will need to plan supplemental lessons or activities that will address those needs. As with the checklist for professional development, it should be noted that the sections on the curriculum evaluation checklist are provided in the order of increasing skill development/complexity, and that for the most part, this order mirrors the order provided in the National Reading Panel's report (National Institute of Child Health and Human Development, 2000). Again, too, not all intervention students will receive instruction in every category. Therefore, the checklist is not to be treated as a guide to the scope scope and sequence for instruction.

	Yes	No
Word study		
1. Does the text/program advance students from the most frequent vowel and consonant sounds to more rare sounds?		
2. Does the text/program advance the practice opportunities from blending syllables to onset–rimes to individual phonemes?		
3. Does the text/program advance the practice opportunities from segmenting syllables to onset–rimes to individual phonemes to phoneme deletion?		
4. Does the text/program advance the practice opportunities from blending sounds in single-syllable words to multisyllable words?		
5. Does the text/program advance the practice opportunities from segmenting sounds in single-syllable words to multisyllable words?		
6. Does the text/program introduce the syllable types sequentially?		
7. Does the text/program advance the practice opportunities from applying knowledge of syllable types with single-syllable words to multisyllable words?		
8. Does the text/program offer sufficient practice opportunities with irregular words?		
9. Does the teacher's edition or ancillary material provide instruction and activities in analyzing words by prefixes, roots, and suffixes?		
10. Does the teacher's edition or ancillary material provide activities or instruction in how to use reference materials to "fix up" mispronunciations of words?		
11. Are there suggestions for how to encourage student interaction in applying the skills?		
12. Does the teacher's edition suggest ways to adapt instruction for students who are struggling to learn the concept/strategy?		
Fluency		
1. Does the text/program provide explicit instruction in and activities for building reading rate?		
2. Does the text/program provide explicit instruction in and activities for building reading accuracy?		
3. Does the text/program provide explicit instruction in and activities for reading with proper phrasing, expression, and intonation?		

4. Does the teacher's edition suggest multiple activities, including peer partnering activities, for practicing fluency?		
5. Does the teacher's edition suggest ways to adapt instruction for students who are struggling to improve their fluency?		
Vocabulary		
1. Does the text/program provide explicit instruction in and practice opportunities for independent word-learning strategies?		
2. Does the text/program build students' knowledge of high-frequency and high-utility words?		
3. Does the teacher's edition suggest how to teach words directly?		
4. Does the text/program provide explicit instruction in and activities for using word parts (prefixes, roots, suffixes) to infer word meanings (including low-frequency words)?		
5. Does the text/program provide explicit instruction in and activities for using contextual analysis to infer word meanings (including low-frequency words)?		
6. Does the teacher's edition or ancillary material suggest ways in which words can be related or contrasted?		
7. Are there suggestions for ways to provide multiple exposures to vocabulary words?		
8. Does the teacher's edition or ancillary material provide explicit instruction in and activities for how to use dictionaries to confirm and deepen knowledge of word meanings?		
9. Are there suggestions for how to encourage discussion and use of targeted words?		
10. Does the teacher's edition suggest ways to adapt instruction for students who are struggling to learn build their vocabularies?		
Comprehension		
1. Does the teacher's edition suggest how to explicitly teach comprehension skills such as previewing, finding the main idea, summarizing, and drawing conclusions?		
2. Does the text or supplemental material include methods for activating and building students' prior knowledge of concepts related to those addressed in the passage?		
3. Are there suggestions for how to encourage discussion about the key concepts before, during, and after reading?		
4. Is there specific guidance in the text for students to generate and answer their own questions about what they are reading?		
5. Are the questions provided in the text or supplemental material at different levels of complexity?		
6. Does the teacher's edition suggest how to support the learning of students at lower and higher ability levels by: • Offering alternative texts/passages to read? • Requiring collaboration with peers? • Providing intervention and extension activities?		

7. Does the text or supplemental material consistently organize the information in a given passage in a common text structure (description, sequencing/procedural, cause–effect, problem–solution, persuasion/ position–reason, compare/contrast)?		
8. Does the teacher's edition or ancillary material provide graphic organizers for organizing and relating key information from a passage?		
Writing		
1. Does the text/program provide explicit instruction in and activities for building writing fluency?		
2. Are writing prompts provided that require students to: • Synthesize information? • Communicate ideas to a specific audience? • Demonstrate learning of subject matter concepts?		
3. Does the text/program provide explicit instruction in and activities for prewriting (to include brainstorming, planning, and collaborating/ researching)?		
4. Does the text/program provide explicit instruction in and activities for how to draft a paragraph response versus a multi-paragraph essay?		
5. Does the text/program provide explicit instruction in and activities for how to review a draft for mechanics and content?		
6. Are model responses provided?		
7. Are there suggestions for how to encourage discussion and collaboration among students as they review and revise drafts?		
8. Does the text/program provide explicit instruction in and activities for how to combine sentences?		
9. Does the text/program provide explicit instruction in and activities for how to finalize and publish a written response?		

As in the professional development checklist in the preceding section, you may have noticed that portions of the checklist above (i.e., those on vocabulary, comprehension, and writing) have a high degree of similarity to a checklist in Chapter 2—in this case, the checklist for selecting materials to support cross-curricular literacy instruction (see pp. 42–43). Again, the difference for the intervention classes (on the elements that overlap) relates to the issue of "intensity" addressed in an earlier section and Table 4.4 of this chapter. To see sample applications of strategies appropriate for use in a reading intervention course, refer to Appendices D and E.

SUMMARY

Teaching secondary students in Tiers 2 and 3 requires expertise in meeting the unique needs of students who have difficulty reading to learn and typically do not read for pleasure. In this chapter, we have identified instructional practices associated with improved outcomes for these students, and have discussed the features of effective instruction that all teachers in all tiers should incorporate into their instruction to enhance outcomes for secondary students. To help you think about the information and prepare to apply it, please take a moment to respond to the reflection questions.

REFLECTION QUESTIONS

1. What are some of the features of effective instruction that should be incorporated into Tiers 1, 2, and 3?

2. Why is checking in with a student by simply asking the student whether he or she understands not an effective instructional idea?

3. What is the most important tool for managing off-task behavior?

4. A good teacher will try to give immediate and corrective feedback to all students. Sometimes it is difficult to do this because of the sheer numbers of students in a class or group. What is an alternative way for the teacher to ensure that all students receive immediate and corrective feedback?

5. Monitoring the progress of students should be practical and support making instructional decisions. What are two essential characteristics of a progress-monitoring assessment?

6. Using the professional development checklist on pages 125–127, decide in which areas the teachers in your school are most in need.

ANSWERS TO QUESTIONS ASSOCIATED WITH FIGURE 4.3

1. The teacher is assessing students' ability to:
   - Self-monitor and identify the words or phrases they don't understand.
   - Use particular "fix-up" strategies when their comprehension breaks down (i.e., they encounter a word or phrase they don't understand).
   - Generate main-idea statements.
   - Generate literal-level comprehension questions.
   - Break unfamiliar words into morphemes (prefixes, roots, and suffixes).

2. The teacher has the students read one page of the novel and use only that passage to complete all tasks specific to the five strategies they have been learning. Students are not required to read more text than is necessary or read different passages to complete each task. This design makes the informal CBM efficient as a progress-monitoring instrument.

CHAPTER 5

Step 4

Refining Implementation of RTI

One of the most important steps in successful implementation of an RTI model is the ongoing evaluation and analysis of its implementation. Now that you are familiar with the framework of RTI and the defining characteristics of each tier in a three-tiered model, you may be wondering how you can tell whether your implementation efforts are on the right track. In this chapter, we focus on the managerial concerns that RTI literacy leadership teams typically confront.

ESTABLISHING WHAT IS "NEGOTIABLE" AND WHAT IS "NON-NEGOTIABLE"

Each middle and high school is faced with its own limitations on schedules, teachers, course credits, and material resources. Therefore, there is no one "right way" to implement RTI at the secondary level, and it is expected that RTI models may vary somewhat from campus to campus, in order to meet the needs and address the challenges of each local context. Some flexibility in the procedures and components should be expected, and many of the available options have been addressed in earlier chapters. The "negotiables" are summarized below.

RTI Negotiables

• *Number of tiers.* Districts or schools typically use either a three-tiered or a four-tiered approach to implementing RTI. This decision depends primarily on a school's or district's budget and on the resources it has available to implement the number of tiers it chooses. The decision may also relate to state and district guidance regarding at what tier special education is addressed. See Chapter 1 for further discussion.

- *Amount of teacher collaboration time.* Teachers need opportunities during the day to collaborate on instruction, progress monitoring, and decision making about students' progress, but the amount of time provided varies from campus to campus. See Chapter 2 for further discussion.

- *Specific cross-curricular literacy strategies.* Several key instructional practices in reading are likely to be included in all RTI implementations at the Tier 1 level, including vocabulary instruction and comprehension instruction. However, the literacy practices used to implement these elements may be adjusted to the needs of the students and school context. See Chapter 2 for further discussion.

- *Adaptations of literacy strategies to content areas.* Content-area teachers (such as teachers of social studies, science, and math) obtain improved outcomes for students and provide higher-quality instruction when they provide research-based literacy strategies consistently across these content areas. Incorporating these literacy strategies in their curricula will help ensure that students can access and comprehend upper level expository text—something that all secondary students are expected to do. See Chapter 2 for further discussion.

- *Professional development plans.* Effective implementation of RTI frameworks requires ongoing professional development for all teachers and administrators, so that they are familiar with the research-based practices related to instruction, progress monitoring, and data-based decision making. See Chapters 2 and 4 for further discussion.

- *Approach to diagnostic assessment.* There is no one "right way" to provide diagnostic assessment to those students with ongoing reading difficulties; however, it is helpful to provide a consistent diagnostic assessment procedure to students with reading difficulties, in order to guide educational decision making. Some schools prefer a top-down approach, while others implement a bottom-up approach. See Chapter 3 for further discussion.

- *Method of assigning students to tiers.* Decisions about which students need and will benefit from supplemental reading interventions (Tier 2) or more intensive interventions (Tier 3) require consideration but do not have specific research-established cut points. Assigning students to the intervention tiers is also handled differently in the secondary setting as compared to the elementary setting. See Chapter 3 for further discussion.

- *Group sizes.* One of the practices typically used to increase intensity of instruction is to reduce group size, so that students have greater opportunities to respond and receive instructional feedback. The precise group size to improve outcomes is determined by schools' resources and their students' needs. It is important to keep in mind that reducing the homogeneity of a group and increasing a teacher's ability to group students in pairs when necessary may result in slightly larger classes. See Chapter 3 for further discussion.

- *Course scheduling and credit*. Perhaps no topic affecting secondary education can be adequately addressed without considering the course scheduling and awarding of credits to students. Anyone who has worked at the secondary level knows the importance of finding ways to fit all requirements into the "master schedule." How a school schedules intervention depends on its resources and the local context, so a variety of options can be considered. See Chapter 3 and Appendices A–C for further information.

- *Instructional adaptations*. The types of instructional adaptations needed to meet the needs of students with reading difficulties vary according to the content areas as well as to the students' needs. Teachers may choose to vary the content, activity, materials, or delivery of instruction. See Chapter 4 for further discussion.

- *Approach to progress monitoring*. Ongoing CBMs assist teachers in determining students' progress in reading or acquisition of content, and in making instructional decisions to accelerate student learning. Progress-monitoring assessments should be quick to administer and sensitive to growth. Because available assessment instruments are not as likely to detect small changes in the reading performance of adolescents with serious reading difficulties, progress monitoring is conducted much less frequently on the secondary level than in the elementary grades. See Chapter 4 for further discussion.

- *Specific reading intervention strategies and programs*. The types of reading strategies and intervention programs used may vary, depending on students' needs, instructional goals, and the expertise and resources of the schools. See Chapter 4 for further discussion and Appendix F for additional resources.

The elements of RTI identified above are all essential to successful implementation, but the precise ways in which they are implemented may vary for several reasons. One reason is that the research base related to effective instructional and progress-monitoring practices for adolescents has not yet defined the optimal numbers, processes, or curricula. A second reason is that particular educational curricula, professional training, and student needs are specific to the educational setting in which you are implementing RTI, and thus decision making requires consideration of these factors.

RTI Non-Negotiables

From the available research and from our own observations of promising practices, we have concluded that there are limits to the changes that can be made within the scope of RTI. We refer to those elements as "non-negotiables." For each one we describe in Figures 5.1 and 5.2, it will be important to consider how the administra-

Non-negotiable	Rationale	Steps the administration and RTI literacy leadership team might take

Administrative support	RTI is a general education initiative and, particularly at Tier 1, involves all core academic teachers. Effective implementation will only occur with sufficient administrative support. Faculty members' participation and effectiveness are related to their perception that the initiative has been well thought out and organized, so that the structures are in place to support the educational changes being asked of them.	• Adjust the schedule to provide teachers with protected time during the day to plan high-quality lessons.
		  ○ Designate this time specifically for planning literacy instruction.
		  ○ Coordinate the planning times of teachers in the same grade, subject, or team (as appropriate).
		• Procure the necessary materials for incorporating literacy instruction into content-area lessons.
		• Maintain a conducive learning environment (one that is orderly and focused on academics).
		• Make sure that all key personnel are well informed about RTI.
		  ○ Present information clearly and confidently to staff.
		  ○ Provide leadership for and guidance in implementing the RTI model.

Responsibility assumed by all content-area teachers	To achieve the goal of having an accessible curriculum for all students, including those who are concurrently enrolled in reading intervention, all content-area teachers need to be accountable for the features of effective instruction and the agreed-upon cross-curricular literacy strategies. If only one department is involved in implementing the support, opportunities for accumulating instructional time in literacy across the day are lost, as are opportunities for promoting transfer of reading skills to different contexts, and for increasing the flexibility with which students employ reading strategies to meet the unique demands of different content areas. Similarly, if only one teacher or class within each department is designated as "Tier 1," you could end up creating a lower academic track for some students or redefining "differentiation" as something that is only done for certain students.	• Participate in the designated planning times.
		• Observe in content-area classrooms when literacy instruction is happening.
		  ○ Emphasize to teachers and students the importance of the initiative.
		  ○ Gather data on the next steps for professional development.
		• Plan time during faculty meetings and ongoing professional development to share teachers' examples of success with helping students of different ability levels develop strategies for self-regulating their learning.

Ongoing professional development	Few middle and high school teachers perceive that they are adequately prepared to meet the competing instructional demands of content and literacy. One	• Limit the number of new strategies and techniques introduced at a time. • Collaboratively set goals for teacher mastery and usage.

(cont.)

FIGURE 5.1. Minimum requirements for building and sustaining Tier 1, the base of a multi-tiered RTI model.

	workshop or institute may provide the information for starting Tier 1, but it will not change teacher practice demonstrably and may result in teachers' feeling overwhelmed.	• Plan a sustained program of professional development.
		  ○ Distribute sessions throughout the school year.
		  ○ Allow release time for teachers to observe literacy instruction occurring in colleagues' or exemplar classrooms.
		  ○ Identify "literacy mentor" teachers in each content area who can facilitate collaborative planning times.
		• Provide a mixture of activities such as these:
		  ○ Expert modeling of new techniques.
		  ○ Time for reflecting on information or planning for application.
		  ○ In-class assistance with implementing the practices.
		  ○ Guided analysis of data to plan instruction.
		  ○ Time for individuals or groups to meet with literacy and content experts.

Fidelity to instructional practices	All reading strategies and programs adopted for Tier 1 require evidence of effectiveness from research. To realize the benefits of the selected instructional practices and programs, implementation with fidelity is necessary. Although some adaptations will be necessary to meet the unique needs and reading goals of different content areas and diverse learners, there are usually key components of the strategies related to the features of effective instruction that need to be present in their entirety. It is essential to know whether implemented programs are effective and should therefore be continued or replaced.	• Make routine fidelity observations in content-area classrooms, using information to provide feedback to teachers.
		  ○ Record information on how closely the teachers are adhering to the critical components and procedures.
		  ○ Utilize external consultants or technical assistance providers with expertise in the components and instructional requirements of an adopted commercial program.
		  ○ Develop a system for organizing the data.
		• Use multiple sources of data to evaluate how strategies and/or programs are being implemented.

FIGURE 5.1. *(cont.)*

tion and RTI literacy leadership team will need to communicate the expectations to faculty members. Note that all of the non-negotiables relate either to the support needed to implement RTI or to the features of effective instruction that should be included in all tiers.

 Stop and Think

Throughout this book, we have pointed out the differences between the way that RTI is implemented at the elementary versus the secondary level. As you review the non-negotiables or minimum requirements for Tier 1, be sure you understand how "core instruction" is defined and supported in middle and high schools where there is not a 90-minute reading block. Refer back to Chapter 2 as necessary.

Non-negotiable	Rationale	Steps the administration and RTI literacy leadership team might take
Time per day	To achieve the goal of secondary students' making gains in reading and closing the gap with their higher-achieving peers, sufficient time is needed to conduct lessons, practice different reading components, and make transitions between activities. Intervention periods that are considerably shorter than a typical class period do not demonstrate a strong administrative commitment to tiered instruction. This could have a negative impact on teacher buy-in and students' motivation to take the intervention work seriously.	• Adjust the schedule to accommodate intervention periods of 30–50 minutes each day (see sample schedules in Appendices A–C). 　o Consider flexible options for use of personnel. 　o Consider flexible options for scheduling electives. • Minimize disruptions to the intervention classes. 　o Refrain from pulling students out of intervention for administrative or procedural tasks. 　o Refrain from scheduling assemblies or other events during intervention classes.
Duration of intervention	It can take several months to gather enough data on a student's performance in targeted areas to gauge whether or not he or she is responding to the intervention and making progress. Simply put, skill building takes time. However, students who are *false positives* (students identified through screening measures as in need of intervention but demonstrating adequate reading skill) need not wait for a semester break to have their schedules changed.	• Schedule intervention classes for a minimum of 1 year. Make schedule changes quickly for students who are misplaced in the intervention tiers (i.e., false positives).
Flexibility of grouping	Within intervention classes, teachers need to evaluate student progress continually through formal progress monitoring, informal CBMs, and daily classroom observations. All instructional decisions should be clearly related to the available data.	• Ensure that teachers have appropriate progress-monitoring instruments. 　o Identify and procure formal measures that have established reliability and validity. 　o Provide intervention teachers with professional development in designing CBMs. • Review progress-monitoring data. 　o Verify that measures are being administered at least every other week. 　o Discuss with the intervention teachers how the data are being interpreted. 　o Check for evidence in lesson plans and observations that curricular components, instructional practices, and/or student groupings or pairings are being adjusted after every third formal progress-monitoring data point. 　o Move students needing more or less intensity between Tiers 2 and 3.

(cont.)

FIGURE 5.2. Minimum requirements for building and sustaining reading interventions in Tiers 2 and 3.

Intervention as a supplement	A tiered intervention model is intended to close the gap in students' reading performance while supporting their access to the general curriculum. If students are participating in Tier 1 while they are in intervention, you risk "tracking" students by ability levels.	• Check the schedules of intervention students to ensure that Tier 2 or 3 is provided in addition to (*not* in place of) the Tier 1 ELAR course. • Communicate the purpose of the tiered framework to students, parents, faculty, and other stakeholders.

Fidelity to instructional practices	The components and procedures described in Chapter 4, as well as those identified in adopted reading programs, benefit from implementation, that adheres to the key instructional principles. These require fidelity of implementation with consideration of adaptations for content and student diversity. In the absence of fidelity data, it cannot be determined whether a particular student did not make progress because the intervention was poorly implemented or because it was inappropriate for this student (Bellini, Peters, Benner, & Hopf, 2007; Dane & Schneider, 1998).	• Provide intervention teachers with specialized training to deliver instruction in ways that have been found effective in scientific research.
		• Make routine fidelity observations in reading intervention classes.
		  o Record information on how closely the teachers are adhering to the critical components and procedures.
		  o Utilize external consultants or technical assistance providers with expertise in the components and instructional requirements of an adopted commercial program.
		  o Develop a system for organizing the data.
		• Use multiple sources of data to evaluate how strategies and/or programs are being implemented.

FIGURE 5.2. *(cont.)*

 Stop and Think

Throughout this book, we have also pointed out the differences between the intervention tiers at the elementary versus the secondary level. As you review the non-negotiables or minimum requirements for Tiers 2 and 3 (or a single intervention tier), note the critical components that help distinguish intervention from tutoring, tracking, or test preparation. When you are discussing RTI with colleagues from the elementary level, keep in mind that some of the non-negotiables listed here are structured a bit differently for lower grade levels. Can you identify what those differences might be? Refer back to Chapters 3 and 4 as necessary.

COMMUNICATING THE NON-NEGOTIABLES TO FACULTY MEMBERS

One of the big considerations in initiating a change process like RTI is the way in which teachers' participation in the RTI process is communicated to faculty members. All of us have experienced initiatives in the past that seemed imposed from a higher level of administration in our school or district. We often really didn't understand the rationale or purpose of such changes. We also may have perceived that we were either devalued or threatened by the changes, especially when there was a list of "must-do" tasks for which we had little opportunity to offer input. We might have even been doing many of the items already, but knowing that someone was now checking up on us seemed to imply that we were not trustworthy or professional. As one teacher said, "I started to question myself. I thought maybe I wasn't doing the right thing." These are all legitimate feelings during the process of change.

 Stop and Think

> *If you are responsible for implementing RTI in your school or district, what can you do to ensure that all teachers and staff members are "on board" without making them feel as if you are imposing daunting changes on them?*

Communication is the key to whether the change requested is accepted or perceived as threatening. In particular, most educators are troubled when the non-negotiables appear without their input and/or do not seem to have adequate evidence or rationale to support them. Transforming the culture of a secondary school from its traditional isolationist and protective stance to a more integrated system can yield enthusiasm when communicated effectively, or can yield resentment when communication is inadequate. Therefore, the expectations must be very clearly but carefully communicated. To avoid negative reactions to the non-negotiables for RTI, we suggest that the administration and leadership team take the following steps:

- Generate "buy-in" for the overall initiative before moving into implementation. This can be accomplished in part by explaining the need for RTI and the anticipated benefits with respect to school-level data; involving teachers in observing other schools' efforts; visiting department or grade-level meetings to answer questions; and presenting an organized plan for preparing the teachers and moving through the steps of implementation (see Chapter 1 for additional information).
- Provide adequate rationale and support for decision making, and provide positive communication with adequate support.
- Establish the non-negotiables as the basic keys to success. In other words, present the requirements in a positive way that demonstrates how everyone has an important role in implementing RTI. If everyone works together and maintains some consistency, the work should have positive, worthwhile outcomes.
- Place the non-negotiables alongside the negotiables to show that not all elements are mandated. Then involve teachers in making decisions on the aspects that have more flexibility.
- Emphasize that observations will be used to plan subsequent professional development and use of other resources dedicated to supporting the initia-

tive. It is impractical to present fidelity checks as devoid of an evaluative component. However, what is done as a result of that ongoing evaluation will communicate to teachers whether the observations are intended to punish or help them.

"HOW DO WE KNOW WHEN WE ARE READY TO IMPROVE OUR PLAN?"

Throughout the process of gearing up to implement RTI, as well as creating and sustaining the momentum, administrators and RTI literacy leadership team members frequently want to know: "How are we doing? How do our efforts compare to other schools?" The answers to these questions are important indicators of progress and necessary next steps for refining your plan. Figure 5.3, the Campus Implementation Assessment (CIA) Guide, is designed to help you generate this information.

The CIA Guide is an informal tool for evaluating your school's level of RTI implementation. It is intended to guide you in reflecting on your progress in particular activities related to full RTI implementation. Ideally, your RTI literacy leadership team will use this as a starting point to begin and continue a "conversation" about where you are and in what areas you need to concentrate to enhance your implementation efforts.

You will notice that the CIA Guide is divided into five primary categories, which are essential to building a strong RTI model:

1. Consensus/leadership building
2. Data collection/management
3. Multi-tiered framework of instruction
4. Special education
5. Professional development

These categories should seem familiar to you, since we have addressed them throughout this book. Within each category on the guide are embedded essential activities or behaviors necessary to reaching full implementation of that category. For example, in order to organize and maintain a three-tiered model of reading instruction and intervention, a school must have a well-defined and orchestrated data collection/management system (Category 2). To make that system work, the RTI or literacy leadership team first must identify appropriate assessments to screen students for potential reading difficulties (Activity 2A).

For each activity, the leadership team will use data (e.g., student assessment results, fidelity observations, teachers' perceptions) to determine where along the continuum of four implementation stages the campus falls. These stages are defined below:

1. *Awareness.* In this stage, personnel realize the importance of a particular activity in one of the five RTI categories and may be making some movement toward preparing to implement the activity, but overall have made virtually no effort toward implementing it. They may be continuing to gather information.

2. *Preparation.* In this stage, campus leaders or essential personnel are making efforts toward implementing a particular activity. For example, members of a campus team may have identified a list of possible assessments they would like to use to evaluate their students' reading abilities, but they have not yet narrowed down or finalized the list. They may be considering the logistics of the activity or readying the necessary budget, time, and materials.

3. *Implementation.* In this stage, a particular activity is being implemented, although leaders may be continually evaluating and tweaking what has been put in place. Processes are not very sophisticated yet, and personnel are still working through details and difficulties.

4. *Mastery and integration.* In this stage, an activity is mastered, and no more significant adjustments are necessary. The activity is integrated campus-wide, with the responsible personnel meeting competency and/or fidelity standards. Processes are functioning in a coherent, consistent manner and are considered "the way we do business."

It is important to note that these four stages are a simplified version of a popular implementation framework developed by the National Implementation Research Network (referred to as the State Implementation and Scaling-up of Evidence-based Practices, or SISEP; see Appendix F for a link to the site) and endorsed by the National Center on Response to Intervention and the Center on Instruction. Like similar theories of systemic change, the SISEP framework is built around stages of implementation that represent increasingly sophisticated levels of program use. Research behind the SISEP model identified seven stages: (1) no implementation, (2) exploration, (3) installation, (4) initial implementation, (5) full implementation, (6) innovation, and (7) sustainability (Fixsen, Naoom, Blasé, Friedman, & Wallace, 2005).

The stages of implementation presented in the CIA Guide are based on the SISEP model, but have been revised to meet the purposes of this tool. Examining discrete action steps or behaviors within categories of RTI implementation requires a different approach than looking at the overall adoption of RTI, for which the SISEP model is more appropriate.

The goal is to move from the awareness stage to the mastery and integration stage for each activity in the CIA Guide. However, it is usually not practical to attempt to master all activities simultaneously. Because of resources or logistical issues, a campus that ranks in the awareness stage across many of the RTI categories may need to choose where to focus its initial efforts. By building on early

	Awareness	Preparation	Implementation	Mastery and integration
1. Consensus/leadership building				
A. The administration understands and supports RTI movement and concepts.				
B. A leadership team has been organized and convened to oversee the implementation of RTI (sometimes this team may be referred to as the problem-solving team).				
C. The roles of various personnel are clearly defined and communicated.				
D. Staff members understand and support RTI movement and concepts.				
E. Staff members are meeting in collaborative teams to review data and plan effective instruction.				
F. The campus leaders are promoting a sense of "buy-in."				
G. The campus is including and promoting parent "buy-in" and education on RTI-related issues.				
H. Different sources of funding are being used appropriately to support implementation of all tiers.				
2. Data collection/management				
A. The campus has identified assessments to screen students for potential reading difficulties.				
B. The campus has identified a structure to analyze results.				

(cont.)

FIGURE 5.3. Campus Implementation Assessment (CIA) Guide.

	Awareness	Preparation	Implementation	**Mastery and integration**
C. The campus is using progress-monitoring tools for reading (may also have tools for math and behavior).				
D. Reading intervention teachers are administering progress-monitoring assessments to their students.				
E. Data are organized and analyzed in a timely manner.				
F. Teachers are involved in analyzing data.				
G. Data are easily accessible to teachers and pertinent staff.				
H. A student's data are easily accessible to his or her parents.				
I. Data are examined vertically (from elementary to middle school and from middle to high school) when appropriate and necessary.				
3. Multi-tiered framework of instruction				
A. Clear guidelines are set for referral processes, intervention, and documentation.				
B. Intervention supplements but does not supplant the core instruction.				
C. Tier 1 is differentiated, and various grouping structures are used (not always whole-group instruction).				
D. Instruction in all tiers is evidence-based (may also include behavioral supports).				
E. There are protocols in place for promoting curricular alignment and professional collaboration among the tiers (general education and intervention).				
F. Tier 2 instruction is more intense than Tier 1, and Tier 3 instruction offers the greatest intensity.				

(cont.)

FIGURE 5.3. *(page 2 of 4)*

	Awareness	Preparation	Implementation	Mastery and integration
G. Students move among the tiers effectively and efficiently.				
H. Interventions are individualized to meet identified areas of student need.				
I. Data are routinely used to refine intervention instruction.				
J. The leadership team regularly monitors fidelity of intervention in each tier.				
K. Instructional components of all tiers are being implemented with 80% or better fidelity.				
4. Special education				
A. Data gathered from the RTI model are used to determine special education eligibility and current status.				
B. The administration and leadership team are promoting RTI as a general education initiative.				
C. The number of referrals to special education is decreasing.				
D. The achievement and educational attainment of students in special education are increasing.				
E. There are protocols in place for promoting curricular alignment and professional collaboration between general and special education.				
5. Professional development (PD)				
A. Faculty and support staff participate in ongoing PD on RTI implementation.				
B. Faculty members receive adequate PD about using assessments to plan instruction.				

(cont.)

FIGURE 5.3. *(page 3 of 4)*

	Awareness	Preparation	Implementation	Mastery and integration
C. Faculty and support staff participate in ongoing PD on Tier 1 instruction (i.e., effective instruction and cross-curricular literacy support).				
D. Intervention teachers are provided with specialized PD and ongoing support for addressing the reading difficulties of adolescents.				
E. The PD involves active participation on the part of participants.				
F. There are opportunities during the PD for teachers to apply what they are learning to their own lessons.				
G. The leadership team establishes a means for teachers to observe literacy instruction or intervention occurring in exemplar classrooms.				
H. Technical assistance providers are available to address the unique literacy needs of each content area.				
I. In-class coaching is available for teachers of all tiers.				

FIGURE 5.3. *(page 4 of 4)*

successes in a few high-priority areas, the campus can increase its momentum toward mastery in all categories. For example, a campus in the awareness stage in all five categories may choose to concentrate on the activities within the leadership-building category to ensure that it has a solid foundation for its RTI model. When the leadership team can rank the campus in the implementation or mastery and integration stages for these activities, they may then choose to put effort into some of the other categories.

To help you better understand how the CIA Guide might be used, we present a serial case study in Boxes 5.1 through 5.3. This case study follows the work of the fictitious Lincoln High School as it prepares for and implements RTI in the area of reading. Within each installment of the scenario, use the discussion questions to reflect on what is happening and what steps the school might take next. At the end of each box, you will find a partly-filled in example of the CIA Guide, to show how the Guide might be completed in evaluating a high school's efforts.

The case studies are intended to provide an opportunity for you and your colleagues to refine your knowledge and skills. They will not be able to address all of the potential roadblocks that you might encounter, but they can be used to anticipate some common issues and build your confidence in addressing others.

BOX 5.1. CASE STUDY, PART 1:
LINCOLN HIGH SCHOOL PREPARES TO IMPLEMENT RTI

It is the spring semester at Lincoln High School, and the administrators and counselors are studying RTI models in preparation for implementing the framework during the next school year. They have already participated in an informational webinar hosted by their state department of education, and they have read several publications that explain the rationale and organization of RTI. In addition, they have visited an elementary school in the district that is experiencing success with three tiers of reading instruction and intervention.

The principal of Lincoln High School, Ms. Aleman, convenes a meeting with the two assistant principals and two counselors to discuss what they have been learning. "I like that the intervention is made available to students without having to go through the special education referral process," Mr. LeBreaux, an assistant principal, remarked. "That has always been a complaint of teachers. They identify that a student is struggling, but there is nothing available to help him unless he is in special education. With the tiered model, we can provide the supplemental instruction to any student as soon as we know there is a problem."

"But I still don't understand when the intervention is supposed to take place," comments the head counselor, Mr. Tamil. "Most of the information we have is about elementary schools. Our students have required courses, and we can't deny them the opportunity to earn their credits within the 4-year completion plan. The elementary school has a 90-minute block for reading instruction and another 30 to 45 minutes of supplemental instruction for the students who are struggling. That would be two or three class periods at our school."

"That is a good point," responded Ms. Aleman. "Working Tier 2 and Tier 3 intervention classes into our master schedule will be difficult. We have to find classrooms and qualified teachers, as well as juggle all the credits students need at each grade level."

Mr. LeBreaux becomes worried that his colleagues are giving up on implementing RTI before they have even started. "But if we don't make this happen, the same students will continue to fail our state assessment. They end up in test remediation classes, after-school tutoring, and intensive summer preparation programs all the way through their senior year," he reminds them. "If we can find a way to schedule all of that, surely we can find a way to schedule classes that will prevent the students from repeatedly failing."

Check Your Understanding

1. What other benefits of RTI should Mr. LeBreaux point out to his colleagues? (See Chapter 1 for ideas.)
2. What resources (e.g., financial, organizational, personnel-related) might the Lincoln High School administrators and counselors consider using to create and staff the intervention classes? (See Chapter 3 for ideas.)
3. What other components of RTI at the secondary level have the administrators and counselors not yet considered? (See Chapters 2 and 4 for ideas.)

After more discussion, the assistant principals offer to work on devising a master schedule that will accommodate Tier 2 and Tier 3 reading intervention classes. The principal agrees to review the credentials and interests of the existing faculty to identify potential interventionists. And the counselors offer to research course credit options for the Tier 2 and Tier 3 classes.

Before closing the meeting, Ms. Aleman remarks, "All of our discussion today has been about scheduling the intervention classes. What we have not addressed is Tier 1 of the model. How are we going to ensure strong core literacy instruction to reduce the need for intervention? Before we meet again, I think we all need to do some additional studying and thinking about what Tier 1 looks like in a high school."

The administrators and counselors review the available resources on Tier 1 instruction and commit themselves to preparing for that discussion, in addition to continuing the work on scheduling the intervention classes.

Sample CIA Guide: Lincoln High School's Progress in Implementing RTI (*Note.* Only the information provided in the scenario has been used to complete this guide.)

	Awareness	Preparation	Implementation	Mastery and integration
1. Consensus/leadership building				
A. The administration understands and supports RTI movement and concepts.		×		
B. A leadership team has been organized and convened to oversee the implementation of RTI (sometimes this team may be referred to as the problem-solving team).		×		
C. The roles of various personnel are clearly defined and communicated.	×			
D. Staff members understand and support RTI movement and concepts.				

E. Staff members are meeting in collaborative teams to review data and plan effective instruction.				
F. The campus leaders are promoting a sense of "buy-in."		×		
G. The campus is including and promoting parent "buy-in" and education on RTI-related issues.				
H. Different sources of funding are being used appropriately to support implementation of all tiers.				
2. Data collection/management				
A. The campus has identified assessments to screen students for potential reading difficulties.				
B. The campus has identified a structure to analyze results.				
C. The campus is using progress-monitoring tools for reading (may also have tools for math and behavior).				
D. Reading intervention teachers are administering progress-monitoring assessments to their students.				
E. Data are organized and analyzed in a timely manner.				
F. Teachers are involved in analyzing data.				
G. Data are easily accessible to teachers and pertinent staff.				
H. A student's data are easily accessible to his or her parents.				
I. Data are examined vertically (from elementary to middle school and from middle to high school) when appropriate and necessary.				
3. Multi-tiered framework of instruction				
A. Clear guidelines are set for referral processes, intervention, and documentation.				
B. Intervention supplements but does not supplant the core instruction.	×			

C. Tier 1 is differentiated ,and various grouping structures are used (not always whole-group instruction).				
D. Instruction in all tiers is evidence-based (may also include behavioral supports).				
E. There are protocols in place for promoting curricular alignment and professional collaboration among the tiers (general education and intervention).				
F. Tier 2 instruction is more intense than Tier 1, and Tier 3 instruction offers the greatest intensity.				
G. Students move among the tiers effectively and efficiently.				
H. Interventions are individualized to meet identified areas of student need.				
I. Data are routinely used to refine intervention instruction.				
J. The leadership team regularly monitors fidelity of intervention in each tier.				
K. Instructional components of all tiers are being implemented with 80% or better fidelity.				
4. Special education				
A. Data gathered from the RTI model are used to determine special education eligibility and current status.				
B. The administration and leadership team are promoting RTI as a general education initiative.	✕			
C. The number of referrals to special education is decreasing.				
D. The achievement and educational attainment of students in special education are increasing.				
E. There are protocols in place for promoting curricular alignment and professional collaboration between general and special education.				

5. Professional development (PD)				
A. Faculty and support staff participate in ongoing PD on RTI implementation.				
B. Faculty members receive adequate PD about using assessments to plan instruction.				
C. Faculty and support staff participate in ongoing PD on Tier 1 instruction (i.e., effective instruction and cross-curricular literacy support).				
D. Intervention teachers are provided with specialized PD and ongoing support for addressing the reading difficulties of adolescents.				
E. The PD involves active participation on the part of participants.				
F. There are opportunities during the PD for teachers to apply what they are learning to their own lessons.				
G. The leadership team establishes a means for teachers to observe literacy instruction or intervention occurring in exemplar classrooms.				
H. Technical assistance providers are available to address the unique literacy needs of each content area.				
I. In-class coaching is available for teachers of all tiers.				

You will notice from the sample CIA in Box 5.1 that most of Lincoln High School's efforts at this time are in Category 1 (consensus/leadership building). The administrators and counselors have a few activities that they are preparing to implement (the preparation stage), but in general they are still gathering information on a few issues of importance. Figure 5.4 outlines some suggestions for the steps Lincoln High School might take at this point to advance its implementation of RTI.

Roadblock	Next steps
Strengthening Tier 1/core reading instruction	1. Identify whether the campus currently exhibits the features of a strong "core" (the features are described in Chapter 2). 2. Determine the necessary professional development for Tier 1 reading instruction, or academic literacy (a checklist of professional development topics is introduced in Chapter 2).
Finding qualified teachers	1. Determine the number of teachers needed to staff the intervention classes. 2. Examine teacher certification and training records to determine whether any existing faculty (in general or special education) have expertise in reading intervention (more information on the minimum knowledge and expertise of interventionists is provided in Chapter 3). 3. Identify teachers on the Lincoln High staff who would be willing to receive specialized training in reading intervention. 4. Coordinate with other campuses in the district to determine whether qualified teachers can be shared or transferred.
Adding Tier 2 and Tier 3 reading intervention to the master schedule	1. Determine the numbers of Tier 2 and Tier 3 intervention periods needed (more information on this step is provided in Chapter 3). 2. Examine existing courses to determine whether intervention classes can take the place of other remediation and tutoring. 3. Consider replacing an elective course with intervention (a chart of credit options for intervention classes is provided in Chapter 3). 4. Look for alternative scheduling options, such as a schoolwide enrichment/intervention period (see the sample schedules provided in Appendices A–C).

FIGURE 5.4. Case study, Part 1: Where does Lincoln High School go from here?

In the next installment of our case study (see Box 5.2), we rejoin Lincoln High School in the fall of the next school year. As with the first segment, use the discussion questions to reflect on what is happening and what steps the school might take next. At the end of the box, you will find another sample CIA Guide, to show how one might be completed in evaluating a high school's additional efforts.

BOX 5.2. CASE STUDY, PART 2: LINCOLN HIGH SCHOOL EVALUATES ITS EARLY RTI IMPLEMENTATION

It is the beginning of November, and the RTI literacy leadership team at Lincoln High School is holding its monthly meeting. In addition to the principal, assistant principal, and head counselor, the team that was formed over the summer also includes the reading intervention teacher, special education coordinator, AP calculus teacher, and ESL teacher. The seven members have completed their second round of fidelity observations for the semester and are collectively reviewing those data, as well as student progress-monitoring data.

Mr. LeBreaux suggests that they start by discussing the observations in content-area classrooms. "I am seeing more English and social studies teachers implementing literacy instruction than science or math teachers," he offers. "I was in six math classes last week, and I only saw one teacher using a vocabulary strategy. That was you, Ms. Graber! You did a great job with that!"

"To be honest," Ms. Graber replied, "it is really difficult to work the strategies we learned last August into math lessons. You caught me on a good day when I was starting a new unit on curves. We can use the vocabulary strategies with lessons like that, but I don't think I will ever be able to use the comprehension strategies. The physics teacher said something similar to me the other day. We don't have a lot of reading, like they do in the English and social studies classes."

The ESL teacher, Ms. Ploss, reminds the group that there was a similar reaction after the faculty participated in professional development last year on how to build students' English language proficiency. "We never followed up on that," she cautions, "and we are still having difficulty improving the academic performance of our ELLs. We need to find a way to help teachers get more comfortable with the strategies and learn to integrate them into their lesson plans better."

"I would be happy to help teachers with the vocabulary and comprehension strategies," the reading interventionist offers. "I don't mind meeting with them during my conference period or showing them some of the things we have been doing. I try to use the students' content-area textbooks for some of our practice lessons, anyway. But who is going to help me with the word study lessons? Ms. Aleman observed my Tier 3 classes, and I know I need better fidelity! I was overwhelmed during my training on the program last summer."

Check Your Understanding

1. How might the RTI literacy leadership team increase the buy-in among content-area teachers and provide more support for them to integrate high-quality literacy instruction into their lessons?
2. What forms of support should the team consider for improving the reading interventionist's word study instruction?
3. What other issues of fidelity has the group not yet considered?

After more discussion about the fidelity observation data, the head counselor suggests that they start looking at the student progress-monitoring data. "Ms. Ploss brought up a good point earlier when she mentioned that the performance of our ELLs might be linked to the low implementation of the English language proficiency strategies. I'm wondering if we will have a similar issue with the students who are in reading intervention. We only have 4 months before state testing."

The leadership team first reviews the schoolwide benchmark results from the October administration and notices that about 15 freshmen are starting to struggle. They passed their state reading assessment in spring of their eighth-grade year, but did not meet grade-level expectations on the most recent benchmark. These 15 are in addition to the students who are enrolled in reading intervention this fall on the basis of their percentile ranks, according to the state department of education's guidance on using the assessment as a screener. Overall, the students in Tier 2 are showing improvement on the reading benchmark. However, they are not yet at grade-level standards. Ms. Urquiza, the reading interventionist, also refers to the biweekly progress-monitoring data she is gathering. "With one or two exceptions per class, the Tier 2 students have mastered literal comprehension with main ideas and details. But they are not applying their skills to grade-level text yet. We are getting there gradually. The students need a lot more work on making inferences and on their vocabulary knowledge."

"The Tier 3 students don't seem to be making much progress," Mr. Tamil comments.

"No," Ms. Urquiza agrees, "they are really struggling. I think a lot of that has to do with my word study instruction. It's hard for me to admit, but the fact that no student in either Tier 3 class is making noticeable improvements has to mean there is a problem with my instruction. Ms. Aleman's fidelity observation has just confirmed that for me, because I have been looking at the progress-monitoring data for a while. I've tried making changes, but I just don't know enough about the syllable types and morphemes."

The principal tries to reassure Ms. Urquiza. "Don't forget that you have a lot of strengths with effective instruction, as well as the strategies for vocabulary and comprehension. That is making a difference for your students, and it will probably help your colleagues as well. I respect you for recognizing your weakness with word study instruction, and I want you to know we are going to help you with that. Please don't get discouraged."

Ms. Aleman sets up a time to meet with the reading interventionist the next day to discuss next steps in Ms. Urquiza's professional development. Ms. Graber offers to meet with Ms. Ploss and the assistant principal to plan how to increase implementation of the literacy strategies in content-area classes.

"What are we going to do about the students who don't have any data?" Mr. Fung, the special education coordinator, asks. He is concerned that some students who are newly enrolled in Lincoln High School have not come with any test scores. "This has been my question since we established the state test as the screener. If we have a student from another state or another country, how do we know if they meet the criteria for Tier 2 or 3? We have several students who enrolled in September and failed the benchmark in October. Do we have to wait until January to get them into an intervention class?"

The head counselor offers to meet with Mr. Fung to work on an alternative method of screening transfer students. In addition, they will devise a plan for enrolling the transfer students, as well as the freshmen who are starting to struggle in reading intervention.

Sample CIA Guide: Lincoln High School's 8-Month Progress in Implementing RTI (*Note.* Only the information provided in the scenario has been used to complete this guide.)

	Awareness	Preparation	Implementation	Mastery and integration
1. Consensus/leadership building				
A. The administration understands and supports RTI movement and concepts.			×	

B. A leadership team has been organized and convened to oversee the implementation of RTI (sometimes this team may be referred to as the problem-solving team).			×	
C. The roles of various personnel are clearly defined and communicated.			×	
D. Staff members understand and support RTI movement and concepts.		×		
E. Staff members are meeting in collaborative teams to review data and plan effective instruction.	×			
F. The campus leaders are promoting a sense of "buy-in."		×		
G. The campus is including and promoting parent "buy-in" and education on RTI-related issues.				
H. Different sources of funding are being used appropriately to support implementation of all tiers.				
2. Data collection/management				
A. The campus has identified assessments to screen students for potential reading difficulties.			×	
B. The campus has identified a structure to analyze results.			×	
C. The campus is using progress-monitoring tools for reading (may also have tools for math and behavior).			×	
D. Reading intervention teachers are administering progress-monitoring assessments to their students.			×	
E. Data are organized and analyzed in a timely manner.			×	
F. Teachers are involved in analyzing data.	×			
G. Data are easily accessible to teachers and pertinent staff.	×			
H. A student's data are easily accessible to his or her parents.				

I. Data are examined vertically (from elementary to middle school and from middle to high school) when appropriate and necessary.				×	
3. Multi-tiered framework of instruction					
A. Clear guidelines are set for referral processes, intervention, and documentation.					
B. Intervention supplements but does not supplant the core instruction.				×	
C. Tier 1 is differentiated ,and various grouping structures are used (not always whole-group instruction).					
D. Instruction in all tiers is evidence-based (may also include behavioral supports).			×		
E. There are protocols in place for promoting curricular alignment and professional collaboration among the tiers (general education and intervention).					
F. Tier 2 instruction is more intense than Tier 1, and Tier 3 instruction offers the greatest intensity.				×	
G. Students move among the tiers effectively and efficiently.	×				
H. Interventions are individualized to meet identified areas of student need.			×		
I. Data are routinely used to refine intervention instruction.				×	
J. The leadership team regularly monitors fidelity of intervention in each tier.				×	
K. Instructional components of all tiers are being implemented with 80% or better fidelity.	×				
4. Special education					
A. Data gathered from the RTI model are used to determine special education eligibility and current status.					
B. The administration and leadership team are promoting RTI as a general education initiative.				×	

C. The number of referrals to special education is decreasing.				
D. The achievement and educational attainment of students in special education are increasing.				
E. There are protocols in place for promoting curricular alignment and professional collaboration between general and special education.				
5. Professional development (PD)				
A. Faculty and support staff participate in ongoing PD on RTI implementation.		×		
B. Faculty members receive adequate PD about using assessments to plan instruction.				
C. Faculty and support staff participate in ongoing PD on Tier 1 instruction (i.e., effective instruction and cross-curricular literacy support).		×		
D. Intervention teachers are provided with specialized PD and ongoing support for addressing the reading difficulties of adolescents.			×	
E. The PD involves active participation on the part of participants.	×			
F. There are opportunities during the PD for teachers to apply what they are learning to their own lessons.	×			
G. The leadership team establishes a means for teachers to observe literacy instruction or intervention occurring in exemplar classrooms.	×			
H. Technical assistance providers are available to address the unique literacy needs of each content area.	×			
I. In-class coaching is available for teachers of all tiers.	×			

You will notice from the sample CIA Guide in Box 5.2 that Lincoln High School has advanced to the implementation stage in several areas and to the preparation stage in others. These mostly relate to Category 1 (consensus/leadership building) and Category 2 (data collection/management). There are more efforts under way in Category 3 (multi-tiered framework of instruction) than during the first installment of the case study. Similarly, there is greater awareness of the Category 5 (professional development) activities needed for successful implementation of RTI. The category with the least amount of attention right now is Category 4 (special education).

Figure 5.5 outlines some suggestions for the steps Lincoln High School might take at this point to advance its implementation of RTI.

In the final installment of our case study (see Box 5.3), we rejoin Lincoln High School in the spring as it ends its first year of RTI implementation. We encourage you to continue using the discussion questions to reflect on what is happening and what steps the school might take next. At the end of the box, you will find another sample CIA Guide to show how one might be completed in evaluating a high school's continuing efforts.

Roadblock	Next steps
Low buy-in and implementation of literacy strategies in Tier 1	1. Offer ongoing professional development in the cross-curricular literacy strategies (see Chapter 2 for more explanation). a. Have a content-area expert meet with each department to assist with adapting the literacy strategies to the unique needs of math, science, social studies, and ELAR. b. Provide time during the next professional development day for teachers to work collaboratively on planning lessons that incorporate the literacy strategies. c. Have a literacy expert provide select content-area teachers with in-class coaching, and allow other teachers in the department to observe during this time. 2. Involve content-area teachers in analyzing the benchmark and other progress-monitoring data to increase their awareness of the need for instructional changes.
Low fidelity to word study instruction in Tier 3	1. Provide ongoing professional development in the key components of reading intervention (see Chapter 4 for more explanation). a. Have a consultant provide the interventionist in-class coaching on using the adopted program for word study instruction. b. Allow the interventionist to observe word study instruction occurring in exemplar classrooms. 2. Identify a reading expert in the district who could collaborate with the interventionist in planning lessons.
Freshmen and transfer students identified as struggling on the October benchmark	1. Determine scheduling options for moving students into intervention (see Chapter 3 and Appendices A–C for more information). 2. Identify other screening instruments (see Chapter 2) or develop CBMs (see Chapter 4) to use between formal benchmark testing times.

FIGURE 5.5. Case Study, Part 2: Where does Lincoln High School go from here?

BOX 5.3. CASE STUDY, PART 3: LINCOLN HIGH SCHOOL EVALUATES ITS FIRST YEAR OF RTI IMPLEMENTATION

The academic year at Lincoln High School is drawing to a close. It is May, and the RTI literacy leadership team is meeting to review the state assessment results that just arrived this week. The goals for today's meeting are to determine the number of Tier 2 and Tier 3 classes needed next year and the aspects of the RTI plan that are ready to be refined.

"I know that not all of the intervention students passed," Ms. Urquiza says, "but I am really pleased to see the progress they made! There are only two students in my Tier 3 class who really concern me. I think the others will continue to improve with more time in intervention next year, but these two have not responded to the very individualized instruction the consultant helped me plan and deliver."

Mr. Fung looks at the names of the students and their test scores. "They haven't been identified for special education yet?" he asked.

"I was surprised by that, too," Ms. Urquiza responds. "I know we don't refer many students at this age, but these kids are struggling to pass all their classes. One of them spent every morning and afternoon in tutoring."

Ms. Ploss seems concerned. "We need to be very careful about the reasons we give for referring students to special education. The students in my ESL classes spend a lot of time in tutoring, often do not pass the state assessment, and appear to be struggling with reading. However, I would not want them all referred for special education."

"So do students have to be in Tier 3 reading intervention to be newly referred?" asks Mr. LeBreaux.

Check Your Understanding

1. What other indicators are taken into consideration in determining whether to refer a student for special education?
2. How can the RTI literacy leadership team members increase their knowledge and understanding of the special education referral process within an RTI framework?

The team continues to discuss the appropriate integration of special and general education. Mr. Fung adds his concerns about the performance of students in special education who are not concurrently enrolled in intervention. "The students in special education who are in Ms. Urquiza's classes are making progress, particularly those in Tier 2," he said. "But the ones who are not enrolled in intervention are not doing any better than they did last year. There are several students who were barely above the 35th percentile last year, so they did not get placed in Tier 2. Again this year, they are just barely above the 35th percentile."

Ms. Aleman brings up the fidelity observations the team has been conducting. "Were we seeing a lot of effective instruction happening in the Tier 1 classes?" she asks.

"I was in every math teacher's room," Ms. Graber responds, "and I know they were working really hard to adapt the vocabulary and comprehension strategies to their math lessons. They didn't concentrate on including the features of effective instruction when they were using the literacy strategies. I think they might have misunderstood that. Some teachers think that using literacy strategies is all they have to do to differentiate instruction. Others think they are supposed to do either literacy strategies or the effective instructional practices. They're still figuring all this out."

"Parents are a little confused about the RTI processes as well," adds Mr. Tamil. "When we made schedule changes for the ninth graders who were struggling or for transfer students, some parents wanted to know why their students were taken out of an elective for a reading class. I think we are going to have more of those concerns when we start making schedule changes based on these state assessment results."

Ms. Aleman offers to work with Mr. Tamil on how to communicate information about the RTI framework to parents. Mr. LeBreaux asks Ms. Graber whether she would be willing to meet about next fall's professional development plans for content-area teachers. Ms. Urquiza, Mr. Fung, and Ms. Ploss arrange a time to explore the special education referral process further.

Sample CIA Guide: Lincoln High School's 14-Month Progress in Implementing RTI (*Note.* Only the information provided in the scenario has been used to complete this guide.)

	Awareness	Preparation	Implementation	Mastery and integration
1. Consensus/leadership building				
A. The administration understands and supports RTI movement and concepts.			×	
B. A leadership team has been organized and convened to oversee the implementation of RTI (sometimes this team may be referred to as the problem-solving team).				×
C. The roles of various personnel are clearly defined and communicated.			×	
D. Staff members understand and support RTI movement and concepts.			×	
E. Staff members are meeting in collaborative teams to review data and plan effective instruction.		×		
F. The campus leaders are promoting a sense of "buy-in."			×	

G. The campus is including and promoting parent "buy-in" and education on RTI-related issues.	×			
H. Different sources of funding are being used appropriately to support implementation of all tiers.				
2. Data collection/management				
A. The campus has identified assessments to screen students for potential reading difficulties.			×	
B. The campus has identified a structure to analyze results.			×	
C. The campus is using progress-monitoring tools for reading (may also have tools for math and behavior).			×	
D. Reading intervention teachers are administering progress-monitoring assessments to their students.			×	
E. Data are organized and analyzed in a timely manner.				×
F. Teachers are involved in analyzing data.	×			
G. Data are easily accessible to teachers and pertinent staff.	×			
H. A student's data are easily accessible to his or her parents.	×			
I. Data are examined vertically (from elementary to middle school and from middle to high school) when appropriate and necessary.			×	
3. Multi-tiered framework of instruction				
A. Clear guidelines are set for referral processes, intervention, and documentation.	×			
B. Intervention supplements but does not supplant the core instruction.			×	
C. Tier 1 is differentiated ,and various grouping structures are used (not always whole-group instruction).	×			
D. Instruction in all tiers is evidence-based (may also include behavioral supports).		×		

E. There are protocols in place for promoting curricular alignment and professional collaboration among the tiers (general education and intervention).	×			
F. Tier 2 instruction is more intense than Tier 1, and Tier 3 instruction offers the greatest intensity.				×
G. Students move among the tiers effectively and efficiently.			×	
H. Interventions are individualized to meet identified areas of student need.			×	
I. Data are routinely used to refine intervention instruction.			×	
J. The leadership team regularly monitors fidelity of intervention in each tier.				×
K. Instructional components of all tiers are being implemented with 80% or better fidelity.		×		
4. Special education				
A. Data gathered from the RTI model are used to determine special education eligibility and current status.	×			
B. The administration and leadership team are promoting RTI as a general education initiative.			×	
C. The number of referrals to special education is decreasing.				
D. The achievement and educational attainment of students in special education are increasing.		×		
E. There are protocols in place for promoting curricular alignment and professional collaboration between general and special education.	×			
5. Professional development (PD)				
A. Faculty and support staff participate in ongoing PD on RTI implementation.			×	
B. Faculty members receive adequate PD about using assessments to plan instruction.	×			

C. Faculty and support staff participate in ongoing PD on Tier 1 instruction (i.e., effective instruction and cross-curricular literacy support).			×	
D. Intervention teachers are provided with specialized PD and ongoing support for addressing the reading difficulties of adolescents.				×
E. The PD involves active participation on the part of participants.			×	
F. There are opportunities during the PD for teachers to apply what they are learning to their own lessons.			×	
G. The leadership team establishes a means for teachers to observe literacy instruction or intervention occurring in exemplar classrooms.		×		
H. Technical assistance providers are available to address the unique literacy needs of each content area.		×		
I. In-class coaching is available for teachers of all tiers.	×			

The sample CIA Guide in Box 5.3 indicates that Lincoln High School has advanced to the mastery and integration stage with some activities and has more implementation in Category 2 (data collection/management) and Category 5 (professional development) than on its previous evaluation. It is also more aware of activities in Category 4 (special education). Notice that there are some activities related to Category 2 (data collection/management) and to Category 3 (multi-tiered framework of instruction) on which the school has not made much progress over the past 6 months. This is important to acknowledge. A school may not be moving into different stages of implementation every time the CIA Guide is completed.

Figure 5.6 outlines some suggestions for the steps Lincoln High School might take to advance its implementation of RTI in the next school year.

Roadblock	Next steps
Confusion over the special education referral process	1. Seek guidance from the state department of education on the required procedures. 2. Use multiple sources of data, particularly progress-monitoring data, to track students' level of performance and rate of growth against grade-level standards (see Chapter 3 for more information). 3. Clearly outline the processes for staff and parents (see Chapter 1 for more information). 4. Remember, RTI can provide data to assist with identifying students for special education and determining their progress once placed in special education, but RTI does not replace any of the "due process" responsibilities outlined by federal and state regulations.
Lack of progress for special education students enrolled in Tier 1 only	1. Provide ongoing professional development to content-area teachers in the features of effective instruction (see Chapter 2 for more explanation). a. Have a consultant provide in-class coaching on differentiating the literacy instruction. b. Provide release time for teachers to observe in exemplar classrooms. 2. Create a structure for special and general education teachers to work more collaboratively on planning lessons. 3. Provide ongoing professional development on co-teaching in inclusive classrooms.
Parents are not well-informed about the RTI framework and processes	1. Hold an informational meeting for parents. 2. Create informational brochures in all languages represented in the community. 3. Include parents in meetings to evaluate an individual student's progress and placement in intervention.

FIGURE 5.6. Case study, Part 3: Where does Lincoln High School go from here?

REFLECTION QUESTIONS

1. Review the negotiables and non-negotiables listed at the beginning of the chapter and in Figures 5.1 and 5.2. How will your school determine the negotiables? How will you oversee the non-negotiables? Are there any non-negotiables you think you will need to add?

2. Having read about Lincoln High School's literacy leadership team, which administrators and faculty/staff members would you select to serve on the team at your school?

3. How do the concerns, questions, and experiences of Lincoln High School compare to those of your own school? How do you plan to start addressing your own roadblocks?

4. Using the CIA Guide (Figure 5.3), rate your campus on each current stage of implementation. Use the results to decide where you would put your initial efforts at this point to implement an RTI model.

Epilogue

In this book, we have reviewed the background of RTI as developed for elementary schools and have explored its application in the area of reading for adolescents. We have discussed each of the three tiers in detail, addressed how they might be implemented in middle and high schools, and raised issues concerning the different conceptualization of RTI at the secondary level as compared to the elementary level. We have also identified some of the administrative issues of moving to this systems approach. As the extended case study in Chapter 5 highlights (see Boxes 5.1–5.3), it may be best to focus on manageable pieces and resolve the issues with those before moving on to the next step. In this way, you can achieve full implementation in a series of successive approximations of the model. Along the way, return to this book to revisit the information and tools you need for your next steps, as well as to reflect on your progress.

Although we have focused on implementing tiered instruction in the area of reading, we acknowledge that this may be occurring in combination with similar efforts focused on behavior (as briefly addressed in Chapter 2) or mathematics. Many of the components we have addressed here will be similarly applicable to the other areas. However, we encourage you to seek more thorough guidance specific to behavior and/or mathematics models, just as you have studied our recommendations for reading and the differences between the way the components are structured at the elementary and secondary levels. There are increasing numbers of resources on RTI available to support your efforts, as outlined in Appendix F.

Our own reflections after writing this book are that this work is complex—perhaps even more so in middle and high schools than in lower grade levels—and that there are no neat and definitive answers for many of the components. You have only to reread the statistics on the state of adolescents' reading (provided in Chapter 1) to remind yourself of how important it is that we collectively take up the challenge and persevere through the roadblocks. When you witness the difference effective and orchestrated instruction can make in your students' achievement and outlook on life, we are confident you will agree that the benefits are worth it.

Sample Middle School Schedules: Grades 6–8

Schedule 1 in this appendix is the master schedule for a medium-sized middle school serving grades 6–8. In this schedule, two teachers provide reading intervention (classes highlighted with solid circles). One teacher is a special education teacher who also provides inclusion services as part of her day (highlighted with dashed circles). The majority of her schedule, however, is dedicated to the reading class that serves as a supplement to the general education ELAR course. Because the teacher is in the general education classrooms daily, she is able to help her students make connections between the ELAR and intervention work. In addition, she can reinforce particular skills and strategies being learned in the intervention class as they are applied to reading authentic material in the ELAR course. Students are enrolled in the appropriate tier of intervention for their identified skill needs, regardless of their grade level. This enables the school to be more flexible in its scheduling options.

The other teacher providing intervention is primarily an ESL and Spanish teacher. However, she offers one Tier 2 intervention course for ELLs who exhibit reading difficulties that do not seem attributable to the students' primary language status. These are students who are classified as intermediate or advanced in their English skills and are able to be tested in English. Although they continue to receive ESL services and are enrolled in the general education ELAR course, they are provided with additional supplemental instruction to address identified reading skill deficits. The RTI literacy leadership team has decided that the ESL teacher is the most appropriate person to assist these students, because she is familiar with their language abilities and can distinguish between what is needed to improve their reading abilities and what is needed simply to improve their English. In addition, the teacher believes that the specialized training she has received in preparation for the intervention course offering will be beneficial to her ESL teaching as well.

The teachers' positions are funded through a combination of Title I, Title III, and IDEA allotments. Given their roles, the master schedule has been devised to include them in the ELAR departmental planning period (Period 6). This provides another opportunity for the teachers to ensure that the general education and reading intervention courses are supporting and reinforcing each other. The teachers of core curriculum courses have two common planning times in their schedules: They have the departmental preparation period (which allows for vertical alignment of the curriculum, including the reading components), and they have a grade-level preparation period. The latter is used for planning lessons that integrate information across the curriculum and for implementing a tiered behavioral support system for students.

Very large middle schools often have an easier time incorporating intervention periods because they have more teachers and more class offerings overall. However, they face challenges in coordinating services and ensuring that teachers are able to meet collaboratively. **Schedule 2** in this appendix is actually a set of schedules for a large campus serving grades 6–8. There are four interdisciplinary teams at each grade level. Two teams have an assigned inclusion teacher who usually assists across the disciplines, including in the general education ELAR classes (highlighted in with dashed circles). The special education teachers dedicated to particular teams share the same lunch and collaborative planning period as their team colleagues. In addition, there is a campus literacy coach (highlighted with underlining) available to assist any teacher at any grade level in the classroom, provide additional training during collaboration meetings, or help with the diagnostic and progress-monitoring assessments of students in intervention.

The periods designated as "flex" on the schedule allow paired sets of teachers to create and agree upon a system for extending the consecutive periods on alternating days. For example, the sixth-grade schedule shows Teachers A and B paired, with a flex period between their Period 1 and Period 3 classes. The teachers might agree to extend Period 1 on Monday and Tuesday to a double block (lasting for periods 1–2), but then to extend Period 3 on Wednesday and Thursday (lasting for Periods 2–3). The two teachers are empowered to alter this flex period as necessary, and they are able to make their plans for this during the collaborative planning time (in these teachers' case, during Period 5).

All features of the schedule described here help strengthen Tier 1 and build in opportunities for teachers to support each other in implementing literacy strategies across the curriculum. They supplement the intervention courses offered for both math (highlighted with dotted circles, but not discussed for the purposes of this book) and reading (highlighted in with solid circles). Given the larger number of students needing Tier 2 supplemental reading instruction, those courses are offered specifically to each grade level and are restricted to no more than 15 students per class. The Tier 3 courses combine students in grades 6–8 to enable more homogeneous grouping by skill need, and to create more flexibility for maintaining a teacher–student ratio of no greater than 1:6.

SCHEDULE 1. Master Schedule for a Medium-Sized Middle School (Grades 6–8)

Teacher	Period 1	Period 2	Period 3	Period 4	Period 5	Period 6	Period 7
Teacher A	8th English	8th English	8th English	8th English	8th English	Dept. Prep.	Grade-Level Prep.
Teacher B	8th Algebra 1	8th Algebra 1	Dept. Prep.	8th Math	8th Math	8th Grade Math	Grade-Level Prep.
Teacher C	8th Earth Sci.	Dept. Prep.	8th Earth Sci.	8th Earth Sci.	8th Earth Sci.	8th Earth Sci.	Grade-Level Prep.
Teacher D	Dept. Prep.	8th Soc. Stud.	8th Soc. Stud.	8th Soc. Stud.	8th Soc. Stud.	8th Soc. Stud.	Grade-Level Prep.
Teacher E	7th English	7th English	7th English	Grade-Level Prep.	7th English	Dept. Prep.	7th English
Teacher F	7th Pre-Alg.	7th Pre-Alg.	Dept. Prep.	Grade-Level Prep.	7th Math	7th Math	7th Math
Teacher G	7th Life Sci.	7th Life Sci.	7th Life Sci.	Grade-Level Prep.	7th Life Sci.	7th Life Sci.	7th Life Sci.
Teacher H	Dept. Prep.	7th Soc. Stud.	7th Soc. Stud.	Grade-Level Prep.	7th Soc. Stud.	7th Soc. Stud.	7th Soc. Stud.
Teacher I	6th English	6th English	6th English	6th English	Grade-Level Prep.	Dept. Prep.	6th English
Teacher J	6th Math	6th Math	Dept. Prep.	6th Math	Grade-Level Prep.	6th Math	6th Math
Teacher K	6th Phys. Sci.	Dept. Prep.	6th Phys. Sci.	6th Phys. Sci.	Grade-Level Prep.	6th Phys. Sci.	6th Phys. Sci.
Teacher L	Dept. Prep.	6th Soc. Stud.	6th Soc. Stud.	6th Soc. Stud.	Grade-Level Prep.	6th Soc. Stud.	6th Soc. Stud.
Teacher M	8th Art	8th Art	8th Math Inclusion	8th Math Inclusion	8th Art	Gifted Advisory	Grade-Level Prep.
Teacher N	7th Science Inclusion	Guitar Music	Guitar Music	Grade-Level Prep.	7th Math Inclusion	7th Math Inclusion	7th Science Inclusion
Teacher O	Phys. Ed.	Phys. Ed.	Phys. Ed.	Phys. Ed.	Phys. Ed.	Phys. Ed.	Phys. Ed.
Teacher P	Phys. Ed.	Phys. Ed.	Phys. Ed.	Phys. Ed.	Phys. Ed.	Phys. Ed.	Prep.
Teacher Q	7th Ag. Explor.	8th Ag. Sci.	7th Ag. Explor.	7th Ag. Explor.	7th Ag. Explor.	Prep.	8th Ag. Sci.
Teacher R	Prep.	6th Word Proc.	7th Gen. Comp.	6th Word Proc.	7th Gen. Comp.	Journalism/Yearbook	6th Word Proc.
Teacher S	Spanish 1	Tier 2 Reading	Spanish 1	Intermediate ESL	English for Beginners	Dept. Prep.	Advanced ESL
Teacher T	ELAR Inclusion	ELAR Inclusion	Tier 3 Reading	Tier 3 Reading	Tier 2 Reading	Dept. Prep.	Tier 2 Reading

SCHEDULE 2. Schedules for a Large Middle School (Grades 6–8). Grade levels, electives, and intervention classes are provided in separate tables.

Sixth-Grade Master Schedule

Teacher	Period 1	Period 2	Period 3	Period 4	Period 5	Period 6	Period 7	Period 8	Period 9
Teacher A	English GT	Flex	English	Lunch	Collaboration	Prep.			
Teacher B	Soc. Stud.	Flex	Soc. Stud.	Lunch	Collaboration	Prep.			
Teacher C	Prep.				Collaboration	Lunch	Science	Flex	Science
Teacher D	Prep.				Collaboration	Lunch	Math	Flex	Math
Teacher E	English	Flex	English	Lunch	Collaboration	Prep.	English	Flex	English
Teacher F	Soc. Stud.	Flex	Soc. Stud.	Lunch	Collaboration	Prep.	Soc. Stud.	Flex	Soc. Stud.
Teacher G	Science	Flex	Science	Lunch	Collaboration	Prep.	Science	Flex	Science
Teacher H	Math	Flex	Math	Lunch	Collaboration	Prep.	Math	Flex	Math
Teacher I	Math Inclusion	Math/ Soc. Stud. Inclusion	Soc. Stud. Inclusion	Lunch	Collaboration	Prep.	English Inclusion	English/ Science Inclusion	Science Inclusion
Teacher J	English	Flex	Prep.	Lunch	Collaboration	English	English	Flex	English
Teacher K	Soc. Stud.	Flex	Prep.	Lunch	Collaboration	Soc. Stud.	Soc. Stud.	Flex	Soc. Stud.
Teacher L	Science	Flex	Prep.	Lunch	Collaboration	Science	Science	Flex	Science
Teacher M	Math	Flex	Prep.	Lunch	Collaboration	Math	Math	Flex	Math
Teacher N	Soc. Stud. Inclusion	Soc. Stud./ Science Inclusion	Prep.	Lunch	Collaboration	Science Inclusion	Math Inclusion	English/Math Inclusion	Math Inclusion
Teacher O	English	Flex	English	Lunch	Collaboration	Prep.	English	Flex	English
Teacher P	Soc. Stud.	Flex	Soc. Stud.	Lunch	Collaboration	Prep.	Soc. Stud.	Flex	Soc. Stud.
Teacher Q	Science	Flex	Science	Lunch	Collaboration	Prep.	Science	Flex	Science
Teacher R	Math	Flex	Math	Lunch	Collaboration	Prep.	Math	Flex	Math

Seventh-Grade Master Schedule

Teacher	Period 1	Period 2	Period 3	Period 4	Period 5	Period 6	Period 7	Period 8	Period 9
Teacher A	Collaboration	English	Flex	English GT	Lunch	English	Prep.	Flex	English
Teacher B	Collaboration	Soc. Stud.	Flex	Soc. Stud.	Lunch	Soc. Stud.	Prep.	Flex	Soc. Stud.
Teacher C	Collaboration	Science	Flex	Science	Lunch	Science	Prep.	Flex	Science
Teacher D	Collaboration	Algebra	Flex	Math	Lunch	Math	Prep.	Flex	Algebra GT
Teacher E	Collaboration	Science Inclusion	Science/Math Inclusion	Science Inclusion	Lunch	English Inclusion	Prep.	English/Soc Stud Inclusion	Soc Stud Inclusion
Teacher F	Collaboration	English	Flex	English	Lunch	English	Flex	English	Prep.
Teacher G	Collaboration	Soc. Stud.	Flex	Soc. Stud.	Lunch	Soc. Stud.	Flex	Soc. Stud.	Prep.
Teacher H	Collaboration	Science	Flex	Science	Lunch	Science	Flex	Science	Prep.
Teacher I	Collaboration	Math	Flex	Math	Lunch	Math	Flex	Math	Prep.
Teacher J	Collaboration	Soc. Stud. Inclusion	English/Soc. Stud. Inclusion	English Inclusion	Lunch	English Inclusion	English Inclusion	Soc. Stud. Inclusion	Prep.
Teacher K	Collaboration	Prep.	English	Flex	Lunch	English	English	Flex	English
Teacher L	Collaboration	Prep.	Soc. Stud.	Flex	Lunch	Soc. Stud.	Soc. Stud.	Flex	Soc. Stud.
Teacher M	Collaboration	Prep.	Science	Flex	Lunch	Science	Science	Flex	Science
Teacher N	Collaboration	Prep.	Math	Flex	Lunch	Math	Math	Flex	Math
Teacher O							English	Flex	English
Teacher P							Soc. Stud.	Flex	Soc. Stud.
Teacher Q	Prep.	Science	Flex	Science	Team Lunch for Study Skills	Lunch Elective			
Teacher R	Prep.	Math	Flex	Math	Team Lunch for Study Skills	Lunch Elective	7th Tier 2 Reading Intervention	7th Tier 2 Reading Intervention	7th Tier 2 Reading Intervention

171

Eighth-Grade Master Schedule

Teacher	Period 1	Period 2	Period 3	Period 4	Period 5	Period 6	Period 7	Period 8	Period 9
Teacher A	English GT	English	English	English	Lunch	Study Skills	Collaboration	Prep.	English
Teacher B	Soc. Stud.	Prep.	Soc. Stud.	Soc. Stud.	Lunch	Study Skills	Collaboration	U.S. History	Soc. Stud.
Teacher C	Science	Science	Science	Science	Lunch	Study Skills	Collaboration	Science	Prep.
Teacher D	Math	Math	Math GT	Math	Lunch	Study Skills	Collaboration	Algebra	Prep.
Teacher E	Science Inclusion	Science/English Inclusion	English Inclusion	Science Inclusion	Lunch	Float/Study Skills	Collaboration	Soc. Stud. Inclusion	Prep.
Teacher F	English	English	English	Study Skills	English	Lunch	Collaboration	Prep.	English
Teacher G	Soc. Stud.	Prep.	Soc. Stud.	Study Skills	Soc. Stud.	Lunch	Collaboration	Soc. Stud.	Soc. Stud.
Teacher H	Science	Science	Science	Study Skills	Science	Lunch	Collaboration	Science	Prep.
Teacher I	Math	Math	Algebra	Study Skills	Algebra	Lunch	Collaboration	Math	Prep.
Teacher J	English	Collaboration	English	English	English	Lunch	Prep.	Study Skills	English
Teacher K	Soc. Stud.	Collaboration	Soc. Stud.	Soc. Stud.	Soc. Stud.	Lunch	Soc. Stud.	Study Skills	Prep.
Teacher L	Science	Collaboration	Science	Science	Science	Lunch	Science	Study Skills	Prep.
Teacher M	Prep.	Collaboration	Algebra	Math	Math	Lunch	Algebra	Study Skills	Math
Teacher N	English Inclusion	Collaboration	Science Inclusion	Math Inclusion	Soc. Stud. Inclusion	Lunch	Float/Team	Float/Study Skills	Prep.
Teacher O	6th–8th Tier 3 Intervention	8th Tier 2 Reading Intervention	6th–8th Tier 3 Intervention	Lunch	6th Tier 2 Reading Intervention	6th Tier 2 Reading Intervention	Collaboration	8th Tier 2 Reading Intervention	Prep.

Electives Master Schedule

Teacher	Period 1	Period 2	Period 3	Period 4	Period 5	Period 6	Period 7	Period 8	Period 9
Teacher A	7th Athletics	7th Phys. Ed.	Prep.	Duty B	6th Phys. Ed.	Team Sports	Prep.	8th Phys. Ed.	8th Athletics
Teacher B	7th Athletics	ISS* Relief Prep.	6th Phys. Ed.	Lunch	6th Phys. Ed.	6th Phys. Ed.	Team Sports	Prep. ISS Relief	8th Athletics
Teacher C	7th Athletics	Team Sports	Prep. Supervision	Lunch	6th Phys. Ed.	6th Phys. Ed.	Team Sports	Prep.	8th Athletics

172

Teacher	Period 1	Period 2	Period 3	Period 4	Period 5	Period 6	Period 7	Period 8	Period 9
Teacher D	7th Athletics	Prep. ISS Relief	7th Phys. Ed.	Lunch	6th Phys. Ed.	6th Phys. Ed.	8th Phys. Ed.	ISS Relief Prep.	8th Athletics
Teacher E	Symphonic Band 0735	Concert Band 0736	Sax 0625	Lunch	Clarinet 0637	Flute 0636	Honor Band 0733	Prep.	Prep.
Teacher F	Symphonic Band 0735	Concert Band 0736	Fr. Horn 0625	Lunch	Low Brass 0626	Trumpet 0639	Honor Band 0733	Prep.	Prep.
Teacher G						Beg. Perc. 0638	Percussion 0734		
Teacher H	Symphonic Orch. 0802	Concert Orch. 0803	6th Choir	Lunch	Treble 0666	Cello 0665	Adv. Orch. 0801	Prep.	Prep.
Teacher I	7th–8th Theatre								7th–8th Choir 0752
Teacher J	7th–8th Theatre	7th–8th Art	6th Art	Lunch	6th Theatre	6th Theatre	7th–8th Art	Prep.	7th–8th Art
Teacher K	7th–8th Art	8th Art	Prep.	Lunch Duty A Lunch B	6th Art	7th–8th Art	Adv. Art	Prep.	7th–8th Art
Teacher L	7th–8th Theatre	8th Theatre	Prep.	Lunch Duty A Lunch B	6th Theatre	6th Theatre	7th–8th Theatre	Prep.	7th–8th Theatre
Teacher M	Multi-Media	Multi-Media	Prep.	Multi-Media	Lunch Duty D Lunch E	Prep.	Multi-Media	Multi-Media	Multi-Media
Teacher N	Tech. 1	Tech. 1	Prep.	Prep.	Tech. 2	Lunch D Lunch Duty E	Tech. 1	Tech. 1	Tech. 1

ESL/Intervention/Special Education Master Schedule

Teacher	Period 1	Period 2	Period 3	Period 4	Period 5	Period 6	Period 7	Period 8	Period 9
Teacher A	Spanish 1A	Spanish 1A	Spanish 1B	Prep.	Spanish 1B	Lunch D Lunch Duty E	Spanish 1A	Prep.	Spanish 1A

Teacher									
Teacher B	Spanish 1A	Spanish 1B	Prep.	Spanish 1	Lunch Duty D / Lunch E	Prep.	Spanish 1B	Spanish 1B	Spanish 1A
Teacher C	French 1A	French 1B	Exp. FLA**	Lunch	Exp. FLA	6th Phys. Ed.	French 1A	Prep.	Prep.
Teacher D	In-Class ESL Support	7th–8th Enrich. ESL	In-Class ESL Support	Prep.					
Teacher E	English for Beginners	Intermed. ESL/Prep.	Advanced ESL	Prep.	In-Class ESL Support	Lunch	Intermed. ESL	Intermed. ESL	In-Class ESL Support
Teacher F	In-Class ESL Support	In-Class ESL Support	In-Class ESL Support	Prep.	Lunch Duty C	Lunch	In-Class ESL Support	In-Class ESL Support	English for Beginners
Teacher G	6th Math Intervention	6th Math Intervention	6th Math Intervention	Lunch	Collaboration	6th Math Intervention	6th Math Intervention	Prep.	6th Math Intervention
Teacher H	Collaboration	7th Math Intervention	7th Math Intervention	Lunch	7th Math Intervention	7th Math Intervention	7th Math Intervention	Prep.	7th Math Intervention
Teacher I	8th Math Intervention	8th Math Intervention	Prep.	8th Math Intervention	Lunch	8th Math Intervention	Collaboration	Prep.	8th Math Intervention
Teacher J	Literacy Coach	Literacy Coach	Literacy Coach	Literacy Coach	Lunch	Literacy Coach	Literacy Coach	Literacy Coach	Prep.
Teacher K	ARD***	ARD	ARD	Inclusion	Lunch	ARD	Inclusion	Inclusion	Inclusion
Teacher L	Applied Science	Applied Math	Applied Math	Prep.	Prep.	Lunch	Applied English	Applied English	Applied Soc. Stud.

*ISS, In-School Suspension; **Exp. FLA, Explorations: French Language; ***ARD, Annual Review and Dismissal Committee.

Sample Junior High School Schedules: Grades 7–8

The primary challenge for small junior high schools, such as the one serving grades 7–8 featured in **Schedule 3**, is that they have little flexibility. Schedule 3 shows that this school has only one teacher for each core subject area, covering both grade levels, and that co-curricular teachers are shared with a high school (HS in the schedule) and with upper elementary grades (5th and 6th in the schedule). To allow for teacher collaboration during the day, the district has had to coordinate the schedules of careers, technology, and band teachers, so that all are available to offer the junior high school classes during fifth period. The special education teacher and reading intervention teacher are included in these collaborative meetings, so that they can contribute to the lesson planning. In a campus of this size, all teachers share the same set of students, so the teachers have an advantage in implementing agreed-upon literacy strategies schoolwide. In particular, the special education teacher plays an important role in strengthening the Tier 1 literacy support, because she provides inclusion services to all subjects (highlighted with dashed circles).

A second common preparation period for core academic teachers is only made possible by having all physical education or athletics classes offered during first period. Often this time is used to pull students for small-group or one-on-one interventions or tutorials. The designated Tier 2 and Tier 3 intervention courses are offered through facilitated labs. One teacher hosts the reading lab (highlighted with solid circles), which is supplemental to the general education ELAR course. The lab offers individualized instruction to students through the use of a grant-funded computerized program. The teacher also works with small groups on other reading skills and provides a multisensory dyslexia program. The learning lab (highlighted with dotted circles) offers support to all subject areas through a combination of computerized programs, volunteer tutors from the community, and a paid professional trained in basic reading intervention strategies.

Schedule 4 is a set of schedules for a large junior high serving grades 7–8. This junior high has been able to group electives by grade level, so that all seventh-grade teachers have three consecutive common planning periods at the beginning of the day, and all eighth-grade teachers have three consecutive common planning periods at the end of the day. This allows for a great deal of job-embedded professional development and ongoing support in implementing RTI. To maximize this opportunity, the campus has developed very clear protocols to guide the meetings and has designated facilitators in each of the three teams per grade level. Because the special education teachers also teach elective courses, they are unable to participate in the full collaboration time with the colleagues to whom they are assigned for inclusion services (highlighted in with dashed circles). However, priority has been placed on including them in the grade-level preparation period so that the teachers can still coordinate services and plan for co-teaching.

The mathematics interventionist has been grouped with the eighth-grade teachers for the collaboration time, even though he provides supplemental math intervention to both grade levels (highlighted with dotted circles, but not discussed for the purposes of this book). Similarly, the reading interventionist has been grouped with the seventh-grade teachers but provides supplemental reading intervention to both grade levels (highlighted with solid circles). As in the other schools' schedules, the Tier 2 courses are specific to grade, but the Tier 3 courses are based on specific need to ensure a more homogeneous class. In addition to the dedicated intervention courses, the school hosts a reading and a math lab (highlighted with underlining) throughout the day. These are used to support all three tiers of instruction as necessary. The labs offer computerized programs, tutors, and paraprofessionals specially trained to support reading or math. Again, some co-curricular teachers are shared with other schools—in this case, another junior high (Other JH in the schedule) and an elementary school's sixth grade (6th in the schedule).

SCHEDULE 3. Master Schedule for a Small Junior High School (Grades 7–8)

Teacher	Period 1	Period 2	Period 3	Period 4	Period 5	Period 6	Period 7	Period 8
Teacher A	7th–8th Boys' Athletics	7th Careers	HS	HS	7th Careers	Prep.	HS	Athletics
Teacher B	7th–8th Boys' Athletics	7th Tech.	6th Phys. Ed.	5th Phys. Ed.	8th Tech.	Reserved	Prep.	Athletics
Teacher C	Prep.	8th English	8th English	8th English	Collaboration	7th English	7th English	8th Homeroom
Teacher D	Prep.	8th Math	7th Math	7th Math	Collaboration	8th Math	8th Math	7th Homeroom
Teacher E	HS	HS	HS	HS	HS	Algebra 1	HS	HS
Teacher F	7th Girls' Athletics	8th Science	8th Science	7th Science	Collaboration	8th Science	7th Science	7th Homeroom
Teacher G	Prep.	7th History	7th History	8th History	Collaboration	8th History	8th History	8th Homeroom
Teacher H	8th Girls' Athletics	Reading Lab	Reading Lab	Reading Lab	Collaboration	Reading Lab	Reading Lab	Reading Lab
Teacher I	Reserved	Inclusion	Inclusion	Inclusion	Collaboration	Inclusion	Special Ed.	Special Ed.
Teacher J	HS Band	Reserved	6th Band	5th Band	7th–8th Band	Reserved	5th Band	Prep.
Teacher K	Prep.	Learning Lab	Learning Lab	Learning Lab	Learning Lab	Learning Lab	Learning Lab	7th–8th Girls' Athletics
Teacher L	7th–8th Phys. Ed.	Prep.	8th Health	8th Health	HS Athletics	Reserved	8th Health	Athletics

SCHEDULE 4. Schedules for a Large Junior High School (Grades 7–8). Grade levels and electives are provided in separate tables.

Seventh-Grade Master Schedule

Teacher	Period 1	Period 2	Period 3	Period 4	Period 5	Period 6	Period 7
Teacher A	Grade-Level Prep.	Dept. Prep.	Prep.	English Pre-AP	English	English Pre-AP	English
Teacher B	Grade-Level Prep.	Dept. Prep.	Prep.	Math	Math Pre-AP	Math	Math Pre-AP
Teacher C	Grade-Level Prep.	Dept. Prep.	Prep.	Science	Science Pre-AP	Science Pre-AP	Science
Teacher D	Grade-Level Prep.	Dept. Prep.	Prep.	Soc. Stud.	Soc. Stud. Pre-AP	Soc. Stud.	Boys' Athletics
Teacher E	Tech. Apps.	Tech. Apps.	Tech. Apps.	Soc. Stud.			

Teacher						
Teacher F	Grade-Level Prep.	Dept. Prep.	Prep.	English	English Pre-AP	English	English Pre-AP
Teacher G	Grade-Level Prep.	Dept. Prep.	Prep.	Math Pre-AP	Math	Math Pre-AP	Math
Teacher H	Grade-Level Prep.	Dept. Prep.	Prep.	Soc. Stud. Pre-AP	Soc. Stud.	Soc. Stud.	Soc. Stud. Pre-AP
Teacher I	Grade-Level Prep.	Dept. Prep.	Prep.	Science Pre-AP	Science	Science	Science Pre-AP
Teacher J	Grade-Level Prep.	Dept. Prep.	Prep.	English Pre-AP	English	English	English Pre-AP
Teacher K	Grade-Level Prep.	Dept. Prep.	Prep.	Math	Math Pre-AP	Math Pre-AP	Math
Teacher L	Grade-Level Prep.	Dept. Prep.	Prep.	Soc. Stud. Pre-AP	Soc. Stud.	Soc. Stud. Pre-AP	Soc. Stud.
Teacher M	Grade-Level Prep.	Dept. Prep.	Prep.	Science	Science	Science	Science Pre-AP
Teacher N	Grade-Level Prep.	Dept. Prep.	Prep.	(8th Tier 2 Reading Intervention)	(7th–8th Tier 3 Reading Intervention)	(7th Tier 2 Reading Intervention)	(7th–8th Tier 3 Reading Intervention)

Eighth-Grade Master Schedule

Teacher	Period 1	Period 2	Period 3	Period 4	Period 5	Period 6	Period 7
Teacher A	English Pre-AP	English	English	English Pre-AP	Grade-Level Prep.	Dept. Prep.	Prep.
Teacher B	Math	Algebra	Algebra	Math	Grade-Level Prep.	Dept. Prep.	Prep.
Teacher C	Soc. Stud.	Soc. Stud. Pre-AP	Soc. Stud. Pre-AP	Soc. Stud.	Grade-Level Prep.	Dept. Prep.	Prep.
Teacher D	Athletics	Science	Science	Science Pre-AP	Grade-Level Prep.	Dept. Prep.	Prep.
Teacher E	Athletics	English	English Pre-AP	English	Grade-Level Prep.	Dept. Prep.	Prep.
Teacher F	Algebra	Math	Math	Math	Grade-Level Prep.	Dept. Prep.	Prep.

Teacher G	Soc. Stud.	Athletics	Soc. Stud.	Soc. Stud. Pre-AP	Grade-Level Prep.	Dept. Prep.	Prep.
Teacher H	Science Pre-AP	Science Pre-AP	Science	Science	Grade-Level Prep.	Dept. Prep.	Prep.
Teacher I	English	English Pre-AP	English	English	Grade-Level Prep.	Dept. Prep.	Prep.
Teacher J	Math	Math	Math	Algebra	Grade-Level Prep.	Dept. Prep.	Prep.
Teacher K	Athletics	Soc. Stud.	Soc. Stud. Pre-AP	Soc. Stud.	Grade-Level Prep.	Dept. Prep.	Prep.
Teacher L	Science Pre-AP	Athletics	Science Pre-AP	Science	Grade-Level Prep.	Dept. Prep.	Prep.
Teacher M	8th Math Intervention	7th Math Intervention	7th Math Intervention	8th Math Intervention	Grade-Level Prep.	Dept. Prep.	Prep.

Electives Master Schedule

Teacher	Period 1	Period 2	Period 3	Period 4	Period 5	Period 6	Period 7
Teacher A	Boys' Athletics	Boys' Athletics	Teen Leadership	Prep.	Boys' Phys. Ed.	Boys' Phys. Ed.	Boys' Phys. Ed.
Teacher B	Girls' Athletics	Girls' Athletics	Teen Leadership	Prep.	Girls' Phys. Ed.	Girls' Phys. Ed.	Girls' Athletics
Teacher C	Boys'/Girls' Phys. Ed.	Boys'/Girls' Phys. Ed.	Boys'/Girls' Phys. Ed.	Prep.	Boys'/Girls' Phys. Ed.	Boys'/Girls' Phys. Ed.	Boys'/Girls' Phys. Ed.
Teacher D	Choir	Choir	Choir	Prep.	Other JH	Other JH	6th Choir
Teacher E	Band	Orchestra	Orchestra	Prep.	6th Band	Orchestra	Orchestra
Teacher F	Grade-Level Prep.	Band	Band	Prep.	Inclusion	Inclusion	Inclusion
Teacher G	Inclusion	Inclusion	Inclusion	Prep.	Grade-Level Prep.	AVID	AVID
Teacher H	AVID	Teen Leadership	AVID	Prep.	Teen Leadership	Teen Leadership	Teen Leadership
Teacher I	Other JH	Other JH	Other JH	Prep.	Health	Health	Health
Teacher J	Other JH	Other JH	Other JH	Prep.	Spanish	Spanish	Spanish
Teacher K	Tech. Apps.	Tech. Apps.	Tech. Apps.	Prep.	7th Soc. Stud.	7th Soc. Stud.	
Teacher L	Other JH	Other JH	Other JH	Prep.	Tech. Apps.	Yearbook	Yearbook
Teacher M	Art	Art	Theater Arts	Prep.	Art	Theater Arts	Theater Arts
Teacher N	Reading Lab	Reading Lab	Reading Lab	Prep.	Reading Lab	Reading Lab	Reading Lab
Teacher O	Math Lab	Math Lab	Math Lab	Prep.	Math Lab	Math Lab	Math Lab

Sample High School Schedule:
Grades 9–12

High school schedules tend to be very complex, for several reasons: the greater number of courses offered, the requirements for teacher certification in each course, and the credit requirements for student graduation. However, the medium-sized high school featured in **Schedule 5** has been able to reallocate resources to create reading intervention classes (highlighted with solid circles), math intervention classes (highlighted with dotted circles, but not discussed for the purposes of this book), and a common planning period for teachers. Approximately half of the intervention periods have replaced the state test remediation classes typically offered for students who had not met grade-level standards. This has been a campus decision, supported by the district, as part of the school improvement plan. The other half of the intervention courses has been made possible by streamlining the school's curricula. Prior to implementing RTI, the school had 13 fragmented English and reading programs. Several of these were computerized tutorials with high annual maintenance costs. The literacy leadership team reviewed all the programs to identify which were meeting the needs of students, which were redundant, and which were not being used at all. In coordination with the English and special education departments, the team members have now clearly defined the general education and intervention curricula. They have been able to eliminate eight programs and free up both budget money and a learning lab teacher to host additional reading intervention periods.

In scheduling the classes, the administration has intentionally overlapped a Tier 2 and Tier 3 course during fourth period. This has created flexibility in the schedule to move some students between the intervention tiers as necessary. Although the interventionists do not share the official common planning time, they do have the same preparation period to allow them time during their workday to coordinate plans. The administration feels it is important to include the interventionists in the interdisciplinary collaboration periods for grades 9 and 10, where higher numbers of students have been failing courses and performing poorly on the state assessment. All teachers participate in the common preparation time. As much as possible, teachers are assigned to groups according to the grade level of the teachers' students. Each teacher mentors a group of students from his or her designated grade of the common planning time. Mentoring activities include (but are not limited to) monitoring students' grades in all classes, offering homework help before or after school, checking-in with parents, providing encouragement during benchmark and annual testing, and explaining the state assessment results. Once a month, the campus operates an early-release schedule to give teachers a 2-hour block of time to spend with the groups of students they mentor for team building, college and career advising, leadership training, or improving academic engagement.

One day a week, the common planning time is devoted to preparing for mentoring activities. The remaining 4 days are reserved for teachers to focus on analyzing data and planning instruction. Each group has a self-selected facilitator who participates in the literacy leadership team meetings and acts as a liaison between the leadership team and his or her planning team. This helps keep the staff informed and involved in the school's RTI efforts. It also provides an avenue for feedback to the administration on how the implementation of different components is progressing or whether there are obstacles to resolve.

SCHEDULE 5. Master Schedule for a Medium-Sized High School

Teacher	Period 1	Period 2	Period 3	Period 4	Period 5	Period 6	Period 7
Teacher A	9th Common Prep.	Driver's Ed.	Driver's Ed.	Driver's Ed.	Prep.	Math Inclusion	Math Inclusion
Teacher B	9th Common Prep	Dual-Credit Biology	Integrated Science	Integrated Science	Dual-Credit Biology	Integrated Science	Prep.
Teacher C	Geometry	Prep.	10th Common Prep.	Trig./Analytic Geom.	Trig./Analytic Geom.	Geometry	Geometry
Teacher D	Modern U.S. History	11th Common Prep.	Modern U.S. History	Government/Economics	Modern U.S. History	Modern U.S. History	Prep.
Teacher E	Spanish III	Spanish II	Spanish II	12th Common Prep.	Prep.	Spanish I/Comm.*	Spanish I/Comm.
Teacher F	Basic Foods	Child Development	Culinary Arts	12th Common Prep.	FCCLA**	Advanced Foods	Prep.
Teacher G	Auto Service	11th Common Prep.	Intro. Auto Shop	Intro. Auto Shop	Intro. Auto Shop	Prep.	Auto Service
Teacher H	Woodworking	Prep.	Adv. Carpentry	12th Common Prep.	CAD Design	Drafting	Woodworking
Teacher I	Chemistry	11th Common Prep.	Chemistry	Science Inclusion	Prep.	Inclusion Science	Chemistry
Teacher J	At Middle School	Prep.	Piano	12th Common Prep.	Chorus	Marching Band	Contemp. Band
Teacher K	9th Common Prep.	10th English	10th English	9th English	9th English	Journalism	Prep.
Teacher L	Algebra I	Prep.	Geometry	12th Common Prep.	Geometry	Algebra I	Algebra I
Teacher M	12th English	12th English	10th Common Prep.	12th English 12th	Prep.	10th English	10th English
Teacher N	9th Common Prep.	State History	State History	State History	Government/Economics	Prep.	Government/Economics
Teacher O	9th Common Prep.	ELAR Inclusion	Tier 2 Reading	Tier 3 Reading	ELAR Inclusion	ELAR Inclusion	Prep.
Teacher P	12th English	11th English	ELAR Inclusion	12th Common Prep.	Creative Writing	Prep.	ELAR Inclusion

Teacher							
Teacher Q	ELAR Inclusion	Tier 3 Reading	10th Common Prep.	Tier 2 Reading	Work–Study Supervision	Tier 2 Reading	Prep.
Teacher R	World History/Geog.	Government/Economics	10th Common Prep.	World History/Geog.	World History/Geog.	Prep.	World History/Geog.
Teacher S	Biology	Biology	10th Common Prep.	Prep.	Biology	Anatomy & Physiology	Biology
Teacher T	Weightlifting	Phys. Ed.	10th Common Prep.	Weightlifting	Phys. Ed.	Prep.	Football/Weightlifting
Teacher U	9th Common Prep.	Prep.	Math Inclusion	Math Inclusion	Phys. Ed.	Phys. Ed.	Individual Sports
Teacher V	Math Inclusion	11th Common Prep.	Tier 2 Math	Prep.	Math Inclusion	Tier 2 Math	Tier 2 Math
Teacher W	Computer Graphics	Prep.	10th Common Prep.	Computer Literacy	General Computer	Computer Literacy	Yearbook
Teacher X	Tier 3 Math	ISS Relief***	Tier 3 Math	12th Common Prep.	Prep.	Math Inclusion	Math Inclusion
Teacher Y	Algebra II	11th Common Prep.	Dual-Credit Calculus	Algebra II	Prep.	Algebra II	Algebra II
Teacher Z	9th Common Prep.	Business Math	Algebra II	Business Math	Business Math	Prep.	Business Math
Teacher AA	Ceramics/Pottery	11th Common Prep.	Creative Art Drawing	Prep.	Ceramics/Pottery	Intro. Art	Intro. Art
Teacher BB	Agricult. Leader	Intro Agricult.	10th Common Prep.	Wildlife Mgmt.	Welding I	Prep.	Intro. Agricult.
Teacher CC	ISS	11th Common Prep.	ISS	ISS	ISS	ISS	Prep.
Teacher DD	9th English	11th Common Prep.	9th English	11th English	11th English	11th English	Prep.
Teacher EE	9th Common Prep.	Spanish I	Prep.	Foreign Lang. & Lit.	Spanish I/Comm.	Spanish I/Comm.	Spanish I/Comm.
Teacher FF	Soc. Stud. Inclusion	Science Inclusion	Soc. Stud. Inclusion	12th Common Prep.	Soc. Stud. Inclusion	Prep.	ISS Relief
Teacher GG	Life Skills	Resource	Life Skills	12th Common Prep.	Resource	Work–Study Supervision	Prep.

*I/Comm., Interpersonal Concepts and Competencies; **FCCLA, Family Career and Community Leaders of America; ***ISS, In-School Suspension.

Examples of Vocabulary and Comprehension Strategies for Content-Area Instruction

Text Structure

Graphic Organizers for Text Structures

Vocabulary Instruction: Frayer Model

Word Map: Physical Geography

Notes Log: Summarization
English Language Arts/Reading (ELAR) Sample

Topic/Title: *The Watsons go to Birmingham—1963*, Chapter 12	**Pages:** 162–168

Main Ideas	**Notes**
p. 162 Kenny wakes up and joins the guys in the back yard.	• Kenny and Byron have a hard time sleeping because they are not used to the heat in Alabama • As soon as he wakes up, Kenny runs out to talk with Dad, Byron, and Mr. Robert
p. 163 Mr. Robert and Toddy are too old to hunt.	• Mr. Robert explains that he and Toddy still dream of hunting, but their bodies are too old • Toddy used to be the best coon dog in all of Alabama • Mr. Robert used to get $100 to breed Toddy
p. 164 Mr. Robert saved Toddy after a raccoon tried to drown him.	• Toddy chased a raccoon and followed him into a lake • The raccoon held Toddy's head under the water to drown him • Mr. Robert dragged Toddy out of the water and blew into his nose to resuscitate him • Kenny and Byron are impressed with this story
p. 165 Kenny goes back inside to eat breakfast.	• Momma, Grandma Sands, and Joey are in the kitchen • Grandma Sands' laugh sounds like the Wicked Witch of the West • Kenny is not used to the Southern style of talking
p. 166 Momma and Grandma Sands are talking and catching up.	• Momma is asking Grandma Sands a lot of questions • They are oohing, aahing, laughing, and catching up on people having trouble with white people, getting married, having babies, and going to jail
p. 167 Momma asks Grandma Sands about Mr. Robert.	• Momma clearly does not approve of Grandma and Mr. Robert living together • Grandma says that Mr. Robert is her dearest friend • Kenny sees that Grandma can make a few words very powerful, just like Byron does • Kenny loves seeing his mom in her role as daughter
p. 168 Kenny walked to the lake and then took a nap.	• Even though he didn't have the energy to walk, Dad and Byron coerced Kenny to walk with them to the lake • Byron seemed to be having a great time, talking and joking with Dad and Mr. Robert • When they got back from the lake, Kenny took a nap under a fan

Main Idea of Section: Kenny's first morning in Alabama is spent listening to Mr. Robert and then to Grandma Sands.

Summary

After a long night of trying to get used to the Alabama heat, Kenny wakes up and joins his Dad, Byron, and Mr. Robert in the back yard. Mr. Robert explains that he and his dog, Toddy, are too old to hunt anymore. He then tells the story about how he saved Toddy's life after a raccoon tried to drown him. After listening to this cool story, Kenny goes back inside to eat breakfast and finds Momma and Grandma Sands catching up at the kitchen table. Momma clearly does not approve of Mr. Robert living with Grandma Sands, and she confronts Grandma about this. Grandma Sands says that Mr. Robert is her dearest friend, and the way she says this makes Momma quiet. Mr. Robert, Dad, and Byron convince Kenny to walk with them to the lake so Momma and Grandma can talk alone. Kenny goes reluctantly and then comes home to take a nap under a fan.

TEXT SOURCE: Curtis, C. P. (1995). *The Watsons go to Birmingham—1963*. New York: Random House.

Reprinted with permission from Meadows Center for Preventing Educational Risk. (2009). *Texas adolescent literacy academies*. Austin, TX: Author.

Notes Log: Summarization
Completed Science Sample

Topic/Title: What is a Tropical Rainforest?		Pages: 1–3
Main Ideas	**Notes**	

Tropical rainforests are found near the equator.	• Tropical rainforests are mostly found between the Tropic of Cancer and the Tropic of Capricorn
	• The largest rainforests are found in:
	  – Brazil (South America)—the Amazon is the largest tropical rainforest, 2/3 the size of the U.S.
	  – The Democratic Republic of Congo (Africa)
	  – Indonesia (islands near the Indian Ocean)
	• Other tropical rainforests found in: Southeast Asia, Hawaii, and Caribbean islands	

Tropical rainforests are called "rainforests" because of the rainfall they receive.	• Tropical rainforests see 160–300 inches of rain per year • The city of Los Angeles sees 10–20 inches of rain per year • Tropical rainforests have a year-round temperature of 75–80 degrees	

Tropical rainforests consist of four layers and hundreds of different species.	• Four layers:
	  – Emergent trees: the few trees that poke out to reach the sun
	  – Canopy: most of the plant growth and animals are here
	  – Understory: young trees and shrubs
	  – Forest floor: has very little sunlight and a thin carpet of wet, rotting leaves
	• Tropical rainforests are unique because they are home to hundreds of different plant and animal species	

Plants and animals of the rainforest are interdependent.	• Interdependent = depend on each other for survival • If one type of plant or animal becomes extinct, other plants and animals are also in danger of extinction	
Rainforests recycle everything.	• When leaves, flowers, or an animal dies on the forest floor, they decay and are recycled back into the soil and roots • Roots are shallow to collect all of the nutrients from the decay • Rain is recycled as water evaporates, forms clouds, and rains again onto the forest	
Rainforests are essential to everyone on Earth.	• Rainforests help control the world's climate • Many medicines come from plants that grow in tropical rainforests • Logging and gold mining threaten to destroy the rainforest	
People live in the rainforest.	• Indigenous people have lived in the rainforest for thousands of years and help sustain the forest • Recently, many people have moved to the rainforest and do not use the resources carefully	
Rainforests cannot grow back once they have been destroyed.	• Plants and animals that are interdependent cannot rebuild their community • Rainforests are 70–100 million years old and have species found nowhere else on Earth	

Main Idea of Section:
It is essential that we protect our tropical rainforests.

Summary
Tropical rainforests are found near the equator between the Tropic of Cancer and the Tropic of Capricorn. The name "rainforests" was chosen because they receive a lot of rain, about 160–300 inches per year, and have four layers of vegetation called emergent trees, canopy, understory, and forest floor. The rainforest is home to hundreds of different species of plants and animals that are interdependent, or dependent on each other for survival. This means that if one plant or animal becomes extinct, other plants or animals may be in danger of extinction. Rainforests recycle everything, including leaves, flowers, animals, and even water. A rainforest cannot grow back once it has been destroyed, so it is important that we protect our tropical rainforests. Without them, we would lose sources of medicines and experience major changes in climate around the world. Rainforests are essential to everyone on Earth.

Reprinted with permission from Meadows Center for Preventing Educational Risk. (2009). *Texas adolescent literacy academies*. Austin, TX: Author.

Notes Log: Summarization
Completed Social Studies Sample

Topic/Title: American Revolution	**Pages:** 252–278

Main Ideas	Notes
British taxes caused resentment among the colonists.	• Stamp tax (1765): tax on all printed documents • Townshend Acts: tax on glass, lead, paper, paint, and tea • Taxes resulted in the colonists boycotting British goods, so Britain repealed many of the taxes • The colonists' resentment toward the British increased
Violence between the British and the colonists led to war.	• Boston Massacre (1770): battle between British soldiers and Boston townspeople; several townspeople were killed • Boston Tea Party (1773): in protest of the Tea Act, members of a militant group (The Sons of Liberty) took over a British ship and dumped all of the tea into the Boston Harbor • Intolerable Acts issued: authorized British officials to use all means necessary to control the colonies; in response, the colonies formed the Continental Congress
The Revolutionary War started in Lexington, Massachusetts.	• 1775: first shots fired • July 4, 1776: colonies approved the Declaration of Independence • Violent war battles: British won several battles near New York City; colonists won several battles in New Jersey and Connecticut
There were two major turning points for the colonists.	• October 7, 1777: colonists defeated British forces at Saratoga, New York • February 6, 1778: colonists signed Treaty of Alliance with France; France agreed to provide the colonists with soldiers, generals, and arms
After many battles, the British forces surrendered in 1781.	• British army had control of the southern colonies, but British forces were depleted • September 28, 1781 (Yorktown, Virginia): the British navy under Charles Cornwallis surrendered to the French and American forces under George Washington • The colonists had finally won their independence
American independence was recognized when the Treaty of Paris was signed.	• Surrender at Yorktown ended all major battles • September 3, 1783: Treaty of Paris signed

Main Idea of Section:

After six years of war, the colonists won their independence.

Summary

In the 1760s, the British issued taxes on items such as glass, lead, paper, tea, and paint. This angered the colonists, so they boycotted British goods. The boycotts caused the British to repeal many of the taxes, but the colonists were still resentful. This resentment led to fights between the British and the colonists. Violence such as the Boston Massacre and the Boston Tea Party led the British to issue the Intolerable Acts, which stated that the British could use any means necessary to control the colonists. The colonists responded by forming the Continental Congress. These events eventually led to war. The first shots of the Revolutionary War were fired in 1775, and the colonists approved the Declaration of Independence on July 4, 1776. The British forces were better trained and better equipped than the colonists, but after many bloody battles and a Treaty of Alliance with France, the British forces were depleted. The British were forced to surrender in 1781, ending all major battles. However, American independence wasn't recognized until the Treaty of Paris was signed in 1783.

Reprinted with permission from Meadows Center for Preventing Educational Risk. (2009). *Texas adolescent literacy academies*. Austin, TX: Author.

Notes Log: Summarization
Notes Log Template (One Page)

Topic/Title	Pages

Main Ideas	Notes

Main Idea of Section

Summary

Notes Log: Summarization
Notes Log Template (Two Pages)

Topic/Title	Pages

Main Ideas	Notes

Main Ideas (cont.)

Notes (cont.)

Main Idea of Section

Summary

Promoting Comprehension: Anticipation–Reaction Guides
Completed English Language Arts/Reading (ELAR) Sample

Before reading: Think about whether you agree or disagree with each statement written below. Make a checkmark in the appropriate column.

During reading: Look for evidence that either confirms your opinion of each statement or makes you want to change it. Write your evidence in the box next to the statement and record the page number where you found it.

Agree	Disagree	Statement	Evidence	Page #
✗	✓	1. In the United States, people from different cultures are all treated the same.	The Watsons have to carefully plan their trip and pack extra supplies. Because of discrimination in the 1960s, they cannot count on having places to eat or sleep when they cross into the southern United States.	129–133
	✓	2. "What goes around comes around." In other words, if you do bad things, they will eventually catch up to you.	The bullies who picked on Kenny and Rufus in Flint do not get punished. The people who set the bomb in the church do not get punished until many years later (not during the time of the story).	27, 43, 60 203, 209
✓		3. You can always rely upon your family to help you in difficult times.	Byron saves Kenny from drowning at Collier's Landing. Kenny tries to save his sister from the church. Byron helps Kenny get over the bombing.	178–179 184–185 199–203
	✓	4. People should not be afraid to stand up for what is right.	The Watsons decided to return to Flint right after the bombing. They might have been killed if they stood up to the racists.	92, 209–210

After reading: Look over your evidence and decide whether you want to change your opinion of any statement. Mark any changes in the Agree/Disagree columns.

Text source: Curtis, C. P. (1995). *The Watsons go to Birmingham—1963*. New York: Random House.

Reprinted with permission from Meadows Center for Preventing Educational Risk. (2009). *Texas adolescent literacy academies*. Austin, TX: Author.

Promoting Comprehension: Anticipation–Reaction Guides
Completed Mathematics Sample

Before reading: Think about whether you agree or disagree with each statement written below. Make a checkmark in the appropriate column.

During reading: Look for evidence that either confirms your opinion of each statement or makes you want to change it. Write your evidence in the box next to the statement and record the page number where you found it.

Agree	Disagree	Statement	Evidence	Page #
✓		1. When calculating the sum of the angles in a quadrilateral, it is helpful to think of the properties of triangles.	*A diagonal in a quadrilateral cuts the figure into two triangles. If the sum of the angles in each triangle is 180°, then the sum of the angles in the quadrilateral equals 360° (triangle 1 + triangle 2).*	*1*
	✓	2. You would expect the opposite sides of a quadrilateral to be congruent.	*If the quadrilateral were a parallelogram, square, rhombus, or rectangle, the opposite sides would be congruent. However, trapezoids are also quadrilaterals with opposite sides that may not be congruent.*	*1*
✓	✗	3. It is easy to see how a trapezoid is different from a parallelogram.	*A quadrilateral is a parallelogram if it has two pairs of parallel and congruent sides. A trapezoid has exactly one pair of sides that is parallel (called bases), but does not have to have any congruent sides.*	*1*
✓		4. When working on word problems involving quadrilaterals, it is helpful to make a drawing.	*The word problem may give the length of sides or the measure of angles, and it may use symbols. Knowing how to construct the quadrilateral from that information might help determine what information is known and what still needs to be solved. It could help check the accuracy of the work.*	*1*

After reading: Look over your evidence and decide whether you want to change your opinion of any statement. Mark any changes in the Agree/Disagree columns.

Reprinted with permission from Meadows Center for Preventing Educational Risk. (2009). *Texas adolescent literacy academies*. Austin, TX: Author.

Promoting Comprehension: Anticipation–Reaction Guides
Completed Social Studies Sample

Before reading: Think about whether you agree or disagree with each statement written below. Make a checkmark in the appropriate column.

During reading: Look for evidence that either confirms your opinion of each statement or makes you want to change it. Write your evidence in the box next to the statement and record the page number where you found it.

Agree	Disagree	Statement	Evidence	Page #
✗	✓	1. It is harder to be a child today than it was in the early 20th century.	In the early 20th century, children had chores like cleaning oil lamps. Also, going to the grocery store took all day! Sometimes, because there were not schools in every town, children had to live apart from their parents to attend school.	315–316
✓		2. Women should be allowed to do anything a man is allowed to do.	Women were not allowed to fight in World War I, but many women went to work as farmers, telegraph messengers, and office managers.	312, 316
	✓	3. Husbands and wives should vote for the same candidates.	When women were first allowed to vote in 1920, some men said that if their wives voted, the men would leave their wives. But some men encouraged their wives (and daughters) to vote their conscience.	312–313
✓		4. Voting is exciting. I can't wait until I am old enough to vote.	In 1920, women were excited to finally get to vote, and many fathers and husbands were excited, too. One father took his daughter to the polls and told everyone about it. Voting is a privilege. Effie Hobby has voted in every election since 1920.	313–314

After reading: Look over your evidence and decide whether you want to change your opinion of any statement. Mark any changes in the Agree/Disagree columns.

Reprinted with permission from Meadows Center for Preventing Educational Risk. (2009). *Texas adolescent literacy academies.* Austin, TX: Author.

Sample: Vocabulary and Comprehension in Social Studies
The Civil War, Lesson 1
Lesson Plan

Big Idea: Conflicts over rights and economic issues lead to a violent civil war.

Standards	7.5A Explain reasons for the involvement of Texas in the Civil War 7.21B Analyze information by sequencing and identifying cause-and-effect relationships
Lesson Topic	Texas Joins the Confederacy

Objectives	Key Vocabulary
CONTENT—Students will: • Learn why Texas seceded and what steps it took to achieve this goal. **LANGUAGE—Students will:** • Use key vocabulary in reading, writing, listening, and speaking throughout the lesson. • Watch and listen to the video, write their responses in their notebooks, and contribute in whole-class discussion. • Listen and/or read the lesson passage and write question responses in their notebooks. • In the review/assessment activity, discuss the events that led Texas to join the Confederacy, and predict what will happen next.	• *Confederacy* • *ordinance* • *secede/ secession* • *sovereignty*
Materials	**Preparation**
• Student notebooks • Overhead projector and transparency markers • Video: "Beginning of the Civil War" • Passages: "Southern States Vow to Secede (pp. 343–344), "The Convention Votes on Secession" (pp. 344–345) and "The Confederacy Is Formed" (until . . . protection of slavery) (p. 345) • Transparency: *Abolish/Abolition* Vocabulary • Transparency: Map of Free and Slave States • Transparency: Questions	• Post the objectives • Links to background

---

Motivation (Engagement/Linkages)   3 min.

• Review the previous week's lesson.
  —"So far, we have learned that the Northern and Southern states clashed because of slavery. The Northern states were against slavery for moral, religious, and political reasons, and they wanted to abolish the practice."
• Display transparency: *Abolish/Abolition* Vocabulary. Review the word *abolition*.
  —"On the other hand, the Southern states were pro-slavery and were fighting to maintain the practice for economic reasons."
• Display transparency: Map of Free and Slave States.
  —"Texas originally was considered a Union state. But with the ongoing division over slavery, which the Dred Scott decision intensified, the Texans decided to leave the Union and join the slave states. Today we will look at the steps the Texans took to leave the Union and join the Confederacy."

Presentation **35 min.**

Vocabulary **(10 min.)**

- Introduce today's vocabulary and discuss "Turn and Talk" questions among pairs and/or whole group. Students write vocabulary terms and synonyms in their notebooks.

Video: "Beginning of the Civil War" **(5 min.)**

- Introduce the video.
  —"Let's watch a short video about how Texas joined the Confederacy (slave states). Listen for the answers to the following questions: What was the statewide dispute about? What decision was reached after the voting?"
- Students watch the video clip.
- Students write their responses in their logs. They may discuss the answers in their pairs.
- Teacher summarizes the video, highlighting the question above by using a few responses from the students.

Teacher-Led Reading: "Southern States Vow to Secede" (pp. 343–344)
"The Convention Votes on Secession" (pp. 344–345)
"The Confederacy Is Formed" (until . . . protection **(20 min.)**
of slavery) (p. 345)

- State the big idea of the reading.
- Preview the reading by asking questions to help activate background knowledge and guide students' thinking about what they will learn.
- Read the questions (on transparency) that students will focus on during the reading.
  —"Some Texans, like Sam Houston and other slave owners, opposed secession. What were their reasons?"
  —"As part of the Confederacy, how did most of Texas feel about slavery? Why?"
- Model thinking aloud as you read in order to make sense of text.
- As you read, demonstrate how to generate different types of questions, while allowing them to respond to these questions.

Practice **5 min.**

- After the reading, in pairs, have students discuss and write responses to the above question(s) in their notebooks.
- Once students are done, begin discussion of the questions while helping students to center on the big idea(s) in the selection.

Review/Assessment **5 min.**

- Introduce the activity.
  —"Today we read about the disputes between the North and the South. We know that the states thought their differences were so great that there could be no compromise, only war. So the Southern states decided to secede from the United States and form the Confederacy."
- Discuss the events that led Texas to join the Confederacy.
- Ask students to write their responses to the questions on their graphic organizer.
- Students contribute their answers in a whole-group discussion.

Texas Secedes from the Union		Texas Joins the Confederacy		Texas as Part of the Confederacy
Why did Texas secede from the United States?	→	How did the Constitution of the Confederacy differ from the Constitution of the United States?	→	What do you think will happen next?

Adapted with permission from Center for Research on Educational Achievement and Teaching of English Language Learners (CREATE) at the Meadows Center for Preventing Educational Risk. (2009). *Texas history lessons* (Grant No. R305A050056, U.S. Department of Education, Institute of Education Sciences). Austin, TX: Author.

Sample: Vocabulary and Comprehension in Social Studies
The Civil War, Lesson 1
Key Vocabulary: Confederacy

Confederacy
(Confederación)
The group of 11 Southern states that withdrew from the United States in 1860–1861

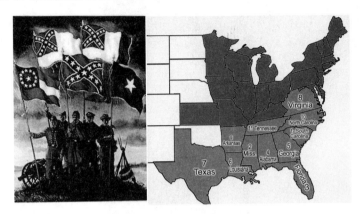

Synonym: *alliance*

Texas joined the *Confederacy* and became a slave state.

The Northern states refused to recognize the *Confederacy.*

Turn and Talk
- Imagine if all the states that border Mexico (Texas, New Mexico, Arizona, California) wanted to form a new confederacy—the "Border Confederacy"—and to start charging extra money for trucks going to and from the United States and Mexico. Do you think the people in these states would vote for this plan? Why or why not?

Adapted with permission from Center for Research on Educational Achievement and Teaching of English Language Learners (CREATE) at the Meadows Center for Preventing Educational Risk. (2009). *Texas history lessons* (Grant No. R305A050056, U.S. Department of Education, Institute of Education Sciences). Austin, TX: Author.

Sample: Vocabulary and Comprehension in Social Studies
The Civil War, Lesson 1
Key Vocabulary: Ordinance

ordinance
(ordenanza)
An official rule or law

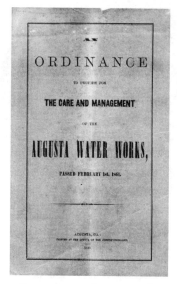

Synonyms: *decree, rule*

The delegates adopted an *ordinance* of withdrawal on February 1.

An *ordinance* signed into law last year banned smoking in most public areas in Austin.

Turn and Talk
- Mention two ordinances for students at your school.

Adapted with permission from Center for Research on Educational Achievement and Teaching of English Language Learners (CREATE) at the Meadows Center for Preventing Educational Risk. (2009). *Texas history lessons* (Grant No. R305A050056, U.S. Department of Education, Institute of Education Sciences). Austin, TX: Author.

Sample: Vocabulary and Comprehension in Social Studies
The Civil War, Lesson 1
Key Vocabulary: Secede/Secession

secede/secession
(separarse/separación)
To withdraw formally from a partnership or association

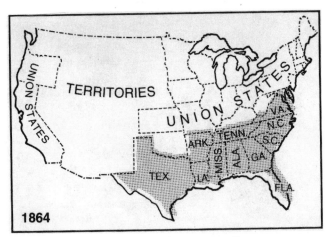

Synonyms: *break away, pull out*

Texas became the seventh state to *secede* from the United States.

The Jackson family decided to *secede* from their current church and join another one.

Turn and Talk
- **Imagine that you were a member of your favorite club or team (e.g., a football or basketball team, fan club, etc.). What are some things that might make you secede?**

Adapted with permission from Center for Research on Educational Achievement and Teaching of English Language Learners (CREATE) at the Meadows Center for Preventing Educational Risk. (2009). *Texas history lessons* (Grant No. R305A050056, U.S. Department of Education, Institute of Education Sciences). Austin, TX: Author.

Sample: Vocabulary and Comprehension in Social Studies
The Civil War, Lesson 1
Key Vocabulary: Sovereignty

sovereignty
(soberania)
Having supreme power or freedom from external control

The Confederate Constitution emphasized the *sovereignty* of the states and the right of people to hold slaves.

Many Christians see God as having *sovereignty* over their lives.

Turn and Talk
- **The school has the sovereignty to limit student cell phone use on school grounds. Can you think of two other things the school has sovereignty over?**

Adapted with permission from Center for Research on Educational Achievement and Teaching of English Language Learners (CREATE) at the Meadows Center for Preventing Educational Risk. (2009). *Texas history lessons* (Grant No. R305A050056, U.S. Department of Education, Institute of Education Sciences). Austin, TX: Author.

Sample: Vocabulary and Comprehension in Social Studies
The Civil War, Lesson 2
Lesson Plan

Big Idea: Conflicts over rights and economic issues lead to a violent civil war.

Standards	7.5A Explain reasons for the involvement of Texas in the Civil War
	7.21B Analyze information by sequencing and identifying cause-and-effect relationships
Lesson Topic	Texans Join the War

Objectives	Key Vocabulary
CONTENT—Students will: • Learn how the people of the Northern and Southern states responded to the war. **LANGUAGE—Students will:** • Use key vocabulary in reading, writing, listening, and speaking throughout the lesson. • Watch and listen to the video, write their responses in their notebooks, and contribute in whole-class discussion. • Listen and/or read the lesson passage and write question responses in their notebooks. • In the review/assessment activity, in groups, explain whether they think their assigned personality (e.g., Tejanos) would answer the Confederacy's call to arms, and explain why.	• *brigade* • *call to arms* • *civil war* • *conscription/draft*
Materials	**Preparation**
• Student notebooks • Overhead projector and transparency markers • Video: "Texans in the War" • Passage: "Many Texans Become Soldiers" (pp. 347–348) and "Most Texans Support the South" (p. 348) • Transparency: Questions • Transparency: The Confederacy's Call to Arms	• Post the objectives • Links to background • Set up for review activity

Motivation (Engagement/Linkages)	**3 min.**

• Provide overview/background information for today's lesson.
  —"We have learned that the Southern states, which were pro-slavery, did not vote for Abraham Lincoln for President because they feared he would abolish slavery. We also learned that Texas, which supported slavery, left the Union and joined the Confederacy when Lincoln became president."
  —"Today we will look at how the people in the South, and specifically Texans, responded to the war."

Presentation	**25 min.**
Vocabulary	**(10 min.)**

• Introduce today's vocabulary, and discuss "Turn and Talk" questions among pairs and/or whole group. Students write vocabulary terms and synonyms in their notebooks.

Partner Reading: "Many Texans Become Soldiers" (pp. 347–348) and "Most   **(10 min.)**
Texans Support the South" (p. 348)

- State the big idea of the reading.
- Preview the reading by asking questions to help activate background knowledge and guide students' thinking about what they will learn.
- Read the questions (on transparency) that students will focus on during the reading.
  —"How many people responded to the need for soldiers, and who were they?"
  —"Why do you think Texas decided to fight for the Confederacy?"
- Remind students why it is important to ask and answer different types of questions during reading.
- Pairs take turns reading paragraphs and asking and answering pair-generated questions. For example, Partner A reads the first paragraph and asks Partner B one question about the reading. Then Partner B reads the next paragraph and asks Partner A one question about the reading. (Students can write and answer the questions as they read.)

Video: "Texans in the War"   **(5 min.)**

- Introduce the video.
  —*The reading introduced us to how the state of Texas responded to the call for soldiers. Now let's watch a video about how the people of Texas responded to the war. You'll also see the fate of those who chose not to fight in the Confederate Army. Listen for the answers to the following questions: What procedure was used to draft men to fight in the war? What was the consequence for not supporting the South/Confederacy?"*
- Students watch the video clip.
- Students write their responses in their logs. They may discuss the answers in their pairs.
- Teacher summarizes the video, highlighting the questions above by using a few responses from the students.

Practice   5 min.

- After the reading, in pairs, have students discuss and write responses to the above question(s) in their notebooks.
- Once students are done, begin discussion of the questions while helping students to center on the big idea(s) in the selection.

Review/Assessment   15 min.

- Introduce the activity.
  —"Today we've talked about the people who fought in the Civil War. Let's put ourselves in their shoes and decide what we would do."
- Assign different personalities to groups of students (e.g., Tejano, African American slave, Anglo slaveholder, German Texan, etc.).
- Ask each group to complete its graphic organizer section saying whether their character would answer the Confederacy's call to arms and to explain why. Students in the group may have differing opinions, but they need to explain why they disagree with their group members.

Groups	Call to Arms: Yes/No	Why?
Tejanos		
African American slaves		
Anglo slaveholders		
European settlers		

- Review responses in a whole-group discussion.

Adapted with permission from Center for Research on Educational Achievement and Teaching of English Language Learners (CREATE) at the Meadows Center for Preventing Educational Risk. (2009). *Texas history lessons* (Grant No. R305A050056, U.S. Department of Education, Institute of Education Sciences). Austin, TX: Author.

Sample: Vocabulary and Comprehension in Social Studies
The Civil War, Lesson 2
Key Vocabulary: Brigade

brigade
(brigada)
A group of people organized for a specific purpose

Synonyms: *regiment, unit, battalion*

At the beginning of the Civil War, Texans joined *brigades* from their hometowns or counties.

The town organized a fire *brigade* in case the dry fields caught fire.

Turn and Talk
- What are some other natural disasters that might cause groups of people to form into brigades?

Adapted with permission from Center for Research on Educational Achievement and Teaching of English Language Learners (CREATE) at the Meadows Center for Preventing Educational Risk. (2009). *Texas history lessons* (Grant No. R305A050056, U.S. Department of Education, Institute of Education Sciences). Austin, TX: Author.

Sample: Vocabulary and Comprehension in Social Studies
The Civil War, Lesson 2
Key Vocabulary: Call to Arms

call to arms
(el llamado a las armas)
A request to report for active military duty

Synonym: *invitation to combat*

Thousands of Texans responded to the *call to arms* in the Mexican War.

After September 11, 2001, many young people in the United States responded to the *call to arms* and joined the military.

Turn and Talk
- **What would persuade you to follow a call to arms from your country?**
- **What reasons would you give if you did not want to follow a call to arms?**

Adapted with permission from Center for Research on Educational Achievement and Teaching of English Language Learners (CREATE) at the Meadows Center for Preventing Educational Risk. (2009). *Texas history lessons* (Grant No. R305A050056, U.S. Department of Education, Institute of Education Sciences). Austin, TX: Author.

Sample: Vocabulary and Comprehension in Social Studies
The Civil War, Lesson 2
Key Vocabulary: Civil War

civil war
(guerra civil)
A war between groups of people living in the same country

The disagreement over slavery was a major cause of the *Civil War* between the northern and Confederate states in the United States.

After the downfall of Moammar Gadahfi in Libya, there was a debate about whether rival militias were in a *civil war*.

Turn and Talk
- What are some reasons that would make people go to war against people of the same country?

Adapted with permission from Center for Research on Educational Achievement and Teaching of English Language Learners (CREATE) at the Meadows Center for Preventing Educational Risk. (2009). *Texas history lessons* (Grant No. R305A050056, U.S. Department of Education, Institute of Education Sciences). Austin, TX: Author.

Sample: Vocabulary and Comprehension in Social Studies
The Civil War, Lesson 2
Key Vocabulary: Conscription/Draft

conscription/draft
(reclutamiento)
Forced enrollment into military service

Synonyms: *compulsory recruitment*

More soldiers were needed in the Texas army, so the Confederate Congress passed the *Conscription* Act.

There has not been a *conscription* or *draft* in the United States since the 1970s. Right now, all military service is voluntary.

Turn and Talk
- **Many countries in the world have a conscription or draft where young people are required to serve in the military. What do you think of this idea?**

Adapted with permission from Center for Research on Educational Achievement and Teaching of English Language Learners (CREATE) at the Meadows Center for Preventing Educational Risk. (2009). *Texas history lessons* (Grant No. R305A050056, U.S. Department of Education, Institute of Education Sciences). Austin, TX: Author.

Text Structure

Elements of Narrative Text				
Examples	Fiction Autobiographies Legends	Historical Fiction Biographies Folktales	Science Fiction Fantasies Myths	Plays Mysteries
Purpose	To entertain or inform			
Characteristics	Follow a familiar story structure **Beginning**: Introduction of setting, characters, and conflict **Middle**: Progression of plot, which includes rising action, climax, and falling action **End**: Resolution or solution to the problem			
Narrative Terms (student-friendly definitions)	Exposition	Introduction of setting, characters, background information, and conflict		
	Setting	Time and place		
	Characters	People, animals, or other entities in the text		
	Conflict	Problem		
	Internal Conflict	A character's struggle within himself/herself		
	External Conflict	A character's struggle with another character		
	Rising Action	Events leading up to the climax; trying to solve the problem		
	Climax	Emotional high point of the story; conflict is addressed		
	Falling Action	Consequences or events caused by the climax		
	Resolution	Final outcome		

Reprinted with permission from Denton, C., Bryan, D., Wexler, J., Reed, D., & Vaughn, S. (2007). *Effective instruction for middle school students with reading difficulties: The reading teacher's sourcebook*. Austin, TX: Meadows Center for Preventing Educational Risk. Retrieved from *www.meadowscenter.org/vgc/downloads/middle_school_instruction/_RTS_Complete.pdf*
Based on University of Texas Center for Reading and Language Arts (2003).

Text Structure

Elements of Expository Text		
Examples	Newspapers Textbooks Magazine Articles Brochures Catalogues	
Purpose	To inform	
Characteristics	Titles Headings Subheadings Boldface Words Charts Tables Diagrams Graphics	
Organization	One expository passage may be organized using several different text structures.	
Types of Organization	**Cause-Effect**	How or why an event happened; what resulted from an event
	Chronology/Sequence	The order of events/steps in a process
	Compare/Contrast	How two or more things are alike/different
	Description/ Categorization	How something looks, moves, works, etc.; a definition or characterization
	Problem-Solution	What's wrong and how to fix it
	Position-Reason	Why a point or idea should be supported; what's wrong with an idea

Reprinted with permission from Denton, C., Bryan, D., Wexler, J., Reed, D., & Vaughn, S. (2007). *Effective instruction for middle school students with reading difficulties: The reading teacher's sourcebook*. Austin, TX: Meadows Center for Preventing Educational Risk. Retrieved from *www.meadowscenter.org/vgc/downloads/middle_school_instruction/_RTS_ Complete.pdf*.

Identifying Text Structure

Identifying Text Structure	
If the author wants you to know...	The text structure will be...
How or why an event happened; what resulted from an event	Cause-Effect
The order of events/steps in a process	Chronological Order/Sequencing
How two or more things are alike/different	Compare/Contrast
How something looks, moves, works, etc.; a definition or characterization	Description/Categorization
What's wrong and how to fix it	Problem-Solution
Why a point or idea should be supported; what's wrong with an idea	Position-Reason

Reprinted with permission from Reed, D. K. (2004a). *Identifying text structure*. Unpublished supplememtal material. Austin, TX: Southwest Educational Development Laboratory.

Signal Words

Cause-Effect		
How or why an event happened; what resulted from an event		
Accordingly	For this reason	Next
As a result of	Hence	Resulting from
Because	How	Since
Begins with	If . . . then	So that
Consequently	In order to	Therefore
Due to	Is caused by	Thus
Effects of	It follows	When . . . then
Finally	Leads/led to	Whether

Chronological Order/Temporal Sequencing		
The order of events/steps in a process		
After	Following	On (date)
Afterward	Formerly	Preceding
Around	Immediately	Previously
As soon as	In front of	Second
At last	In the middle	Shortly
Before	Initially	Soon
Between	Last	Then
During	Later	Third
Eventually	Meanwhile	To begin with
Ever since	Next	Until
Finally	Not long after	When
First	Now	While

Compare/Contrast		
How two or more things are alike/different		
Although	Even though	Nevertheless
And	However	On the contrary
As opposed to	In common	On the other hand
As well as	In comparison	Opposite
Better	In contrast	Otherwise
Both	In the same way	Same
But	Instead of	Similar to
Compared with	Just as/like	Similarly
Despite	Less	Still
Different from	Likewise	Whereas
Either	More than	Yet

Reprinted with permission from Reed, D. K. (2004b). *Signal words*. Unpublished supplememtal material. Austin, TX: Southwest Educational Development Laboratory.

Signal Words *(Page 2)*

Description/Categorization

How something looks, moves, works, etc.; a definition or characterization

Above	Down	Near
Across	For example	On top of
Along	For instance	Onto
Appears to be	Furthermore	Outside
As in	Generally	Over
Behind	Identify	Refers to
Below	In addition	Such as
Beside	In back of	To illustrate
Between	In front of	To the right/left
Consists of	Including	Typically
Describe	Looks like	Under

Problem-Solution

What's wrong and how to fix it

Answer	Problem	The problem facing
Challenge	Puzzle	The task was
Clarification	Question	Theory
Difficulty	Reply	This had to be accomplished
Dilemma	Resolution	To fix the problem
How to resolve the issue	Response	To overcome this
Lies	Riddle	Trouble
Obstacles	Solution	Unknown
One solution was	Solved by	What to do
Overcomes	The challenge was	What was discovered
Predicament		

Position-Reason

Why a point or idea should be supported; what's wrong with an idea

Accordingly	It is contended	Therefore
As illustrated by	It is evident that	Thesis
Because	It will be argued that	This contradicts the fact that
Consequently	Must take into account	This must be counterbalanced by
For instance	Since	This view is supported by
For this reason	The claim is limited due to	Turn more attention to
In conclusion	The implication is	What is critical
In order for	The position is	What is more central is
It can be established	The strengths of	

Graphic Organizers for Text Structures
Story Map

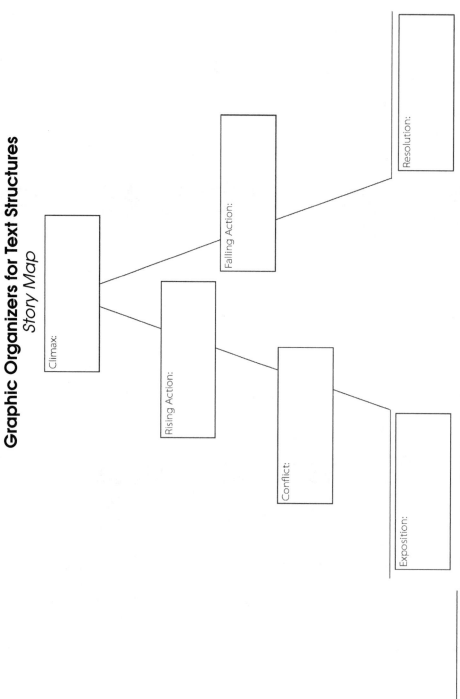

Graphic Organizers for Text Structures
Main-Idea Web

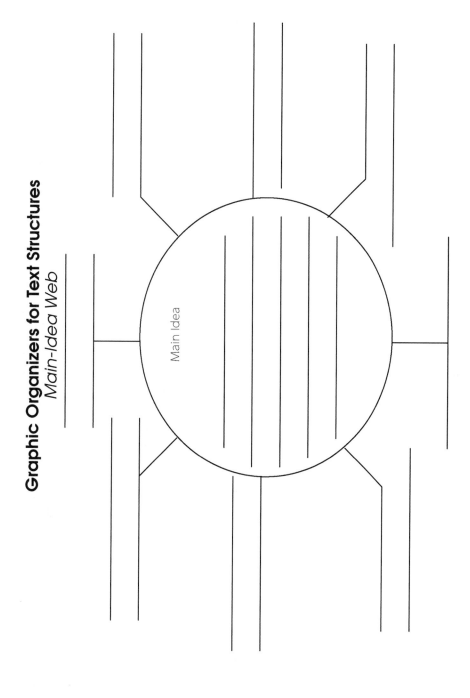

Main Idea

Reprinted with permission from Denton, C., Bryan, D., Wexler, J., Reed, D., & Vaughn, S. (2007). *Effective instruction for middle school students with reading difficulties: The reading teacher's sourcebook.* Austin, TX: Meadows Center for Preventing Educational Risk. Retrieved from *www.meadowscenter.org/vgc/downloads/middle_school_instruction/_RTS_Complete.pdf*

Graphic Organizers for Text Structures
Cause–Effect Chart (Herringbone)

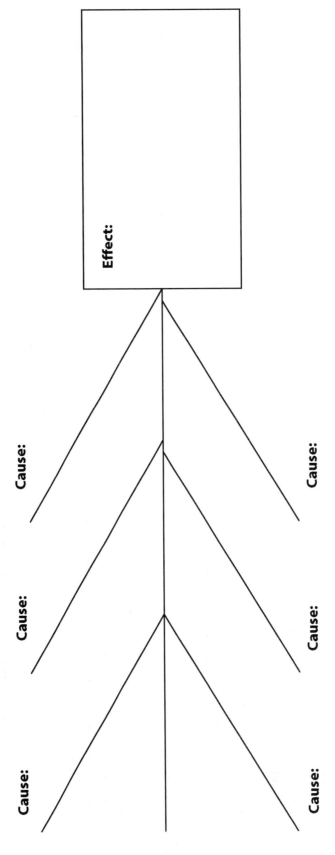

Effect:

Cause:

Cause:

Cause:

Cause:

Cause:

Cause:

Graphic Organizers for Text Structures
Cause–Effect Chart (Semantic Map)

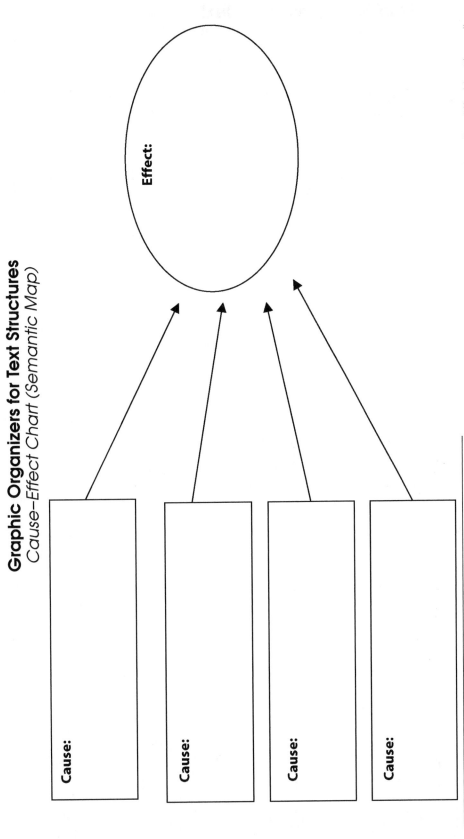

Graphic Organizers for Text Structures
Cause–Effect Chart (Basic)

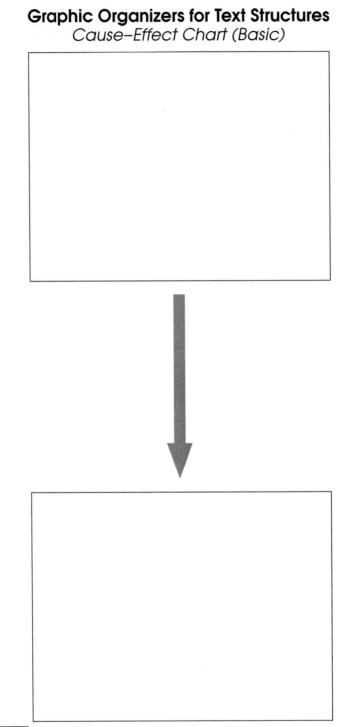

Graphic Organizers for Text Structures
Chronological Ordering/Sequencing

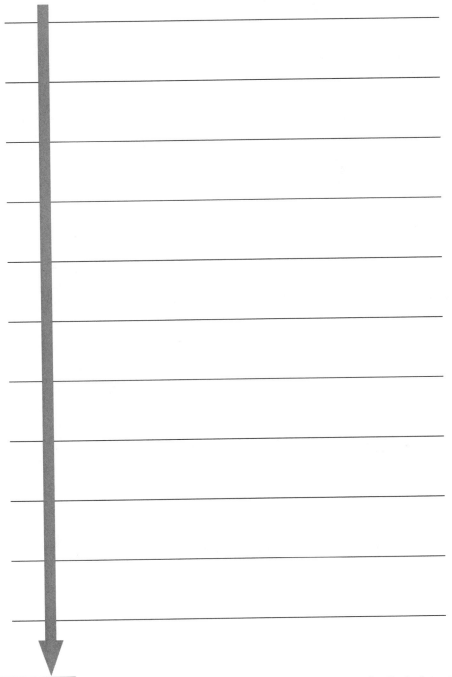

Reprinted with permission from Denton, C., Bryan, D., Wexler, J., Reed, D., & Vaughn, S. (2007). *Effective instruction for middle school students with reading difficulties: The reading teacher's sourcebook*. Austin, TX: Meadows Center for Preventing Educational Risk. Retrieved from *www.meadowscenter.org/vgc/downloads/middle_school_instruction/_RTS_ Complete.pdf*

Graphic Organizers for Text Structures
Temporal Sequencing

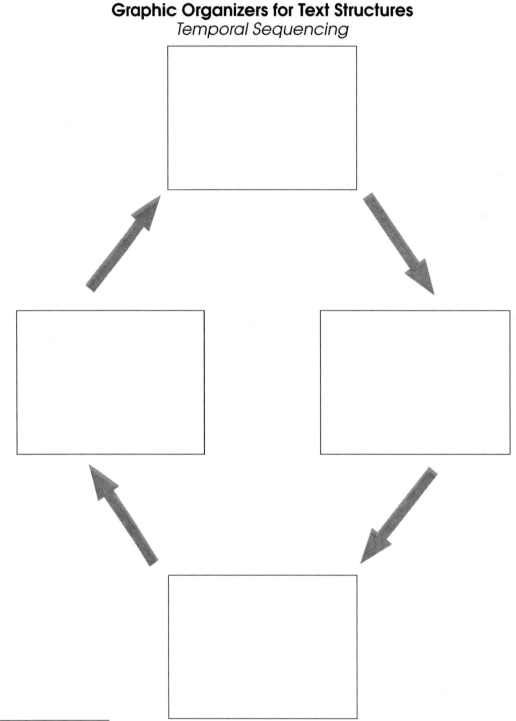

Graphic Organizers for Text Structures
Compare/Contrast

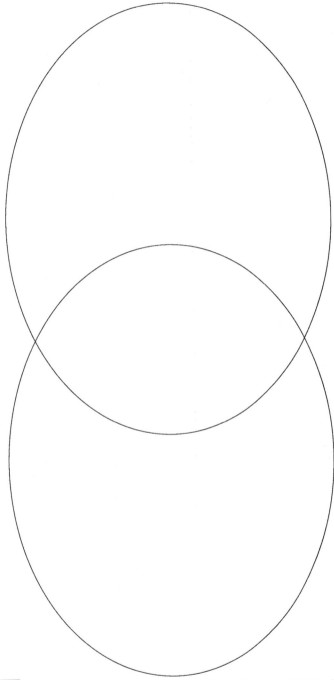

Graphic Organizers for Text Structures
Description (Web)

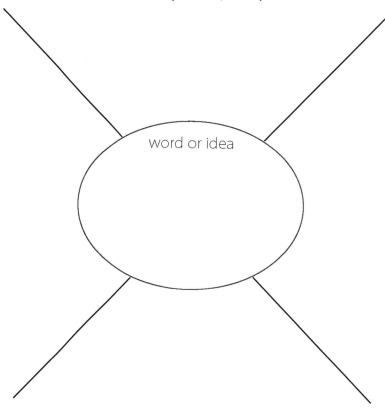

Graphic Organizers for Text Structures
Description (Chart)

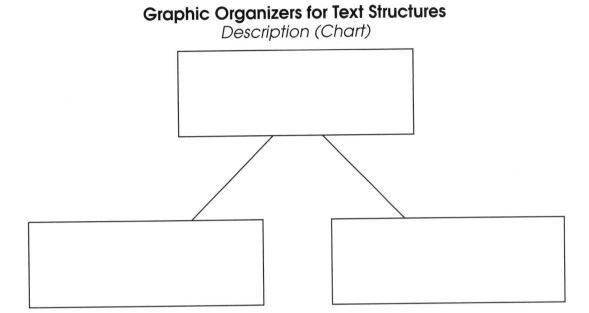

223

Graphic Organizers for Text Structures
Problem–Solution

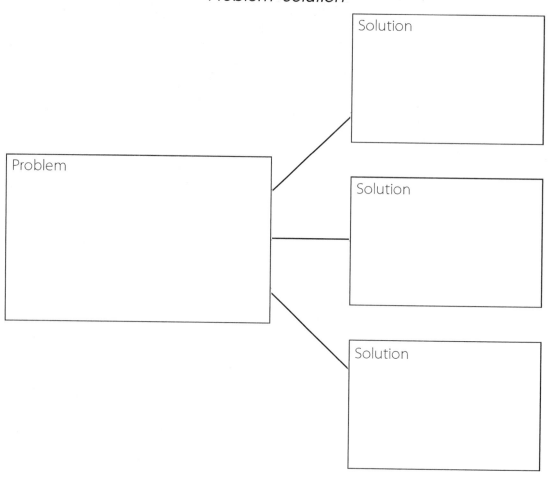

Graphic Organizers for Text Structures
Problem–Solution–Result

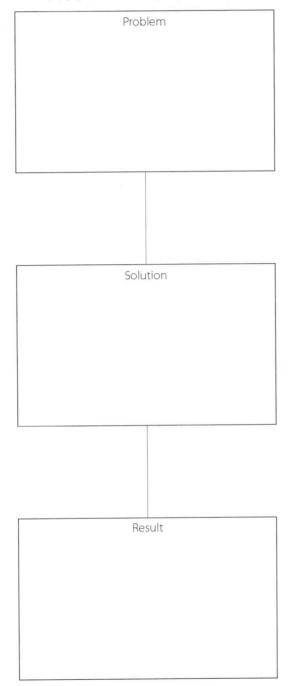

Graphic Organizers for Text Structures
Position–Reason

Position

Reason 1	Reason 2

Vocabulary Instruction: Frayer Model
Mathematics Sample

Definition	Characteristics
a polygon with four sides and four angles	• sum of the angles = 360 degrees • sides may be parallel • sides may be congruent • may contain right angles • has two diagonals

Term
quadrilateral

Examples	Nonexamples
• parallelogram • rhombus • square • rectangle • trapezoid	• circle • triangle • oval • straight line • star • octagon

Reprinted with permission from Meadows Center for Preventing Educational Risk. (2009). *Texas adolescent literacy academies.* Austin, TX: Author.
Frayer model based on Frayer, Frederick, & Klausmeier (1969).

Vocabulary Instruction: Frayer Model
Scaffolding the Frayer Model

- Provide additional examples and nonexamples of concepts, as needed, to support student understanding.

- Always make sure that students have encountered the word and built some conceptual knowledge about it before using the Frayer Model.

- Frequently remind students about characteristics of appropriate examples and nonexamples.

- Try using pictures or manipulatives for examples/nonexamples.

- Return to *I Do*/corrective feedback whenever it is clear that students do not understand the word/concept well enough.

Reprinted with permission from Meadows Center for Preventing Educational Risk. (2009). *Texas adolescent literacy academies*. Austin, TX: Author.

Word Map: *Physical Geography*

3. Does it make sense? Circle the sentence(s) that do(es) not make sense. Underline the part(s) that do(es) not make sense.

1. While Anchorage saw a lot of snow this winter, other parts of the state had plenty.
2. Yet for the past several years, the summers have been shorter and more rainy, melting whatever snow added to the glaciers.
3. The beetles are dying, and therefore expanding their territory.

4.) Context: Make a next-to-self- and/or-world connection.

Physical geography is important to me/the world because:

1. Vocabulary concept word(s):

<u>physical geography</u>

2. Definition: Write the definition in your own words.

5. Assurance word: <u>regions</u>
Write a sentence that uses the assurance word and the vocabulary concept word(s).

7. Debate: Take a stand: Circle the statement you are "for" and provide at least one reason why.

1. Human beings are responsible for new warming trends in our environment, and we should therefore investigate ways to stop this trend.
2. We can't tell exactly who or what is responsible for this warming trend, and we don't know exactly what damage it would cause, so we shouldn't feel responsible to try to stop it at this point in time.

Statement and/or Reasons:

1.

2.

6. Word building: Choose the real word and write another real, related word.

A. geographied
B. geographical

C. _____

Reprinted with permission from Simmons, D., Rupley, W. H., & Vaughn, S. (2009). *Enhancing the quality of expository text instruction and comprehension through content and case-situated professional development* (Final report, Institute of Education Sciences Grant No. R305M050121A). Submitted to U.S. Department of Education, Institute of Education Sciences. This research was supported by Grant No. P50 HD052117 from the Eunice Kennedy Shriver National Institute of Child Health and Human Development. The content is solely the responsibility of the authors and does not necessarily represent the official views of the Eunice Kennedy Shriver National Institute of Child Health and Human Development or the National Institutes of Health.

APPENDIX E

Examples of Reading Intervention Strategies

Promoting Word Reading

Promoting Fluency

Promoting Vocabulary

Promoting Comprehension

Promoting Word Reading
Instruction in Syllable Types

Sequence of types

Closed syllables

Open syllables

Vowel-consonant-*e* syllables

R-controlled syllables

Vowel pair syllables

Consonant-*le* syllables

Irregular words of each syllable structure

Routine for instruction

1. Provide multiple opportunities to practice identifying a syllable type in one-syllable words.
2. Gradually increase practice in a syllable type to include two-syllable words and then multi-syllable words.
3. Ask: Do I need to divide this word into different syllables?
    a. If no: Why not?
    b. If yes: Where? Why?
4. Ask: What is the syllable type?
    a. What are the characteristics of that syllable type?
    b. What does it tell me about the vowel sound?
5. Say each syllable out loud slowly.
6. Put the syllables together and say the whole word.
7. Provide cumulative reviews of the syllable types.
    a. Word sorts
    b. Manipulating words to divide between syllables
    c. Manipulating words to add or remove letters that change the syllable type (e.g., *pin* to *pine*; *so* to *soft*; *bell* to *be*)
    d. Practicing with regular and irregular words

Reprinted with permission from Meadows Center for Preventing Educational Risk. (2009). *Texas adolescent literacy academies.* Austin, TX: Author.

Promoting Word Reading
Scaffolding the Identification of Syllable Types

- Whenever appropriate, have students identify the syllable types when students encounter unfamiliar words in their reading.

- If students do not recognize the syllable types or know the vowel sounds, return to explicitly teaching them.

- Gradually increase the length and complexity of application words on which students practice.

- Challenge students to find additional examples of the syllable types in words the students encounter.

- Teach students how to divide the syllables in a word.

- Teach preskills (e.g., short vowels, long vowels, consonant blends, consonant digraphs, diphthongs, more complex phonics such as *-igh*).

Additional tools and resources available at:
- **www.searchlight.utexas.org**
- **www.fcrr.org/Curriculum/SCAindex.htm**

Reprinted with permission from Meadows Center for Preventing Educational Risk. (2009). *Texas adolescent literacy academies*. Austin, TX: Author.

Promoting Word Reading
Content-Area Word Lists by Syllable Type

CLOSED SYLLABLE

A closed syllable has one vowel that is closed in by a consonant. The vowel sound is short. (VC, CVC, CCVC, CVCC, or CCVCC)

Language Arts:

Index

Poet

Edit

Predict

Concept

Literature

Relationship

Social Studies:

West

Taft

Empire

Modern

Populist

Democratic

Independent

Math:

Sum

Add

Subtract

Figure

Factor

Object

Investigate

Science:

Rust

Energy

Property

Interact

Element

Temperature

Electromagnetic

(cont.)

Reprinted with permission from Meadows Center for Preventing Educational Risk. (2009). *Texas adolescent literacy academies*. Austin, TX: Author.

OPEN SYLLABLE

An open syllable has one vowel that occurs at the end of the syllable. The vowel sound is long. (CV or CCV)

Language Arts:

Poet

Student

Pronoun

Predict

Autobiography

Comprehensive

Relationship

Social Studies:

Triumph

Migrate

Nation

Review

Reform

Develop

Independent

Math:

Meter

Below

Table

Result

Describe

Equation

Denominator

Science:

Science

Lunar

Resource

Climate

Volcano

Reflection

Electromagnetic

(cont.)

VOWEL-CONSONANT-*E* SYLLABLE

A VC-*e* syllable (silent-*e* syllable) ends with an *e*, has one consonant before the *e*, and has one vowel before the consonant. The vowel sound is long, and the *e* is silent. (VC-*e* or CVC-*e*)

Language Arts:

T a l e

W r i t e

T h e m e

D e s c r i b e

I n t r o d u c e

F o r e s h a d o w

V i s u a l i z e

Social Studies:

M i n e

R i s e

E m p i r e

S a f e g u a r d

D e b a t e

P o p u l a t e

E n t e r p r i s e

Math:

C u b e

S c o r e

S h a p e

D i v i d e

A l i k e

E v a l u a t e

I n v e s t i g a t e

Science:

P l a t e

W a v e

E x p l o r e

N a t u r e

C o m b i n e

P o l l u t e

C r e a t e

(cont.)

VOWEL PAIRS or TEAMS

A vowel pair syllable has two vowels together that make one vowel sound.

Language Arts:

<u>Rea</u>d

<u>Goa</u>l

<u>Mea</u>ning

<u>Spea</u>king

De<u>tail</u>

Proof<u>rea</u>d

<u>Mai</u>n Character

Social Studies:

<u>Gree</u>k

<u>Speech</u>

<u>Peace</u>

<u>Laun</u>ch

<u>Free</u>dom

<u>Sweat</u>shop

Bern<u>stein</u>

Math:

<u>Paid</u>

<u>Mean</u>

<u>Speed</u>

<u>Pie</u>

<u>Fea</u>ture

Ex<u>plain</u>

<u>Rea</u>son

Science:

<u>Stream</u>

<u>Toad</u>

<u>Heat</u>

<u>Sea</u>

<u>Beat</u>

<u>Lead</u>

<u>Rain</u>

(cont.)

R-CONTROLLED VOWELS

An *r*-controlled syllable contains a vowel followed by an *r*. This combination makes a unique sound. (V-*r*)

Language Arts:

In<u>for</u>m

Auth<u>or</u>

Thea<u>ter</u>

Narra<u>tor</u>

Charac<u>ter</u>

<u>Per</u>spective

Fig<u>ur</u>ative

Social Studies:

<u>Far</u>m

<u>Mar</u>ket

Ac<u>cord</u>

Mod<u>ern</u>

An<u>ar</u>chist

A<u>part</u>heid

Af<u>firm</u>ative

Math:

<u>Part</u>

<u>Per</u>cent

Pat<u>tern</u>

En<u>large</u>

Fac<u>tor</u>

Simi<u>lar</u>

Perime<u>ter</u>

Science:

Sul<u>fur</u>

<u>Car</u>bon

En<u>er</u>gy

<u>Par</u>ticle

Con<u>ser</u>vation

<u>Zir</u>conium

<u>Ber</u>kelium

(cont.)

CONSONANT-*LE* SYLLABLE

A consonant-*le* syllable has a consonant followed by *le*. The vowel sound in this syllable is the schwa sound followed by the *l* sound. The *e* is silent. (-C+*le*)

Language Arts:

Ti<u>tle</u>

Fa<u>ble</u>

Peo<u>ple</u>

Princi<u>ple</u>

Arti<u>cle</u>

Exam<u>ple</u>

Partici<u>ple</u>

Social Studies:

Set<u>tle</u>

Cat<u>tle</u>

Stru<u>ggle</u>

Bat<u>tle</u>

Set<u>tle</u>ment

Spin<u>dle</u>top

Profita<u>ble</u>

Math:

Sin<u>gle</u>

Dou<u>ble</u>

Cou<u>ple</u>

Mid<u>dle</u>

Pu<u>zzle</u>

Possi<u>ble</u>

Trian<u>gle</u>

Science:

Tur<u>tle</u>

Trem<u>ble</u>

Bee<u>tle</u>

Man<u>tle</u>

Nee<u>dle</u>leaf

Predicta<u>ble</u>

Adapta<u>ble</u>

Promoting Fluency
Partner Reading Routine

Cold Read (use a blue ink pen)	1. Teacher models fluent reading of a passage. 2. All students follow along in a copy of the passage and underline words to review. 3. Teacher and students repeat any words the students underlined. 4. Teacher asks students the main idea of the passage.

Warm Read
(use a black ink pen)
	1. Partner One reads while Partner Two:
	    • Follows along
	    • Underlines errors
	    • Circles last word
	    • Conducts error correction
	    • Calculates WCPM
	2. Partners switch duties.

Hot Read
(use a red ink pen)
	1. Partner One reads while Partner Two:
	    • Follows along
	    • Underlines errors
	    • Circles last word
	    • Conducts error correction
	    • Calculates WCPM
	2. Partners switch duties.
	3. Each partner graphs her/his own hot read WCPM on a fluency chart.

Reprinted with permission from Meadows Center for Preventing Educational Risk. (2009). *Texas adolescent literacy academies*. Austin, TX: Author.
Partner reading based on Bryant et al. (2000); Delquadri, Greenwood, Whorton, Carta, & Hall (1986); and Mathes, Fuchs, Fuchs, Henley, & Sanders (1994).

Partner:

Here are the words I underlined. Let's read them together.

Read the underlined words together.

Partner:

Would you like to review any other words?

If YES, review the words.

If NO, move on to the next step.

Reprinted with permission from Meadows Center for Preventing Educational Risk. (2009). *Texas adolescent literacy academies.* Austin, TX: Author.

Promoting Fluency
Scaffolding Fluency Instruction

Scaffolding steps:

- Move students up a level in text when the lower-ability reader has 2 consecutive days with 95 words correct per minute (WCPM) or better.

- Use progress monitoring data to reconfigure pairs appropriately.

- Implement the routine three to four times per week for 12 to 20 weeks. Then, take a break before returning to Partner Reading three to four times per week.

Caveats about fluency:

- Fluency instruction alone will not close the gap between struggling readers and their normally achieving counterparts.

- Fluency instruction is not always the most appropriate use of time:

  - Consider whether the student demonstrates average or above-average comprehension.

  - Consider a benchmark of 90–100 WCPM with 90% accuracy in grade-level text.

Reprinted with permission from Meadows Center for Preventing Educational Risk. (2009). *Texas adolescent literacy academies*. Austin, TX: Author.

Promoting Vocabulary
Word Map: Food Preservation

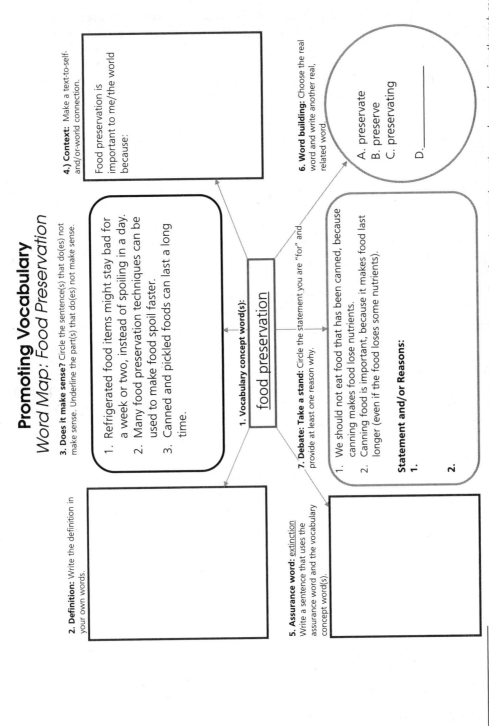

3. Does it make sense? Circle the sentence(s) that do(es) not make sense. Underline the part(s) that do(es) not make sense.

1. Refrigerated food items might stay bad for a week or two, instead of spoiling in a day.
2. Many food preservation techniques can be used to make food spoil faster.
3. Canned and pickled foods can last a long time.

4.) Context: Make a text-to-self-and/or-world connection.

Food preservation is important to me/the world because:

1. Vocabulary concept word(s):

food preservation

2. Definition: Write the definition in your own words.

5. Assurance word: extinction
Write a sentence that uses the assurance word and the vocabulary concept word(s).

6. Word building: Choose the real word and write another real, related word.

A. preservate
B. preserve
C. preservating

D. _____

7. Debate: Take a stand: Circle the statement you are "for" and provide at least one reason why.

1. We should not eat food that has been canned, because canning makes food lose nutrients.
2. Canning food is important, because it makes food last longer (even if the food loses some nutrients).

Statement and/or Reasons:

1.

2.

Reprinted with permission from Simmons, D., Rupley, W. H., & Vaughn, S. (2009). *Enhancing the quality of expository text instruction and comprehension through content and case-situated professional development* (Final report, Institute of Education Sciences Grant No. R305M050121A). Submitted to U.S. Department of Education, Institute of Education Sciences. This research was supported by Grant No. P50 HD052117 from the Eunice Kennedy Shriver National Institute of Child Health and Human Development. The content is solely the responsibility of the authors and does not necessarily represent the official views of the Eunice Kennedy Shriver National Institute of Child Health and Human Development or the National Institutes of Health.

Promoting Comprehension
Does It Make Sense?: Sentence-Level Comprehension Monitoring

Reason for sentence-level comprehension practice: Sometimes it is difficult to understand a chapter that you read from a novel or textbook. Sometimes it is even difficult to understand a paragraph or even one sentence! Comprehending text requires understanding the words, phrases, syntax or grammar, and many other things. We need to practice self-monitoring when we don't understand even at the sentence level.

Directions: Decide if the sentences below make sense. Underline the part that doesn't make sense. Explain or correct the mistake.

English Language Arts/ELAR Examples

1. So maybe he wasn't that fierce in day care, since I'm pretty sure he did hit a kid with his crutch once. Yes ☐ No ☐

2. It's like no rules apply, and that makes everything real safe, if you know what I mean, like let's have a blast and who cares what happens. Yes ☐ No ☐

3. The deal is, we have to wait until daylight, so no one can see us messing with the storm drain. Yes ☐ No ☐

Science Examples

4. Refrigerated food items might stay bad for a week or two, instead of spoiling in a day. Yes ☐ No ☐

5. Many food preservation techniques can be used to make food spoil faster. Yes ☐ No ☐

6. Canned and pickled foods can last a long time. Yes ☐ No ☐

Social Studies Examples

7. While Anchorage saw a lot of snow this winter, other parts of the state had plenty. Yes ☐ No ☐

8. Yet for the past several years, the summers have been shorter and more rainy, melting whatever snow added to the glaciers. Yes ☐ No ☐

9. The beetles are dying, and therefore expanding their territory. Yes ☐ No ☐

This research was supported by Grant No. P50 HD052117 from the Eunice Kennedy Shriver National Institute of Child Health and Human Development. The content is solely the responsibility of the authors and does not necessarily represent the official views of the Eunice Kennedy Shriver National Institute of Child Health and Human Development or the National Institutes of Health.

Resources for Implementing RTI at the Secondary Level

Throughout this book, we have referred to additional resources that are available to guide your implementation of RTI at the secondary level. Therefore, this last appendix is a list of websites that may provide such resources. The sites are grouped by categories, but many have tools and resources in different categories that can be accessed from the initial link.

General Information on RTI with Secondary Students

- National High School Center—*www.betterhighschools.org*
- National Center on RTI—*www.rti4success.org*
- National Center on Learning Disabilities—*www.ncld.org*
- Center on Learning Disabilities—*www.ldonline.org*
- National Dissemination Center for Children with Disabilities—*www.nichcy.org*
- International Reading Association—*www.reading.org*
- Council for Exceptional Children—*www.cec.sped.org*
- Meadows Center for Preventing Educational Risk—*www.meadowscenter.org*
- Council for Administrators of Special Education—*www.casecec.org*
- National Association of School Psychologists—*www.nasponline.org*
- RTI Action Network—*www.rtinetwork.org*
- IDEA Partnership Collection—*www.ideapartnership.org/index.php?option=com_content&view=category&layout=blog&id=15&Itemid=56*
- Secondary Literacy Instruction and Intervention Guide—*www.stupski.org/documents/Secondary_Literacy_Instruction_Intervention_Guide.pdf*
- Tiered Interventions in High Schools—*centeroninstruction.org/files/Tiered%20Inventions%20in%20High%20Schools.PDF*

Assessing Secondary Students' Reading Abilities

- RTI Data Management Tool—*buildingrti.utexas.org/rti/rti-dmt*
- The National Center on Student Progress Monitoring—*www.studentprogress.org*
- Research Institute on Progress Monitoring—*progressmonitoring.org*
- Progress Monitoring in the Context of RTI—*centeroninstruction.org/files/plugin-UsingCBMRTI_powerpoint.pdf*
  - Accompanying manual—*centeroninstruction.org/files/plugin-UsingCBMRTI_manual.pdf*
  - Accompanying handouts—*centeroninstruction.org/files/plugin-UsingCBMRTI_handouts.pdf*
- Assessments to Guide Adolescent Literacy Instruction—*centeroninstruction.org/files/Assessment%20Guide.pdf*
- Reading Assessment Database—*www.sedl.org/reading/rad*

Implementation Fidelity

- What Do We Know about Assessing and Improving Fidelity of RTI?—*centeroninstruction.org/files/Assessing%20and%20Improving%20Fidelity%20of%20RTI.pdf*
- RTI Classification and Self-Assessment Tool—*www.rtictrl.org*
- State Implementation and Scaling-up of Evidence-based Practices (SISEP)—*www.scalingup.org*
- Fidelity tools—*www.rti4success.org/resourcetype/rti-integrity-rubric-and-worksheet*
- Adolescent Literacy Walk-Through for Principals: A Guide for Instructional Leaders—*centeroninstruction.org/files/Adol%20Lit%20Walk%20Through.pdf*

RTI Leadership

- RTI Considerations for School Leaders *iris.peabody.vanderbilt.edu/rti_leaders/chalcycle.htm*
- National Association for State Directors of Special Education—*www.nasdse.org*

State-Level Guidance on RTI

- All states, overview—*secc.sedl.org/orc/rr/secc_rr_00102.pdf*
- All states, database—*state.rti4success.org*
- Alabama—*www.alsde.edu/general/RESPONSE_TO_INSTRUCTION.pdf*
- Alaska—*www.eed.state.ak.us/nclb/pdf/Alaska_RTI_Guidance.pdf*
- Arizona—*www.ade.state.az.us/azrti*
- Arkansas—*www.arstudentsuccess.org/closing-the-achievement-gap/rtIdata-based-problem-solving.html*
- California—*www.cde.ca.gov/nr/el/le/yr08ltr114att.asp*
- Colorado—*www.cde.state.co.us/RtI/LearnAboutRtI.htm*
- Connecticut—*www.sde.ct.gov/sde/cwp/view.asp?a=2618+q=322020*
- Delaware—*www.doe.k12.de.us/infosuites/staff/profdev/rti_docs.shtml*
- Florida—*www.florida-rti.org*
- Georgia—*www.gadoe.org/ci_services.aspx?PageReq=CIServRTI*
- Hawaii—*doe.k12.hi.us/periodicals/csss/2008/CSSS0808.pdf*
- Idaho—*www.sde.idaho.gov/site/rti*
- Illinois—*www.isbe.state.il.us/RtI_plan/default.htm*

- Indiana—*www.doe.in.gov/rti/index.html*
- Iowa—*educateiowa.gov/index.php?option=com.content&task=view&id=801&itemid=1305*
- Kansas—*www.kansasmtss.org*
- Kentucky—*www.education.ky.gov/KDE/Instructional+Resources/Kentucky+System+of+Interventions*
- Louisiana—*www.louisianaschools.net/offices/literacy/rti.html*
- Maine—*www.maine.gov/education/rti/index.shtml*
- Maryland—*www.marylandpublicschools.org/MSDE/programs/rti/?WBCMODE=presen%252*
- Massachusetts—no website specific to RTI
- Michigan—*miblsi.cenmi.org/Home.aspx*
- Minnesota—*www.rtimn.blogspot.com*
- Mississippi—*www.mde.k12.ms.us/RtI/index.html*
- Missouri—*dese.mo.gov/divspeced/RtIpg.html*
- Montana—*www.opi.mt.gov/pub/Resources/RTI/Index.html*
- Nebraska—*rtinebraska.unl.edu*
- Nevada—no website specific to RTI
- New Hampshire—*www.education.nh.gov/innovations/rti/index.htm*
- New Jersey—no website specific to RTI
- New Mexico—*www.ped.state.nm.us/RTI/index.html*
- New York—*www.nysrti.org/*
- North Carolina—*www.ncpublicschools.org/curriculum/responsiveness/rtimaterials*
- North Dakota—*www.dpi.state.nd.us/speced/personnel/index.shtm*
- Ohio—*education.ohio.gov/GD/Templates/Pages/ODE/ODEPrimary.aspx?Page-2+TopicID-844+TopicRelationID-657*
- Oklahoma—*sole.state.ok.us/curriculum/SpecEd/pd/RtI/guidanceDoc.pdf*
- Oregon—*www.ode.state.or.us/search/page/?id=315*
- Pennsylvania—no website specific to RTI
- Rhode Island—*www.ritap.org/rti*
- South Carolina—*www.ed.sc.gov/agency/Standards-and-Learning/Academic-Standards/old/Instructional-Promising-Practices/documents/ResponsetoIntervention.html*
- South Dakota—*doe.sd.gov/oess/sped_RtI.asp*
- Tennessee—*state.tn.us/education/speced/doc/10509rtiguidelines.pdf*
- Texas—*ritter.tea.state.tx.us/special.ed/rti*
- Utah—*www.updc.org/abc*
- Vermont—*education.vermont.gov/new/html/pgm_sped/forms.html*
- Virginia—*www.doe.virginia.gov/instruction/response_intervention/index.shtml*
- Washington—*www.k12.wa.us/RTI/default.aspx*
- West Virginia—*wvde.state.wv.us/osp/RtIOSP.html*
- Wisconsin—*dpi.wi.gov/rti/index.html*
- Wyoming—*edu.wyoming.gov/Programs/rti.aspx*

Tier 1 Instruction

- Improving Literacy Instruction in Middle and High Schools: A Guide for Principals—*www.fcrr.org/Interventions/pdf/Principals%20Guide-Secondary.pdf*
- Improving Adolescent Literacy: Effective Classroom and Intervention Practices—*ies.ed.gov/ncee/wwc/pdf/practiceguides/adlit_pg_082608.pdf*

- Reading at Risk: The State Response to the Crisis in Adolescent Literacy—*centeron-instruction.org/files/Reading_At_Risk_Full_Report.pdf*
- Literacy Instruction in the Content Areas: Getting to the Core of Middle and High School Improvement—*www.all4ed.org/files/LitCon.pdf*
- Evidence-based Decision Making: Assessing Reading across the Curriculum Interventions—*centeroninstruction.org/files/REL_2007-Evidence-based%20decisionmaking%20%20assessing%20reading%20across%20the%20curriculum%20interventions.pdf*
- Bringing Literacy Strategies into Content Area Instruction—*centeroninstruction.org/files/Bringing%20Literacy%20Strategies%20into%20Content%20Instruction.pdf*

Tier 2 and Tier 3 Instruction

- Meeting the Needs of Significantly Struggling Learners in High School: A Look at Approaches to Tiered Intervention—*centeroninstruction.org/files/Meeting%20the%20Needs.pdf*
- Effective Instruction for Adolescent Struggling Readers: A Practice Brief—*centeroninstruction.org/files/Adol%20Struggling%20Readers%20Practice%20Brief.pdf*
- Effective Instruction for Middle School Students with Reading Difficulties: The Reading Teacher's Sourcebook—*www.meadowscenter.org/vgc/materials/middle_school_instruction.asp*
- Adolescent Literacy Intervention Programs: Chart and Program Review Guide—*www.learningpt.org/literacy/adolescent/intervention.pdf*

Funding

- Implementing RTI Using Title I, Title III, and CEIS Funds: Key Issues for Decision Makers—*centeroninstruction.org/files/Implementing%20RTI%20Using%20Title%20I,%20III%20&%20CEIS%20Funds.pdf*

Positive Behavior Support (PBS)

- Technical Assistance Center on Positive Behavioral Interventions and Supports—*www.pbis.org*
- Association for Positive Behavior Support—*www.apbs.org*
- Michigan PBS Implementation Guide—*www.michigan.gov/documents/mde/SchoolwidePBS_264634_7.pdf*
- How the Effective Behavior and Instructional Support Process Works in Secondary Schools—*centeroninstruction.org/files/How%20EBIS-RTI%20Process%20Works%20in%20Secondary%20Schools.pdf*
- Illinois PBS Network—*www.pbisillinois.org*

Miscellaneous

- Professional development resources—*www.learningport.us*
- What Works Clearinghouse—*ies.ed.gov/ncee/wwc*

References

ACT. (2006). *Reading between the lines: What the ACT reveals about college readiness in reading.* Retrieved from *act.org/research/policymakers/pdf/reading_summary.pdf*

ACT. (2009). *ACT profile report—National: Graduating class 2009.* Retrieved from *www.act.org/news/data/09/data.html*

Alfassi, M. (2004). Reading to learn: Effects of combined strategy instruction on high school students. *Journal of Educational Research, 97*(4), 171–184.

Applebee, A. N., Langer, J. A., Nystrand, M., & Gamoran, A. (2003). Discussion-based approaches to developing understanding: Classroom instruction and student performance in middle and high school English. *American Educational Research Journal, 40,* 685–730.

Archer, A., Isaacson, S., & Peters, E. (1988). *Training manual: Effective instruction.* Reston, VA: Council for Exceptional Children.

Ardoin, S. P. (2006). The response in response to intervention: Evaluating the utility of assessing maintenance of intervention effects. *Psychology in the Schools, 43*(6), 713–725.

Barth, A., Stuebing, K. K., Fletcher, J. M., Cirino, P. T., Francis, D. J., & Vaughn, S. (in press). Reliability and validity of the median score when assessing the oral reading fluency of middle grade readers. *Reading Psychology.*

Bellini, S., Peters, J., Benner, L., & Hopf, A. (2007). A meta-analysis of school-based social skills interventions for children with autism spectrum disorders. *Remedial and Special Education, 28*(3), 153–162.

Biancarosa, G., & Snow, C. E. (2004). *Reading next: A vision for action and research in middle and high school literacy. A report from the Carnegie Corporation of New York.* Washington, DC: Alliance for Excellent Education.

Bloom, H. S., Hill, C. J., Black, A. R., & Lipsey, M. W. (2008). *Performance trajectories and performance gaps as achievement effect-size benchmarks for educational interventions.* New York: MDRC.

Bos, C. S., & Anders, P. L. (1992). Using interactive teaching and learning strategies to promote text comprehension and content learning for students with learning disabilities. *International Journal of Disability, Development, and Education, 39*(3), 225–238.

Bradley, R., Danielson, L., & Hallahan, D. P. (2002). *Identification of learning disabilities: Research to practice.* Mahwah, NJ: Erlbaum.

Bryant, D. P., Linan-Thompson, S., Ugel, N., Hamff, A., & Hougen, M. (2001). The effects of professional development for middle school general and special education teachers on implementation of reading strategies in inclusive content area classes. *Learning Disability Quarterly, 24,* 251–264.

Bryant, D. P., Vaughn, S., Linan-Thompson, S., Ugel, N., Hamff, A., & Hougen, M. (2000). Reading outcomes for students with and without reading disabilities in general education middle-school content area classes. *Learning Disability Quarterly, 23*(4), 238–252.

Canter, A., Klotz, M. B., & Cowan, K. (2008). Response to intervention: The future for secondary schools. *Principal Leadership, 8*(6), 12–15.

Carnine, L., & Carnine, D. (2004). The interaction of reading skills and science content knowledge when teaching struggling secondary students. *Reading and Writing Quarterly, 20*(2), 203–218.

Center for Research on Educational Achievement and Teaching of English Language Learners (CREATE) at the Meadows Center for Preventing Educational Risk. (2009). *Texas history lessons* (Grant No. R305A050056, U.S. Department of Education, Institute of Educational Sciences). Austin, TX: Author.

Chall, J. S., & Jacobs, V. A. (1983). Writing and reading in the elementary grades: Developmental trends among low SES children. *Language Arts, 60,* 617–626.

Compton, D. L. (2006). How should "unresponsiveness" to secondary intervention be operationalized?: It is all about the nudge. *Journal of Learning Disabilities, 39,* 170–173.

Conley, S., Fauske, J., & Pounder, D. G. (2004). Teacher work group effectiveness. *Educational Administration Quarterly, 40*(5), 663–703.

Curtis, C. P. (1995). *The Watsons go to Birmingham—1963.* New York: Random House.

Dane, A. V., & Schneider, B. H. (1998). Program integrity in primary and early secondary prevention: Are implementation effects out of control? *Clinical Psychology Review, 18,* 23–45.

Delquardi, J., Greenwood, C. R., Whorton, D., Carta, J. J., & Hall, R. V. (1986). Classwide peer tutoring. *Exceptional Children, 52*(6), 353–542.

Denton, C., Bryan, D., Wexler, J., Reed, D., & Vaughn, S. (2007). *Effective instruction for middle school students with reading difficulties: The reading teacher's sourcebook.* Austin, TX: Meadows Center for Preventing Educational Risk. Retrieved from *www.meadowscenter.org/vgc/downloads/middle_school_instruction/_RTS_Complete.pdf.*

Denton, C. A., Barth, A. E., Fletcher, J. M., Wexler, J., Vaughn, S., Cirino, P. T., et al. (2011). The relations among oral and silent reading fluency and comprehension in middle school: Implications for identification and instruction of students with reading difficulties. *Scientific Studies of Reading, 15,* 109–135.

Denton, C. A., Fletcher, J. M., Anthony, J. L., & Francis, D. J. (2006). An evaluation of intensive intervention for students with persistent reading difficulties. *Journal of Learning Disabilities, 39(5),* 447–466.

Deshler, D. D., Schumaker, J. B., Lenz, B. K., Bulgren, J. A., Hock, M. F., Knight, J., et al. (2001). Ensuring content-area learning by secondary students with learning disabilities. *Learning Disabilities Research and Practice, 16(2),* 96–108.

Donovan, M. S., & Cross, C. T. (Eds.). (2002). *Minority students in special and gifted education* (National Research Council, Committee on Minority Representation in Special Education, Division for Behavioral and Social Sciences and Education). Washington, DC: National Academy Press.

Dunlap, G., Carr, E. G., Horner, R. H., Zarcone, J., & Schwartz, I. (2008). Positive behavior support and applied behavior analysis: A familial alliance. *Behavior Modification, 32,* 682–698.

Edmunds, M., & Briggs, K. (2003). The Instructional Content Emphasis Instrument: Observations of reading instruction. In. S. Vaughn & K. L. Briggs (Eds.), *Reading in the classroom: Systems for the observation of teaching and learning* (pp. 31–52). Baltimore: Brookes.

Edmunds, M., Vaughn, S., Wexler, J., Reutebuch, C., Cable, A., Tackett, K., et al. (2009). A synthesis of reading interventions and effects on reading outcomes for older struggling readers. *Review of Educational Research, 79,* 262–300.

Education Trust. (2005). *Gaining traction, gaining ground: How some high schools accelerate learning for struggling students.* Washington, DC: Author.

Elbaum, B., Vaughn, S., Hughes, M. T., & Moody, S. W. (2000). How effective are one-to-one tutoring programs in reading for elementary students at risk for reading failure?: A meta-analysis of the intervention research. *Journal of Educational Psychology, 92(4),* 605–619.

Fixsen, D. L., Naoom, S. F., Blasé, K. A., Friedman, R. M., & Wallace, F. (2005). *Implementation research: A synthesis of the literature.* (FMHI Publication No. 231). Tampa, FL: University of South Florida, Louis de la Parte Florida Mental Health Institute.

Fletcher, J. M., Coulter, W. A., Reschly, D. J., & Vaughn, S. (2004). Alternative approaches to the definition and identification of learning disabilities: Some questions and answers. *Annals of Dyslexia, 54*(2), 304–331.

Fletcher, J. M., Lyon, G. R., Fuchs, L. S., & Barnes, M. A. (2006). *Learning disabilities: From identification to intervention.* New York: Guilford Press.

Fletcher, J. M., Shaywitz, S. E., Shankweiler, D. P., Katz, L., Liberman, I. Y., Stuebing, K. K., et al. (1994). Cognitive profiles of reading disability: Comparisons of discrepancy and low achievement definitions. *Journal of Educational Psychology, 86,* 6–23.

Fletcher, J. M., & Vaughn, S. (2009). Response to intervention: Preventing and remediating academic deficits. *Child Development Perspectives, 3,* 30–37.

Florida Department of Education. (2009–2010). *Florida Assessments for Instruction in Reading (FAIR).* Tallahassee, FL: Author.

Foorman, B. R., & Torgesen, J. (2001). Critical elements of classroom and small-group instruction to promote reading success in all children. *Learning Disabilities Research and Practice, 16*(4), 203–212.

Frayer, D. A., Frederick, W. C., & Klausmeier, H. G. (1969). *A schema for testing the level of concept mastery* (Technical Report No. 16). Madison: University of Wisconsin Research and Development Center for Cognitive Learning.

Fuchs, L. S., & Fuchs, D. (1998). Treatment validity: A unifying concept for reconceptualizing the identification of learning disabilities. *Learning Disabilities Research and Practice, 13*, 204–219.

Fuchs, L. S., & Fuchs, D. (2007). A model for implementing responsiveness to intervention. *Teaching Exceptional Children, 39*(5), 14–20.

Fuchs, L. S., Fuchs, D., & Compton, D. L. (2010). Rethinking response to intervention at middle and high school. *School Psychology Review, 39*(1), 22–28.

Fuchs, L. S., Fuchs, D., Hosp, M. K., & Jenkins, J. R. (2001). Oral reading fluency as an indicator of reading competence: A theoretical, empirical, and historical analysis. *Scientific Studies of Reading, 5*(3), 239–256.

Gersten, R., Compton, D., Connor, C. M., Dimino, J., Santoro, L., Linan-Thompson, S., et al. (2008). *Assisting students struggling with reading: Response to intervention and multi-tier intervention for reading in the primary grades. A practice guide* (NCEE Publication No. 2009-4045). Washington, DC: National Center for Education Evaluation and Regional Assistance, Institute of Education Sciences, U.S. Department of Education. Retrieved from *ies.ed.gov/ncee/wwc/publications/practiceguides*.

Graves, M.F., Cooke, C.L., & Laberge, M.J. (1983). Effects of previewing short stories. *Reading Research Quarterly, 18*, 262–276.

Griffiths, A. J., Parson, L. B., Burns, M. K., VanDerHeyden, A., & Tilly, W. D. (2007). *Response to intervention: Research for practice*. Alexandria, VA: National Association of State Directors of Special Education. Retrieved from *www.nasdse.org/Portals/0/Documents/ RtI_Bibliography2.pdf*

Guthrie, J. T. (2008). Reading motivation and engagement in middle and high school. In J. T. Guthrie (Ed.), Engaging *adolescents in reading* (pp. 1–16). Thousand Oaks, CA: Corwin Press.

Guthrie, J. T., Wigfield, A., Barbosa, P., Perencevich, K. C., Taboada, A., Davis, M.H., et al. (2004). Increasing reading comprehension and engagement through concept-oriented reading instruction. *Journal of Educational Psychology, 96*, 403–423.

Hammill, D. D., Wiederholt, J., & Allen, E. A. (2006). *Test of Silent Contextual Reading Fluency (TOSCRF)*. Austin, TX: PRO-ED.

Heller, R., & Greenleaf, C. L. (2007). *Literacy instruction in the content areas: Getting to the core of middle and high school improvement*. Washington, DC: Alliance for Excellent Education.

Horner, R. H., Sugai, G., Todd, A. W., & Lewis-Palmer, T. (2005). Schoolwide positive behavior support. In L. M. Bambara & L. Kern (Eds.), *Individualized supports for students with problem behaviors: Designing positive behavior plans* (pp. 359–390). New York: Guilford Press.

Housand, A., & Reis, S. M. (2008). Self-regulated learning in reading: Gifted pedagogy and instructional settings. *Journal of Advanced Academics, 20*(1), 108–136.

Jacobs, V. (2008). Adolescent literacy: Putting the crisis in context. State literacy plans: Incorporating adolescent literacy. *Harvard Educational Review, 78*(1), 7–39.

Jones, B. F., Pierce, J., & Hunter, B. (1989). Teaching students to construct graphic representations. *Educational Leadership, 46*(4), 20–25.

Kamil, M. L., Borman, G. D., Dole, J., Kral, C. C., Salinger, T., & Torgesen, J. (2008). *Improving adolescent literacy: Effective classroom and intervention practices: A practice guide* (NCEE Publication No. 2008-4027). Washington, DC: National Center for Education Evaluation and Regional Assistance, Institute of Education Sciences, U.S. Department of Education. Retrieved from *ies.ed.gov/ncee/wwc*

Klingner, J. K. (2009). Response to intervention. In S. Vaughn & C. S. Bos (Eds.), *Strategies for teaching students with learning and behavior problems* (7th ed., p. 67). Upper Saddle River, NJ: Pearson.

Kosanovich, M. L., Reed, D. K., & Miller, D. H. (2010). *Professional learning for secondary-level teachers.* Portsmouth, NH: RMC Research Corporation, Center on Instruction.

Lang, L., Torgesen, J., Vogel, W., Chanter, C., Lefsky, E., & Petscher, Y. (2009). Exploring the relative effectiveness of reading interventions for high school students. *Journal of Research on Educational Effectiveness, 2,* 149–175.

Langer, J. A. (1981). From theory to practice: A prereading plan. *Journal of Reading, 24,* 152–156.

Langer, J. A. (1984). Examining background knowledge and text comprehension. *Reading Research Quarterly, 19,* 468–481.

Lewis, T. J., Jones, S. E. L., Horner, R. H., & Sugai, G. (2010). School-wide positive behavior support and students with emotional/behavioral disorders: Implications for prevention, identification and intervention. *Exceptionality, 18*(2), 82–93.

Mathes, P. G., Fuchs, D., Fuchs, L. S., Henley, A. M., & Sanders, A. (1994). Increasing strategic reading practice with Peabody classwide peer tutoring. *Learning Disability Research and Practice, 9,* 44–48.

McMaster, K. L., Fuchs, D., & Fuchs, L. S. (2006). Research on peer-assisted learning strategies: The promise and limitations of peer-mediated instruction. *Reading and Writing Quarterly, 22,* 5–25.

Meadows Center for Preventing Educational Risk. (2009). *Texas adolescent literacy academies.* Austin, TX: Author.

Morrissey, K. L., Bohanon, H., & Fenning, P. (2010). Teaching and acknowledging expected behaviors in an urban high school. *Teaching Exceptional Children, 42*(5), 27–35.

National Association of State Directors of Special Education. (2006). *Response to intervention: Policy considerations and implementation.* Alexandria, VA: Author.

National Center for Education Statistics. (2009). *The nation's report card: Reading 2009* (NCES Publication No. 2010-458). U.S. Department of Education, Washington, DC: Institute of Education Sciences.

National Center for Education Statistics. (2010). *The nation's report card: Grade 12 reading and mathematics 2009 national and pilot state results* (NCES Publication No. 2011-455). Washington, DC: Institute of Education Sciences, U.S. Department of Education.

National Center on Student Progress Monitoring. (n.d.). *Common questions for progress monitoring: What are the benefits of progress monitoring?* Retrieved from *www.studentprogress. org/progresmon.asp#3*

National Commission on Adult Literacy. (2008). *Reach higher, America: Overcoming crisis in the U.S. workforce.* New York: Council for Advancement of Adult Literacy.

National High School Center, National Center on Response to Intervention, & Center on Instruction. (2010). *Tiered interventions in high schools: Using preliminary "lessons learned" to guide ongoing discussion.* Washington, DC: American Institutes for Research.

National Institute of Child Health and Human Development. (2000). *Report of the National Reading Panel. Teaching children to read: An evidence-based assessment of the scientific research literature on reading and its implications for reading instruction* (NIH Publication

No. 00–4769). Washington, DC: National Institute of Child Health and Human Development.

National Research Center on Learning Disabilities. (n.d.). *Responsiveness to intervention in the SLD determination process.* Retrieved from *www.osepideasthatwork.org/toolkit/pdf/RTI_SLD.pdf*

Neuman, S. B. (1988). Enhancing children's comprehension through previewing. In J. E. Readence & R. S. Baldwin (Eds.), *Dialogues in literacy research: Thirty-seventh yearbook of the National Reading Conference* (pp. 219–224). Chicago: National Reading Conference.

Nichols, W. D., Young, C.A., & Rickelman, R. J. (2007). Improving middle school professional development by examining middle school teachers' application of literacy strategies and instructional design. *Reading Psychology, 28*(1), 97–130.

O'Connor, R. E. (2000). Increasing the intensity of intervention in kindergarten and first grade. *Learning Disabilities Research and Practice, 15,* 43–54.

O'Connor, R. E., Fulmer, D., Harty, K., & Bell, K. (2005). Layers of reading intervention in kindergarten through third grade: Changes in teaching and student outcomes. *Journal of Learning Disabilities, 38,* 440–455.

O'Connor, R. E., Harty, K. R., & Fulmer, D. (2005). Tiers of intervention in kindergarten through third grade. *Journal of Learning Disabilities, 38*(6), 532–538.

Ogle, D. M. (1986). K-W-L: A teaching model that develops active reading of expository text. *The Reading Teacher, 39,* 564–570.

Organisation for Economic Co-operation and Development (OECD). (2007). *Annual report 2007.* Retrieved from *www.oecd.org/dataoecd/34/33/3852812.3.pdf*

Perfetti, C. A., Landi, N., & Oakhill, J. (2005). The acquisition of reading comprehension skill. In M. J. Snowling & C. Hulme (Eds.), *The science of reading: A handbook* (pp. 227–247). Oxford, UK: Blackwell.

RAND Reading Study Group. (2002). *Reading for understanding: Towards a RAND program in reading comprehension.* Santa Monica, CA: RAND Corporation.

Rayner, K., Foorman, B. R., Perfetti, C. A., Pesetsky, D., & Seidenberg, M. S. (2001). How psychological science informs the teaching of reading. *Psychological Science in the Public Interest, 2,* 31–74.

Reed, D. K. (2004a). *Identifying text structure.* Unpublished supplemental material, Southwest Educational Development Laboratory, Austin, TX.

Reed, D. K. (2004b). *Signal words.* Unpublished supplemental material, Southwest Educational Development Laboratory, Austin, TX.

Reed, D. K. (2009). A synthesis of professional development on the implementation of literacy strategies for middle school content area teachers. *Research in Middle Level Education Online, 32*(10), 1–12.

Reed, D. K., Bryan, D., Denton, C., Dougherty, C., Hotchkiss, K., Novosel, L., et al. (2009). *Texas adolescent literacy academies: Effective instruction for middle school students: Content area instructional routines to support academic literacy.* Austin, TX: Meadows Center for Preventing Educational Risk.

Reed, D. K., & Groth, C. (2009). Academic teams promote cross-curricular applications that improve learning outcomes. *Middle School Journal, 40*(3), 12–19.

Reschly, D. J. (2003, December). *What if LD identification changed to reflect research findings?: Consequences of LD identification changes.* Paper presented at the Responsiveness-to-Intervention Symposium, Kansas City, MO.

Roberts, G., Torgesen, J. K., Boardman, A., & Scammacca, N. (2008). Evidence-based strate-gies for reading instruction of older students with learning disabilities. *Learning Dis-abilities Research and Practice, 23*(2), 63–69.

Saenz, L. M., Fuchs, L. S., & Fuchs, D. (2005). Peer-assisted learning strategies for English language learners with learning disabilities. *Exceptional Children, 71,* 231–247.

Scammacca, N., Roberts, G., Vaughn, S., Edmonds, M., Wexler, J., Reutebuch, C. K., et al. (2007). *Interventions for adolescent struggling readers: A meta-analysis with implications for practice.* Portsmouth, NH: RMC Research Corporation, Center on Instruction.

Shanahan, T., & Shanahan, C. (2008). Teaching disciplinary literacy to adolescents: Rethink-ing content-area literacy. *Harvard Educational Review, 78*(1), 40–59.

Share, D. L., McGee, R., & Silva, P. (1989). IQ and reading progress: A test of the capac-ity notion of IQ. *Journal of the American Academy of Child and Adolescent Psychiatry, 28,* 97–100.

Siebert, D., & Draper, R. (2008). Why content-area literacy messages do not speak to math-ematics teachers: A critical content analysis. *Literacy Research and Instruction, 47,* 229–245.

Simmons, D., Rupley, W., & Vaughn, S. (2009). *Enhancing the quality of expository text instruc-tion and comprehension through content and case-situated professional development* (Final Report, Institute of Education Sciences Grant No. R305M050121A). Submitted to U.S. Department of Education, Institute of Education Sciences

Speece, D. L., & Case, L. P. (2001). Classification in context: An alternative approach to iden-tifying early reading disability. *Journal of Educational Psychology, 93,* 735–749.

Speece, D. L., Case, L. P., & Molloy, D. E. (2003). Responsiveness to general education instruction as the first gate to learning disabilities identification. *Learning Disabilities Research and Practice, 18*(3), 147–156.

Stage, S. A., & Jacobsen, M. D. (2001). Predicting student success on a state-mandated performance-based assessment using oral reading fluency. *School Psychology Review, 30*(3), 407–419.

Stanovich, K. E., & Siegel, L. S. (1994). Phenotypic performance profile of children with read-ing disabilities: A regression-based test of the phonological–core variable–difference model. *Journal of Educational Psychology, 86,* 24–53.

Stanovich, P. J., & Stanovich, K. E. (2003). *Identifying and implementing educational practices supported by rigorous evidence: A user friendly guide.* Washington, DC: Institute for Edu-cation Sciences and National Center for Education Evaluation and Regional Assis-tance. Retrieved from *www.ed.gov/rschstat/research/pubs/rigorousevid/index.html*

State of Washington Office of Superintendent of Public Instruction. (2009). *Washington Assessment of Student Learning.* Olympia: Author.

Stecker, P. M., Fuchs, L. S., & Fuchs, D. (2005). Using curriculum-based measurement to improve student achievement: Review of research. *Psychology in the Schools, 42,* 795–819.

Stewart, R. M., Benner, G. J., Martella, R. C., & Marchand-Martella, N. E. (2007). Three-tier models of reading and behavior: A research review. *Journal of Positive Behavior Inter-ventions, 9*(4), 239–253.

Sturtevant, E. G., & Linek, W. M. (2003). The instructional beliefs and decisions of middle and secondary teachers who successfully blend literacy and content. *Reading Research and Instruction, 43*(1), 74–90.

Sugai, G., & Horner, R. H. (2009). Responsiveness to intervention and school-wide positive behavior supports: Integration of multi-tiered system approaches. *Exceptionality, 17*(4), 223–237.

Tackett, K. K., Roberts, G., Baker, S., & Scammaca, N. (2009). *Implementing response to intervention: Practices and perspectives from five schools. Frequently asked questions.* Portsmouth, NH: RMC Research Corporation, Center on Instruction.

Tolar, T. D., Barth, A. E., Francis, D. J., Fletcher, J. M., Stuebing, K. K., & Vaughn, S. (2011). Psychometric properties of maze tasks in middle school students. *Assessment for Effective Intervention.* Advance online publication. doi: 10.1177/1534508411413913.

Torgesen, J., Houston, D., & Rissman, L. (2007). *Improving literacy instruction in middle and high schools: A guide for principals.* Portsmouth, NH: RMC Research Corporation, Center on Instruction.

Torgesen, J., Wagner, R., & Rashotte, C. (1999). *Test of Word Reading Efficiency (TOWRE).* Austin, TX: PRO-ED.

Torgesen, J. K., Houston, D. D., Rissman, L. M., Decker, S. M., Roberts, G., Vaughn, S., et al. (2007). *Academic literacy instruction for adolescents: A guidance document from the Center on Instruction.* Portsmouth, NH: RMC Research Corporation, Center on Instruction.

University of Texas Center for Reading and Language Arts. (2003). *Special Education Reading Project (SERP) secondary institute: Effective instruction for secondary struggling readers: Research-based practices.* Austin, TX: University of Texas System/Texas Education Agency.

University of Texas Center for Reading and Language Arts. (2005). *3-tier reading model: Reducing reading difficulties for kindergarten through third grade students.* Austin, TX: Author.

U.S. Department of Education. (2004). Individuals with Disabilities Education Improvement Act of 2004, Pub. L. 108–466. *Federal Register, 70,* 35802–35803.

Vaughn, S., & Bos, C. (Eds.). (2000). *Strategies for teaching students with learning and behavior problems* (7th ed.). Upper Saddle River, NJ: Pearson.

Vaughn, S., Cirino, P. T., Wanzek, J., Wexler, J., Fletcher, J. M., Denton, C. A., et al. (2010). Response to intervention for middle school students with reading difficulties: Effects of a primary and secondary intervention. *School Psychology Review, 39*(1), 3–21.

Vaughn, S., Denton, C. A., & Fletcher, J. M. (2010). Why intensive interventions are necessary for students with severe reading difficulties. *Psychology in the Schools, 47*(5), 432–444.

Vaughn, S., & Fletcher, J. M. (2010). Thoughts on rethinking response to intervention with secondary students. *School Psychology Review, 39*(2), 296–299.

Vaughn, S., Fletcher, J. M., Francis, D. J., Denton, C. A., Wanzek, J., Wexler, J., et al. (2008). Response to intervention with older students with reading difficulties. *Learning and Individual Differences, 18,* 338–345.

Vaughn, S., & Fuchs, L. S. (2003). Redefining learning disabilities as inadequate response to instruction: The promise and potential problems. *Learning Disabilities Research and Practice, 18,* 137–146.

Vaughn, S., & Klingner, J. K. (2007). Overview of the three-tier model of reading intervention. In D. H. Haager, S. Vaughn, & J. K. Klingner (Eds.), *Evidence-based reading practices for response to intervention* (pp. 3–9). Baltimore: Brookes.

Vaughn, S., Klingner, J. K., & Bryant, D. P. (2001). Collaborative strategic reading as a means to enhance peer-mediated instruction for reading comprehension and content area learning. *Remedial and Special Education, 22*(2), 66–74.

Vaughn, S., Linan-Thompson, S., & Hickman, P. (2003). Response to intervention as a means of identifying students with reading/learning disabilities. *Exceptional Children, 69*, 391–409.

Vaughn, S., Wanzek, J., Murray, C. S., Scammacca, N., Linan-Thompson, S., & Woodruff, A. L. (2009). Response to early reading interventions: Examining higher responders and lower responders. *Exceptional Children, 75*, 165–183.

Vaughn, S., Wanzek, J., Wexler, J., Barth, A., Cirino, P. T., Romain, M., et al. (2010). The relative effects of group size on reading progress of older students with reading difficulties. *Reading and Writing: An Interdisciplinary Journal, 23*(8), 931–956.

Vaughn, S., Wexler, J., Leroux, A. J., Roberts, G., Denton, C. A., Barth, A. E., et al. (2011). Effects of intensive reading intervention for eighth grade students with persistently inadequate response to intervention. *Journal of Learning Disabilities*. doi: 10.1177/0022219411402692

Vaughn, S., Wexler, J., Roberts, G., Barth, A. E., Cirino, P. T., Romain, M., et al. (2011). The effects of tertiary treatments on middle school students with reading disabilities: Individualized versus standardized approaches. *Exceptional Children, 77*, 391–407.

Vellutino, F. R., Scanlon, D. M., Sipay, E. R., Small, S. G., Chen R., Pratt, A., et al. (1996). Cognitive profiles of difficult-to-remediate and readily remediated poor readers: Early intervention as a vehicle for distinguishing between cognitive and experiential deficits as basic causes of specific reading disability. *Journal of Educational Psychology, 88*, 601–638.

Vellutino, F. R., Scanlon, D. M., Small, S., & Fanuele, D. P. (2006). Response to intervention as a vehicle for distinguishing between children with and without reading disabilities: Evidence for the role of kindergarten and first-grade interventions. *Journal of Learning Disabilities, 39*, 157–169.

Wexler, J., Vaughn, S., Edmonds, M., & Reutebuch, C. K. (2008). A synthesis of fluency interventions for secondary struggling readers. *Reading and Writing: An Interdisciplinary Journal, 21*(4), 317–347.

Wexler, J., Vaughn, S., & Roberts, G. (2010). *Preventing school dropout with secondary students: The implementation of an individualized reading intervention and dropout prevention intervention* (Institute of Education Sciences Grant Contract No. R324A100022).

Wexler, J., Vaughn, S., Roberts, G., & Denton, C. A. (2010). The efficacy of repeated reading and wide reading practice for high school students with severe reading disabilities. *Learning Disabilities Research and Practice, 25*(1), 2–10.

Yep, L. (1977). *Dragonwings*. New York: Harper Trophy.

Zirkel, P. A., & Thomas, L. B. (2010). State laws and guidelines for implementing RTI. *Teaching Exceptional Children, 43*(1), 60–73.

Index

Page numbers followed by f or t indicate figures and tables.